A SHORT HISTORY OF CANADA

Fifth Edition

DESMOND MORTON

M&S

To Gael

First published 1983 (Hurtig Publishers); 1st revd ed. 1987 (Hurtig Publishers); 2nd revd ed. 1994 (McClelland & Stewart); 3rd revd ed. 1997 (McClelland & Stewart)

Canadian Cataloguing in Publication Data

Morton, Desmond, 1937-
    A short history of Canada

5th ed.
Includes index.
ISBN 0-7710-6508-6 (bound)   ISBN 0-7710-6509-4 (pbk.)

1. Canada – History.   I. Title.

FC164.M676 2001   971   C00-933001-1
F1026.M73 2001

We acknowledge the financial support of the Government of Canada through the Book Publishing Industry Development Program for our publishing activities. We further acknowledge the support of the Canada Council for the Arts and the Ontario Arts Council for our publishing program.

Designed by Ingrid Paulson
Typeset in Minion by M&S, Toronto
Maps by VisuTronx
Printed and bound in Canada

McClelland & Stewart Ltd.
The Canadian Publishers
481 University Avenue
Toronto, Ontario
M5G 2E9
www.mcclelland.com

1   2   3   4   5   04   03   02   01

CONTENTS

PREFACE |

A nation, said the French philosopher Ernest Renan, is a people that has done great things together in the past. It is not bound by language or by a common culture but by a shared experience. History is what Canadians have in common.

Canadians believe that their history is short, boring, and irrelevant. They are wrong on all counts. The choices Canadians can make today have been shaped by history. The governors of New France launched arguments that federalists and sovereignists repeat in present-day Quebec. Were the natives who far outnumbered them sovereign allies – or enemies – or were they subjects of the French king? That debate began early. Early fur traders illustrated economic laws that modern-day resource development unconsciously follows. Canadians trying to understand the challenges of political leadership would do well to take a second look at the arts of Sir John A. Macdonald and William Lyon Mackenzie King.

In each generation, Canadians have had to learn how to live with each other in this big, rich land. It has never been easy. If we ignore history, we make it doubly difficult. This book has been written to make it a little easier for Canadians to know and understand their country. It is concerned with politics and economics as well as how Canadians have lived their own lives, because our greatest problems and achievements have come through the entwining of our lives with a community.

This book was first written with the inspiration and support of Mel Hurtig. That inspiration was reinforced – unconsciously and perhaps grudgingly – by generations of students at Erindale College, the Mississauga campus of the University of Toronto. Many were new Canadians, committed to an adopted country, yet puzzled by it and reluctant to take its truths for granted. Because of the enriching flow of new Canadians, there will never be a final history of Canada.

Later, at McGill University in Montreal, students were diverse in a different way. McGill students reflect all of Canada, from Newfoundland to the Lower Mainland of B.C. Many are francophones, and I seldom encountered a class without articulate sovereignists. Some were students from Europe or Asia. I couldn't have designed a better forum to understand Canada and its wonderful complexity.

More than most of my books, this one profited from the perceptiveness and patience of my original editor, Sarah Reid, of my current editor, Alex Schultz, and of my late wife, Jan. They deserve whatever claims the book may have to be readable. Where it fails, they could not prevail over stubbornness. Clara Stewart, Kathie Hill, and Lorna Wreford have laboured on this manuscript at various stages, reminding me that readers deserve clarity as well as facts. The latest edition, the first full revision since 1983, has involved my beloved wife and partner, Gael Eakin. Perhaps only the partners of other authors will have any idea of what she has endured. Meanwhile, Suzanne Aubin and Marie-Louise Moreau have added their wisdom and experience of Canada, protected my time, and absorbed my burdens so that this work could be done. I hope they all accept a share of what is good in the book.

Any new edition of a book is better than its predecessor, if only because colleagues and reviewers have generously suggested corrections and improvements. I particularly benefited from the erudition of Vincent Eriksson of Canmore Lutheran College. Neither he nor the many others bear any responsibility for errors, misinterpretations, and what the Anglican *Book of Common Prayer* calls "invincible ignorance."

This book is a product of its birthplace, a suburban campus in the young city of Mississauga, a place as full of energy as it is of self-doubt. It has been renewed in Montreal, among people passionately committed to a new, sovereign Quebec and others as passionately devoted to the preservation of a tolerant, multicultural Canada. Whatever our future, we should understand how Canada has travelled through its most recent centuries to the present. If we follow that voyage, our history will give us confidence in change and compromise and in some enduring truths about communities and families and human beings. It should also tell us that no ideas, however deeply held, last forever.

Georgeville, Quebec
August 15, 2000

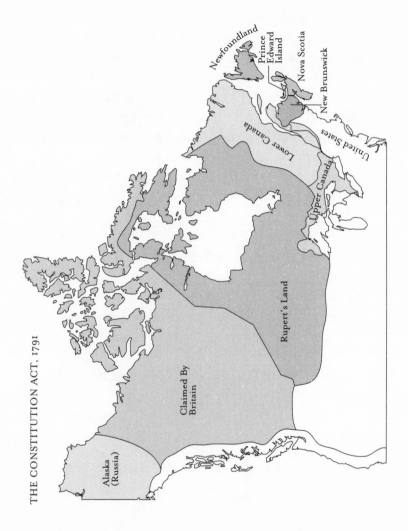

THE CONSTITUTION ACT, 1791

Newfoundland

Prince
Edward
Island

Nova Scotia

New Brunswick

United States

Lower Canada

Upper Canada

Rupert's Land

Claimed By
Britain

Alaska
(Russia)

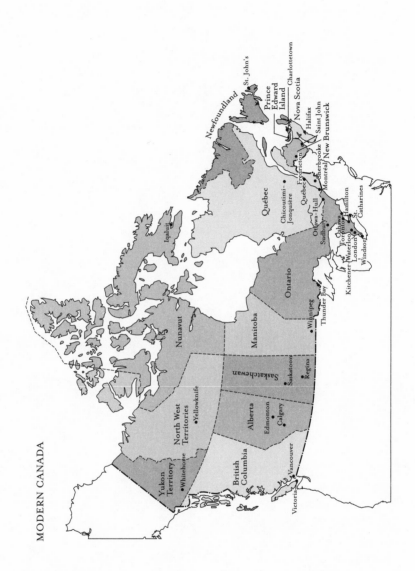

MODERN CANADA

PART I

DIFFERENT HISTORIES

I | NEW NATION

At midnight on July 1, 1867, church bells rang out from Lunenburg to Sarnia. In Ottawa, militia artillery fired the first round of a hundred-gun salute. Crowds cheered the explosions and waited as the militiamen laboured in the dark with rammers and sponges. At dawn, 4 million people awoke as citizens of a new Dominion of Canada. Some of them, in New Brunswick and Nova Scotia, might resent their fate, but a two-day weekend (for July 1 fell on a Monday) was too rare a treat to be shunned. Picnics, lacrosse tournaments, cricket matches, and excursions focused the day's excitement. Farm families united around groaning kitchen tables. On Toronto's waterfront, a huge ox was roasted all day so that dripping hunks of meat could be distributed to the poor.

Carefully respecting the ban on Sabbath labour, George Brown arrived at the offices of his *Globe* at midnight, determined to do editorial justice to events he had helped to bring about. As the morning hours passed, his pen filled page after page with statistics, politics, history, business, and hope for the new Dominion. Only at dawn was Brown finished. Solemnly he pledged that "the teeming millions who shall populate the northern part of this continent, from the Atlantic to the Pacific, shall, under a wise and just Government, reap the fruit of well-directed enterprise, honest industry and religious principles." By then, the express trains that normally carried the *Globe* to readers across the old province of Canada West had departed without it. Brown's aspirations for Canada would go largely unread.

In the summer of 1867, Canada was little more than hopes. Confederation covered only 370,045 square miles (958 416.5 km^2), a mere tenth of British North America. Three colonies had become four provinces, but the northern edge of the new provinces of Ontario and Quebec ran vaguely along the watershed that drained into the St. Lawrence and the Great Lakes. The population – 3,816,680 by official count in 1871 – was a tenth as large as that of the bustling, powerful nation to the south. Many Canadians wondered how long they would survive the American boast that "manifest destiny" would allow them to rule the entire continent.

George Brown's Dominion Day mood allowed no dismay. Small as it was, Canada's population was at least as large as America's had been when the Thirteen Colonies won their independence in 1783. Confederation itself was proof that the divisions between a million French Canadians and two and a quarter million Canadians of British origin could be overcome. If there remained differences of race, region, and religion, prosperity would dissolve them. The *Globe*'s readers that day could share Brown's intoxication with statistics, marvelling at every aspect of the young country's potential, from shipbuilding to the vast deposits of rock oil near Petrolia.

In his day, Brown had flailed at the corruption and waste of railway builders, but now he celebrated their achievements: 2149 miles (3458 km) of track in Quebec and Ontario alone, backed by canals, roads, bridges. The Grand Trunk, with 1277 miles

(2055 km) of track, was the world's largest railway system. Almost two of those miles rumbled across the St. Lawrence River on the world-famous Victoria Bridge at Montreal, completing a line that ran unbroken from Sarnia to Portland, Maine. Soon there would be more. Confederation was nothing if not a guarantee that new rail lines would snake their way east to Halifax and perhaps west across the fabled Rocky Mountains to the Pacific.

Prosperity would depend on the *Globe*'s most faithful readers, the farmers. Across the Dominion, there were more Canadians in farming than in any other occupation. If there was such a thing as an average farmer in 1867, he owned from fifty to one hundred acres, cultivated twenty of them, grew seventy-two bushels of wheat, and kept eight cattle and a team of horses. In reality, soil and climate created vast differences. Quebec farmers were poorer, on average, than those in Ontario or the agricultural regions of the Maritimes, but they were recovering from several grim years of depression. Surplus offspring had left for New England mill towns and were sending home the hard-earned sums that would allow the family farm to diversify into dairying. With soil exhausted and crops ravaged by the Hessian fly, much of Ontario was now sliding into its own rural depression.

Few social scientists and statisticians existed in the 1860s to warn people of national trends. Canadians who gathered for barter or gossip at the local tavern or general store knew only of a neighbour's daughter marrying a man from "the Boston states" or of sons gone homesteading in Kansas. The census, every ten years since 1851, identified trends: Canadians were leaving the land, and many were leaving Canada. Most people, of course, lived their lives within the limits of family and community. They looked to government not for social or economic programs but for bridges, wharves, and post offices, and, quite rarely, for a place on the public payroll.

Some major public programs existed. Egerton Ryerson had campaigned tirelessly to make the rural communities of Upper Canada establish public schools and tax themselves for their support. Ontarians boasted of the results (and grumbled at the cost). Ryerson's counterpart in Lower Canada, Pierre Chauveau, became the first premier of the new province of Quebec. In the lower provinces, only Nova Scotia had a public school system. Across Canada more than 10 per cent of the population – more women than men – could not read. A rural population saw little need for the "charitable and eleemosynary institutions" Canada's new constitution assigned to provinces. Farm families usually made room for their own orphans, elderly, and insane. If the treatment seemed harsh and misguided, were publicly run asylums and orphanages any better?

Outside major cities, police were rare. Magistrates turned to the militia or recruited special constables if criminals defied the majesty of the law. A frightened rural community could make its own laws, as the Black Donnellys of Lucan, near London, Ontario, would discover in 1880. Anonymous gangs of "white caps" punished wife abusers and drunks by whipping, ducking, or snow baths. Even when victims died, rural juries seldom convicted. When their sense of justice was aroused, rural communities could also defend their own. The "Megantic outlaw," Donald Morrison, was hidden from the law for three years in the 1880s because his Eastern Township neighbours refused to believe that his alleged arson and accidental manslaughter were authentic crimes.

Farming lay at the heart of Canadian society and economics in 1867. Closely linked were the other resource industries of fishing and logging. However harsh or inhospitable the coastline, most fishing families cultivated a few acres of vegetables. On the edge of the Canadian Shield, settlers forced the thin soil to grow hay and oats for the logging camps where they and their sons spent the winters. Wheat, square timber, and fish made up most of the $80 million in exports with which the new Dominion hoped to pay its way in the world.

The future, of course, would be different. It lay not so much with the resource frontier as with the cities that controlled the trade and transportation routes. Once rivers and harbours fostered cities; in the 1860s railways confirmed or denied urban ambitions. The Victoria Bridge determined that Montreal would continue for another century as the metropolis of Canada, the first city of one hundred thousand people. Quebec, with 59,699 people, would wither: poor rail connections undermined her claim to be the great port of the St. Lawrence timber trade. Toronto, with 56,092 citizens in 1871, would grow because of the river of railway tracks across her waterfront – the Grand Trunk, the Great Western, and her own creation, the Northern, reaching to Collingwood, Lake Huron, and the West. Halifax with 29,582 people and Saint John with 28,805 were the fourth and fifth cities of the Dominion and dominated their own provinces. Their huge merchant fleets allowed George Brown to boast of Canada as a new maritime power. But in the Victorian mansions where the shipowners displayed their wealth, already there were fears that Confederation would turn great ports into economic backwaters.

If railways decided the fate of cities, they also created arguments for urban growth. The self-sufficiency of small market towns, producing their own tools, furniture, and boots, ended with the railway. Mass markets justified mass production, costly machinery, and armies of persuasive salesmen. Necessities made locally or in the home could now be supplied year-round with a variety, quality, and price local tradesmen could seldom match. In 1867, manufacturing employed 15 per cent of Canadian workers and produced 20 per cent of Canadian wealth. That year, the Massey family's reaper and mower won a prize at the Paris Exposition. What could better typify the hopes of Confederation than a Yankee-style pride in home-grown inventiveness? What was more Canadian than delight at foreign recognition? More significant for Canadian development was the process that would carry Daniel Massey's little foundry at Bond Head to the town of Bowmanville and finally, by 1878, to the growing metropolis of Toronto.

The merchants and industrialists of the expanding cities were, for the most part, self-made men: once-penniless clerks and artisans who had saved their money, seen their chance, and seized it. Some were Americans; a disproportionate number, perhaps because they were apprenticed so young and in such a hard school, were Scots. Few of these hard-bitten achievers (including George Brown) spared much sympathy for those who had failed in the struggle for wealth. Confederation coincided with an era when skilled workers were losing the struggle for both near-equality with their employers and superiority over the unskilled. New technologies undermined ancient crafts, from shoemaking to typography. Luck and strong organization saved the typographers; other occupations would decline in status or, like coopers and cobblers, disappear.

The average worker in Confederation Canada – as mythical a being as the average farmer – learned the rhyme that "a dollar a day is very good pay." That might be true for labourers; a skilled worker expected twice as much or more for a work week of sixty hours over six days. A mixed blessing of industrialism was that women now found paid work, at barely half a man's wage. Children earned far less. An employee, of course, paid for his own holidays – even Dominion Day and Christmas – and took his own risks with old age, sickness, and injuries on the job. A worker's meagre savings tided him and his family through a harsh winter or cyclical bad time. Officials responsible for municipal relief made certain that any applicant considered starvation as a serious alternative.

Urban, industrial workers were a minority. Most Canadians still worked in a wageless, pre-industrial economy. Many, like Gaspé fishermen, were in debt to their merchant suppliers. Rural Canadians had no sympathy with arguments for shorter hours, higher wages, or labour unions. When workers in Hamilton and Toronto imitated British industrial workers by demanding a nine-hour day, the Halifax *Witness* delivered an editorial sermon most of its readers would instinctively echo:

In this new country, where every man who strives may advance in social power and rank, to teach men subordination to class movements is to deprive them of those noble opportunities for personal advancement which are the peculiar glory and advantage of this continent.

Close to half the population was female. Less than a third of women were married, and 6 per cent were widows (double the percentage of widowers). Two-thirds of women were classified as "children or unmarried." The vast majority of them worked hard, but only 11,422 female servants and a handful of laundresses and seamstresses emerge from the occupational census. Women had no share in public life and, legally, no more status than their husbands or fathers permitted. Their official status was hardly higher than that of the 23,035 Indians (or *sauvages*, as the French translation of the census described them). The once-proud aboriginal people of North America now survived largely as wards of an indifferent state. A few generations earlier, Indians had helped save Canada during the War of 1812; now they were heading for extinction. Few Canadians even noticed. They were more aware of over twenty-six thousand blacks, many of them descendants of Loyalists in Nova Scotia. The Underground Railway had brought thirty thousand refugees from American slavery, but many went home after the Civil War, tired of being poor, patronized, or scorned by Canada's white majority.

Although most Canadians professed to ignore class differences, they had developed plenty of alternative divisions. Except for bilingual elites and humbler workers at the linguistic frontiers, the two "founding nations" of French and English had few contacts. In the first Dominion census, only 8 per cent were neither British or French in origin; 202,991 Germans were the largest exception. Census-takers found only 125 Jews, 11 "Hindoos," and 3 Chinese. English-speakers had their own historic differences. The Irish, the largest of the "British" groups, brought with them the divisive hatreds of Green and Orange, to be played out in frequent midsummer riots in Montreal, Toronto, Saint John, or wherever the fires of prejudice could be lit. Immigrant Scots, better educated in village schools and taught a trade, prospered mightily in a land where learning and skills were scarce.

The architects of the new Dominion tried hard to accommodate the bitter quarrels of Catholic and Protestant. Few politicians escaped the temptation of mixing religion and politics, or the risks. Protestants were far from united: early censuses distinguished six varieties of Presbyterian and eight of Methodist. Nor were Canadians entirely united in Christianity: the census also found 1884 "pagans" and 20 atheists, almost all from Ontario.

For Brown's Toronto, for Montreal businessmen with renewed visions of a transcontinental empire, and especially for the twenty thousand people in the sweltering little logging town of Ottawa, Confederation was a triumph. For others, half-devoured by the long struggle with the land, the forest, or the sea, it was a matter of deep indifference. For some, like those who draped the entrance to the Halifax *Chronicle* in black bunting, or who gathered in Montreal's Institut canadien to hatch schemes to bring down that "sellout," George-Étienne Cartier, Confederation was an enemy almost before it was born. It was Cartier, a man of action more than words, who had urged, cajoled, and manoeuvred his fellow French Canadians into Confederation. The man who had composed *Avant tout, soyons Canadiens* ("Before All Else, Let's Be Canadians"), who sang it in his rough, raucous voice whenever the company could endure it, was also the man who insisted that Confederation created a "new nation." It was, Cartier insisted, only within a new political entity of British North America that the cultural nation of French Canada could be safe from American conquest or English assimilation.

The new Canadian nation was not the outcome of a long struggle for liberation or even of the effort, so common in nineteenth-century Europe, to revive a half-buried language and culture. The Dominion had no common language or agreed-upon symbols. Perhaps the beaver qualified best, "a most respectable animal," as Sir William Dawson of McGill University acknowledged, but no revolutionary: "a type of unvarying instincts and old-world traditions. He does not improve and becomes extinct rather than change his ways."

Canadians certainly shared a climate – harsh, interminable winters that might, if one believed the dangerous new doctrines of Charles Darwin, breed out the feeble and the weak-willed. Winters were more popular with the wealthy than with workers, who faced rising costs for food and fuel, wage cuts, and layoffs when frost and snow gripped their communities. Canada's image as "Our Lady of the Snows" would repel the investment and immigration that so preoccupied the Fathers of Confederation.

July 1, 1867, seemed a time of hope and fresh beginnings. In fact, Confederation had broken little with the past. Unlike the American revolutionaries, who deliberately concealed their borrowings from colonial tradition, the Fathers of Confederation built deliberately, pragmatically, and cautiously from their own historical experience. They and their critics carried their memories intact across the narrow divide of the first Dominion Day. The history of Canada as a single transcontinental nation begins from that day; its communities harboured much older history.

2 | FIRST NATIONS

Written history has its limits. It has little to contribute to the first millennia of Canada's human past. Such a circumstance makes a book like this blessedly shorter, but it is aggravating to those whose history, being absent, seems to be scorned. Without writing to give an apparent precision and durability to human memory, all history is what English law used to call "time out of mind," and a period that might seem like eternity may in fact have begun only a few dozen years before.

For pre-Contact America, all time is out of mind. The people who created the great Mayan and Aztec civilizations, or the smaller but hardly less sophisticated cultures of the Iroquois, the Algonquin, and the Haida, mastered some remarkable technologies, but systematic writing was not among them. European priests, travellers, and traders, with a feeble grasp of native languages and with concerns other than the preservation of "pagan" myths, have been the chief historical source; but how precise were their interlocutors or their interpreters?

To know more of pre-Contact history, we must rely on the

evidence of archaeologists, anthropologists, and ethnographers, all of whom draw vast inferences from a few tiny fragments of stone, clay, or bone, from speech and language patterns, or from legends. Increasingly, we are urged to record and respect the tales of native elders, but are such stories, often the sole basis of a land claim or an ancient rivalry, any less self-serving than those our European ancestors accepted when they were told that the Virgin Mary gave her special protection to the town of Montreal or that God, in His infinite wisdom, had invited the British to rule His vast American domain?

When Europeans reached North America in the 1500s, there may have been about a third to half a million people living in what later would be called Canada, though the numbers soon fell rapidly. Native people have a variety of beliefs about their creation. A widespread myth features an Earth Diver who plunges into the primeval ocean to emerge with the mud from which land – "Turtle Island" – forests, animals, and humanity are fashioned. Sometimes a great spirit persuades animals to do the diving. Other native peoples believed in the myth of a Great Transformer, occasionally a form of the Trickster common to many native legends. A sometimes comic figure in nature folklore, the Trickster stole fire, light, water, animals, and even humanity to create the known world. Among the Haida and Tsimshian, it is the Raven; among the Ojibwa, Nanabozo; among the Blackfoot, Coyote. Among the Mi'kmaq, Maliseet, and Abenaki the world was created by a superhero of human character and supernatural powers. Some peoples recognized the opposites of cold and heat, good and evil, summer and winter, and imagined two forces contending to create their universe. Common to all native beliefs was the conviction that their origins were here in North America and that they were in fact, rather than in mere seniority among immigrants, the true First Nations.

Archaeologists would insist that North America's first known human inhabitants arrived in a more pedestrian way. Twelve to twenty thousand years ago, they had made their way across the land bridge between Asia and the Americas that survives as the Aleutians. Then they made their way south, adapting gradually to the enormous diversity of climate and topography of a hitherto uninhabited continent. Scientists have reinforced the claim by comparing the DNA of natives and their alleged ancestors in Manchuria and Mongolia. At least one native leader has claimed that migration flowed the other way. What is certain is that no ancient immigration officer was on hand to document either migration.

Scientific evidence suggests two great waves of prehistoric migration, the first twelve to twenty thousand years ago, and the second, after an intervening ice age, much later. The cold forced native ancestors to migrate southward, and then, as it receded, settlement pushed northward again. A later wave of arrivals helps explain why the Athapaskan-speakers differ completely in language and even physical appearance from the Algonquian-speakers, who inhabit the eastern and central belt of woodlands. The Inuit are part of a circumpolar people who may also be found in Siberia.

Whatever they had in common in their origins, the native peoples whom whites encountered had made an effective adaptation to their environment. Traditionally, native groups were classified by their eleven language families, though a simpler division might be based on differing lifestyles. Across most of Canada, from the Yukon to the Atlantic, were members of two language groups, Algonquian and Athapaskan, sharing a hunting-gathering existence, with small bands, great mobility, and such technological triumphs as the birchbark canoe and the skills in trapping and in curing animal pelts that gave Canada its first staple industry. To their north were the Inuit, amazingly adapted to life in the Arctic desert. To this day, no one else has been better able to survive in a region of dark, bitterly cold winters and short summers, almost wholly dependent on fish and animal life. To the south of the forest-dwelling Algonquin were the Iroquois, people who had learned to farm the soil and to sustain themselves, winter and summer, in substantial villages. Far away on the western plains were people who had adopted the collective organization needed to hunt the huge herds of prairie bison and to survive long prairie winters. Still farther west were people who had adapted to life in the southern plateau regions of the Rockies. Along the Pacific, in the shadow of the coastal mountains, were people who had adapted to a life of fishing, trading, and limited agriculture, and whose towering totem poles and wooden houses bespoke a complex culture and belief system.

Every one of the First Nations had, through millennia of adaptation, found the culture, beliefs, skills, and technology to survive in their part of Canada, whether it was the light snowshoes of the Algonquin, the hunting organization of Blackfoot and Cree, or the Arctic clothing, kayaks, and igloos of the Inuit. All had unique artistic and decorative skills, sophisticated myths and legends to explain their world to themselves and others, and religious beliefs that sustained the human qualities needed for survival. Some made war, but in moderation, preserving captured women for intermarriage and children for adoption.

Whatever their form of life, native North Americans saw themselves as part of nature, not as its masters. Though they fought other bands and nations, they had very little sense of territorial ownership. Even agricultural societies migrated when the soil was exhausted and rebuilt their villages on other sites. Native beliefs found kindred spirits in the animals they hunted, and misfortune befell those who offended such spirits by killing cruelly or to excess. Of course, their lives were hard, and death from hunger, cold, and injury was no stranger. They knew sickness too, though many of the white men's diseases were unknown to them and, in their lack of immunity, contact brought catastrophic death rates.

Human remains and languages show that native people traded long before Europeans arrived, exchanging what they produced in surplus for what they could not supply for themselves. Perhaps their eagerness for new technology was their downfall. A less curious or adaptable people might have ignored the Europeans and their goods and left them to live or, more probably, die on their own. Without the full co-operation and assistance of natives in showing the Europeans their methods of survival, their territory, and their resources, the early explorers and settlers would have perished in even greater numbers and possibly abandoned their quest, much as the Vikings had done five hundred years before.

Instead, with the enthusiasm of natural free traders, Canada's first peoples welcomed the Europeans and their goods into existing trading systems. Any second thoughts came too late.

CARTIER'S QUEBEC | 3

I t was not just the natives whose history began before 1867. For George-Étienne Cartier, or any other *Canadien*, the history of Canada began in 1534, when another Cartier had made his landfall on the Gaspé shore of the Baie des Chaleurs. By erecting a cross and claiming the continent for His Most Christian Majesty Francis I, Jacques Cartier, the veteran navigator from Saint-Malo, had posted the French bid for North America.

The bid ignored the claims of Indians or Inuit, established for thousands of years since their ancestors had crossed the Alaska land bridge from Asia. Even some Europeans had staked an earlier claim: Vikings, driven west from Iceland to the coast of Labrador, Newfoundland, and perhaps even New England, had recorded their discoveries in Norse sagas. Basque and Breton fishermen had come regularly, returning under strict oaths of secrecy about the origins of their rich catches. In 1497, when the boastful John Cabot came back to Bristol to report schools of codfish so dense "they sometimes stayed his shippes," he merely broke a trade secret.

Cartier had come for a different form of wealth. He had been enticed by vague Indian claims of a wealthy "Kingdom of the Saguenay" and by the great river that he hoped would lead past the rapids of Lachine to a western ocean. When the gold he brought home on his third voyage proved to be iron pyrites, the French seaman was discredited. Anyway, France was too deep in the wars between Catholic and Huguenot to care about distant lands. Seventy years would pass before the French came again. This time, Samuel de Champlain would make them stay.

Canada could hardly ask for a nobler founder than Champlain. Navigator, soldier, visionary, a Protestant turned Catholic by conviction, a man of Renaissance curiosity and eternal fortitude, Champlain created New France. A few bleak winters spent on the Bay of Fundy persuaded him to try elsewhere. Fate then took him back to Cartier's great river, the "Father of Waters." Where Cape Diamond rears up to narrow the St. Lawrence River, Champlain and a few men built their *habitation* in the autumn of 1608.

Champlain's business, financed by court favourites and Rouen merchants, was the fur trade. In its name, he made alliances with the Algonquins; fought their dreaded enemies, the Iroquois; journeyed to the Huron country that is now central Ontario; and sent young Frenchmen to learn Indian languages and lifestyles as the first *coureurs de bois*. Champlain has been condemned for provoking the Iroquois, but his intervention only speeded up the inevitable.

Enemies and climate had driven the Iroquois south of the Great Lakes. Their longhouse culture of cornfields and tribal alliances gave them a strength and political stability no other northern Indians possessed. On the other hand, they lacked rich sources of good furs or the swift canoes to carry them to the new European trading posts. Anyone who has tried skinning a rabbit with a stone knife or boiling water in a clay pot will not wonder why Indians were soon eager for the steel knives and copper kettles the Europeans traded for their furs. Lacking furs and canoes, the Iroquois used their military power to become middlemen between the stolid Dutch traders at Albany and the Huron and Algonquin suppliers. If these tribes went to the French, the Iroquois would punish or destroy them.

For almost a century, war with the Iroquois was a recurrent, tragic fact of life for the struggling French settlement. The war made every settler a soldier living under the threat of death by torture or brutal captivity. One result was a legend of an embattled people, defended by heroes such as Adam Dollard des Ormeaux of the Long Sault and such heroines as Madeleine de Verchères. Only divine inspiration could have spared the few hundred colonists or the frail outpost of Montreal, established in 1642 by Paul de Chomédy, Sieur de Maisonneuve. In the legend of French Canadian survival, there was little room for sympathy with the Indians, who were caught between powerful European rivals and using their own ingenuity and courage to defend their interests. But if Canadians are truly North Americans, argues Quebec historian Gérard Bouchard, these are our ancestors as much as the Europeans.

To Champlain and his backers, New France meant more than furs or war. The fur trade was a vital commercial foundation for a higher purpose: the conversion of the Indian people. As part of the price for their furs, the Algonquin and the Huron had to bring black-robed missionaries to their homes, complete with their strange incantations and their epidemic infections. It was a terrible price for European goods. In five years, almost half the Huron had perished, and devastating sickness kept spreading.

If commerce led to conversion, Champlain saw that colonization was vital to both. European settlers would give the

Indian converts a demonstration of the Christian life while they laboured to make New France self-sufficient. The interlocking of commerce, colonization, and conversion was Champlain's plan, sustained against adversity, failures, and the first English conquest by the Kirke brothers in 1629. It was also Maisonneuve's plan when he established Montreal in defiance of the Iroquois peril.

It was the vision that Jesuit missionaries reported in the *Rélations*, the brilliant newsletters that attracted funds for their enterprise from the ladies and gentlemen of the French court. The plan sent Jesuits to Huronia in the 1630s. A generation later, the few Huron survivors of European diseases and Iroquois invasions withdrew from their devastated land. Only in 1662, when a newly powerful Louis XIV finally extended royal government to his remote and embattled subjects, was Champlain's concept altered.

In reality, the three elements of Champlain's scheme never worked together. Traders preferred to leave their customers as they found them. Missionaries were scandalized by trading morals and methods. Colonists rarely measured up as role models for the few Indian converts. As well, they were too attracted to the freedom of the fur trade, too busy defending themselves from the Iroquois, and often too untrained as farmers to be successful producers. The *habitants*, as they proudly called themselves (in distinction from the official term of *censitaire*, or "tenant"), cleared trees and laid out their characteristic strip farms running back from the riverbanks, but even the Iroquois peril could not persuade them to leave their own land and live in forts and villages. With effort and good weather, the settlers could enjoy a rude plenty. At other times, the colony was close to starvation. Always the annual trading fleet had to make room for food and livestock as well as for the cloth, hardware, and brandy the fur trade demanded.

Under royal government after 1662, Quebec's missionary impulse weakened. The autocratic Bishop François Montmorency de Laval established a stern tradition of religious authority in the little colony, but Louis XIV's officials could be certain of royal backing against any bishop's pretensions. It was far harder for them to resolve a dilemma that persisted throughout the French regime and, in some form, has remained with the leaders of French Canada ever since. Were the people of New France to be *habitants* cultivating their small colony in the valley of the St. Lawrence, or were they to be *voyageurs*, carrying the fur trade, Catholicism, and French influence throughout the continent?

The instructions of Louis XIV's minister of colonies, Jean Baptiste Colbert, were clear. His Intendant, or business manager, Jean Talon, must expand the population, improve farming, and develop industries in a compact, self-contained colony. Talon and his successors did their best to obey. Shiploads of women were brought over to marry the settlers and to balance the sexes in the male-dominated colony. Though immigration slowed to a trickle after 1700, impressive rates of natural increase sent the population of New France soaring from only three thousand at the start of royal government to sixty thousand a century later. As in the English colonies to the south, the legal and administrative structures of the old world were simplified and adapted to the new. Seigneurs served as settlement agents, and any who fancied themselves as feudal lords could swiftly be brought to earth by a blunt message from the Intendant.

The seigneuries along the St. Lawrence and its tributaries formed one version of New France. On his farm, the *habitant* could fish or hunt. The long strip of land, rolling back from the river to the forest, would be divided among his sons. Rents and taxes were low. An efficient, reasonably cheap court system allowed the *habitant* to indulge a proverbial delight in lawsuits.

Officials and clergy might seem all-powerful, but they were also paternal. The forest and the fur trade were outlets for the ambitious or the discontented. Since officers' appointments in the colonial garrison were reserved for the sons of influential colonists, there was even access to the lower rungs of the French aristocracy. By the 1750s, visitors from the Old World claimed that a new kind of French people was emerging along the banks of the St. Lawrence – sociable, self-indulgent, independent.

The pressure to expand created another version of New France. As Talon complained, his efforts to create a compact settlement were undone by the unscrupulous but plausible rogue Louis XIV had appointed governor of the colony. Sent to the New World to escape his creditors, Louis de Buade, Comte de Frontenac, saw only one way to rebuild his fortune and return in splendour to court. Whatever it might cost in renewed war or humiliating treaties, Frontenac had to reach past the Iroquois and revive the fur trade. First he built a fort at Cataraqui (now Kingston), where the St. Lawrence becomes Lake Ontario. Then he sent Robert de la Salle to build another fort at Detroit. Soon agents for the trade, missionaries, and *coureurs de bois* reached out along the Great Lakes, the Ohio and the Mississippi rivers, and north to Hudson Bay to find new Indian bands, new converts, and, above all, new sources of fur.

For governors, soldiers, and ordinary *habitants*, there was really no other source of wealth. A journey to the West, with its dangers and back-breaking labour, netted a *voyageur* enough to buy the livestock or land that might turn subsistence farming into a chance to keep a wife and family in crude comfort. A successful licence at a trading fort could give a young officer the quick fortune he wanted to support the status of minor nobility in France. Governors and even Intendants took their cut of fur-trade revenue, from selling licences to taking a share of the fur price. Nothing else was as profitable. Talon developed shipbuilding and the iron deposits at Saint-Maurice near Trois-Rivières, but never with commercial success. Only when the French king poured a fortune into fortifying Louisbourg and into wartime garrisons could corruption provide an alternative source of wealth. By then, the fate of the French regime was sealed.

In 1701, the "Great Peace," signed between the French and their Indian neighbours, symbolized the end of one phase of expansion, but it led to a much more dangerous rivalry than the Iroquois or the Dutch had represented. The English colonies, sheltered behind the Appalachians, looked as compact and settled as the seigneuries on the St. Lawrence. In fact, they were quarrelsome, divided, and, by the 1750s, ready to explode beyond their borders.

Long before, two dissident *coureurs de bois*, Pierre Radisson and Médard Chouart des Groseillers, bedevilled by Talon's restrictions on the fur trade, had managed to interest English merchants in the opportunities of Hudson Bay. In 1670, the English established the Company of Adventurers Trading into Hudson's Bay. There is now no doubt that the French were better at trading with the Indians than the English. Their goods, from Europe's leading manufacturing nation, were superior to most that the English could supply. The long Indian wars had forced the *Canadiens* to become tough, efficient wilderness warriors. What the French lacked in the developing struggle for North America was a powerful navy and the will to match the thousands of English emigrants who left annually for the Thirteen Colonies. Embattled in Europe, France was forced to treat her remote colonies as valued but sacrificial pawns.

In a game of historical might-have-been, the compact colony of New France might have escaped conquest by a sort of armed neutrality. That never seemed possible. Frontier wars, with their lightning raids, burnings, and massacres, cried out for vengeance. A legacy of fear and hatred of the Iroquois and their American backers grew up in New France, to be matched with equally horrifying memories in New England and northern New York. Even more significant was the role that the expansionist fur trade came to play in French strategic thinking.

At the French court, New France was merely a pawn in a European power game. Louis XIV's decision to occupy New Orleans and the later plan in the 1750s to build a belt of French forts along the Ohio and Mississippi rivers were part of complex schemes to help France's Spanish allies and to distract the British. They owed nothing to the commercial needs of the fur trade, for there were few pelts to be gained from the Ohio region. The French-Canadian militiamen who struggled and died in the brutally mismanaged expedition to build Fort Duquesne (at present-day Pittsburgh) were expendable pieces in a board game played far away at Versailles. When first Virginians under George Washington, and then British troops under General George Braddock, were routed from the Ohio valley, the French congratulated themselves. In fact, by provoking the stronger British, the French strategists had sealed the fate of New France.

Blockaded by the Royal Navy, preoccupied by wars with its European neighbours, France could spare only a few thousand regular troops to back its gamble in the New World. Louisbourg, the fortress built on Cape Breton Island to protect the approaches to the St. Lawrence, fell in 1758 because France had too few warships to relieve it. The French military commander in New France, the Marquis de Montcalm, detested his superior, the Canadian-born governor, Pierre de Rigaud, Marquis de Vaudreuil. Their rivalry, far more than the gross corruption of the last Intendant, François Bigot, doomed the colony. Montcalm's regulars won frequently against incredible odds, notably at the battle of Carillon or Ticonderoga in 1758. But when the British besieged Quebec in 1759, and General James Wolfe clambered up to the Plains of Abraham on September 12, Montcalm's insistence on mixing Canadian militia with his soldiers led to confusion in the French ranks, panic flight, and a sudden end to resistance. In the struggle for Quebec, French and *Canadiens* discovered how little they still had in common.

In September 1760, with Quebec in British hands and Montreal surrounded, the surviving French troops burned their standards, boarded ships, and went home. So did most of the leaders and merchants of the colony. The remaining *Canadiens*, abandoned to the mercy of their enemies, would retain an enduring suspicion of remote imperial strategies and their bloody consequences.

It had taken a century and a half to create New France, but the French were now finished with it. To the French Ministry of Marine, the colony had represented huge costs, small returns, and no advantage that fishing concessions off Newfoundland could not match. Voltaire's blunt dismissal of Canada as "several acres of snow" became the official consensus. The British seemed hardly more interested. His Majesty's new Province of Quebec would be made as hospitable to British settlers as the imposition of English law and an elected assembly reserved for Protestants could make it. Narrow boundaries for the new colony cut off the fur-trading hinterland. The Royal Proclamation of 1763 threatened *habitants* with assimilation and promised native inhabitants substantial sovereignty under the Crown, a guarantee to be recalled centuries later. Incoming British merchants would have to find other ways to become rich. The conquered *Canadiens*, the British assumed, would undoubtedly accept the blessings of the new regime and become English-speaking, if not necessarily Anglican.

Not for the last time, however, the *Canadiens* defied the inevitable. The first British governor, General James Murray, and his successor, Sir Guy Carleton, detested each other, but their aristocratic souls both rejoiced in the ordered, rural, and seemingly dutiful society that had survived the capitulation of 1760. Under its Catholic clergy and a scattering of remaining seigneurs and merchants it was, claimed Murray, "perhaps the bravest and best race upon the Globe." To both governors, it was intolerable that the handful of shifty merchants and camp followers who had accompanied the British army to Montreal and Quebec should now monopolize power simply because British law excluded Catholics. Murray's goodwill was immediately apparent. The Catholic bishop of Quebec had died on the eve of the conquest. Without a bishop, no new clergy could be ordained. With Murray's help, a successor was chosen, sent to France to be consecrated (since the Catholic church was illegal in Britain), and returned to Quebec. The British gained a staunch clerical ally.

The British had imagined that a flood of settlement would soon help anglicize Quebec. Few people came. By 1772, Sir Guy Carleton had absorbed an obvious point: "barring a catastrophe shocking to think of [Carleton probably meant smallpox], this country must, to the end of time, be peopled by the Canadian race." A more troublesome principle followed logically: they must be governed by institutions and practices familiar to them. Carleton's arguments convinced the British government. The Quebec Act of 1774 restored the kind of regime Quebec's clergy and seigneurs desired. The Church regained its legal right to tithes, and the seigneurs regained the old civil law. The earlier promise of an elected assembly vanished. If the community of English-speaking merchants at Montreal raged at this betrayal, they were adequately compensated. The huge fur-trading hinterland to the west, removed from Quebec in 1763, was restored in 1774. Indians and traders would not be disturbed by American settlers.

Carleton could not foresee that his Quebec Act would help drive the Thirteen Colonies to open revolt, but he was certainly confident that the Act would rally both the Indians and gratified *habitants* to the British side. He was disappointed. When Americans invaded Quebec after the Declaration of Independence in 1775, the clergy and seigneurs appealed almost in vain for people to rally to Carleton's aid. The Americans, as they advanced to besiege Quebec City, had a little better success in winning over the *Canadiens*. Only when starving Americans began to raid livestock and food supplies, leaving worthless paper from the Continental Congress as payment, did the *habitants* choose sides. By the spring of 1776, the Americans had been driven away.

To the south, however, the Revolution prevailed. Carleton's prediction was challenged. Quebec might not be forever *Canadien*. Ten thousand Loyalist refugees poured up the old invasion route of the Richelieu River and across the Niagara River into British territory. Beyond the seigneury of Longueuil, Loyalists and German veterans of the war were granted land.

The cataclysm of the American Revolution forced the British to reconsider the government of the scattered colonies that remained to them. Once again it was Carleton (now Lord Dorchester) who offered his ingenuity: the old province of Quebec would be split. Beyond Longueuil, Upper Canada would develop a model British society that *Canadiens* and Americans could admire and perhaps even ask to join. The eastern portion, Lower Canada, would also have an elected Assembly, an appointed upper house or council, and an executive – replicas of the British Commons, Lords, and cabinet – but the *Canadiens* would keep their language, civil law, and religious institutions. In 1791, the Constitutional Act confirmed the arrangements.

Certainly the *Canadiens* seemed to prosper. If a high birth rate is a symptom of a nation's well-being, rarely has a people been happier. The 60,000 *habitants* of 1760 were 110,000 by 1784 and 330,000 by 1812. The Colbert-Talon dream of a compact, prosperous rural society was fulfilled. The methods were primitive – farmers piled their manure on the ice to float downriver at the spring breakup – but wheat production climbed and seigneurial fortunes rose. The long war between Britain and revolutionary and Napoleonic France that began in 1793 awakened few old loyalties among Lower Canadians. Instead, wartime scarcities promoted wheat exports and a growing timber trade from the St. Lawrence. The Church opened colleges to train its clergy. Wealthier *habitants* sent their sons to train for such professions as law and medicine.

The avocation of these newly educated *Canadiens* would be politics. The aging anglophile seigneurs and local notables who had represented the *Canadiens* in the Assembly in its early years gave way to younger, more critical men. Elections gave an outlet for new grievances. Despite their dramatic population growth, the *Canadiens* felt threatened. Land that their children might someday need was being granted to Americans who had not even been Loyalists. Quebec's new Anglican bishop, Jacob Mountain, made no secret of his hope that, through its schools, a state-endowed "Royal Institution" would systematically anglicize the French.

In spite of *Canadien* predominance, visitors saw signs that Lower Canada was becoming anglicized. By 1812, most of the thirty thousand Montrealers spoke English. So did a majority in Quebec City. Whether French-speaking merchants vanished through a preference for seigneurial life, intermarriage, or because of brutal competition, the business of Lower Canada was being done in English. Except for those who purchased seigneuries as a source of income, few merchants cared about the overpopulation or shrinking harvests in rural districts. Opportunities depended on the fur trade or improving a St.

Lawrence River route to the wheat and potash trade of Upper Canada. Financing canals to get past the St. Lawrence rapids was expensive, and Montreal merchants wanted others in Britain or rural Canada to foot the bill.

Lower Canada's Assembly soon became the battleground where *Canadiens* could challenge the harsh verdict of the Conquest. A journalist, Étienne Bédard, taught young notaries, doctors, and lawyers that *Canadiens* could win their fight by using the institution the British themselves most admired: Parliament. By 1810, Bédard's determination had led him to prison. With war imminent on the American frontier, the British removed his antagonist, Sir James Craig, replacing him with a more sympathetic (and bilingual) governor, Sir George Prévost. In French Canada, Craig's name survives as a symbol of English oppression of the *Canadiens*.

The War of 1812 seldom crossed the Lower Canadian border. When it did, *Canadiens* could take pride in their patriotic role. Colonel Charles de Salaberry, a French Canadian in the British army, beat the Americans at Châteauguay in 1813, and Louis-Joseph Papineau was a militia officer. Handsome, eloquent, seemingly self-confident, Papineau was the logical choice for Speaker of the Assembly in 1815. A professed believer in British institutions, Papineau was also a proud and grasping seigneur, with good reason to preserve French Canada's most basic social institution. Above all, Papineau was a man of words, concealing a tragic streak of indecision behind billowing rhetoric.

When the War of 1812 boom subsided, much that was seriously wrong in Lower Canada surfaced – crop failures, declining yields, and infestations meant that the seigneuries could no longer support their populations. Montreal's merchants urged a reunion of the Canadas and expensive canal-building on the St. Lawrence route; Papineau and the *Canadien*-dominated

Assembly refused. In 1822, after the merchants won over Lower Canada's unelected council and executive, Papineau and his allies set out for England to defeat the reunion plan. Though the delegation succeeded, Papineau came home disillusioned by Britain and her institutions. Now every issue was reduced to an uncompromising conflict between Papineau and his *patriotes* and those he denounced as a "Château Clique" or *bureaucrates*. Leaving more moderate allies in his wake, Papineau set an increasingly radical course, halting all public works, barring funds for official salaries, and making administration of Lower Canada almost impossible.

Papineau's goals were unclear. In religion he was almost a freethinker; as a seigneur, he was highly conservative. At times he preached the merits of an American-style republic. Mostly, he denounced the control of appointments by the governor's appointed advisers. This had strong appeal for the educated professionals of the *Canadien* elite. Without government jobs, they were condemned to spend their lives as impoverished village notaries and doctors. Constitutional arguments also aroused English-speaking followers like Wolfred and Robert Nelson, ready to believe that British liberties were at stake. George-Étienne Cartier, a law student and precocious member of Montreal's French-speaking elite, was one of scores of ardent young men who took up the *patriote* cause.

In the Lower Canadian countryside, the mood was grimmer. Overpopulation had become a terrible burden. The narrow strips of land, subdivided for the sons in each generation, could be split no more. With no Intendant to restrain them, seigneurs, French and English, became oppressive landlords. Wheat fly and exhausted soil reduced yields. For the first time, a class of landless labourers emerged.

Meanwhile, a tide of immigration swept up the St. Lawrence, bearing economic refugees from Britain's acute post-war slump.

Most of these had moved on to Upper Canada or the United States; often only the poorest remained. So did cholera. The first major epidemic invaded Lower Canada in 1832. Hundreds died miserably from a plague no medical knowledge could cure. Many applauded the *patriote* orators who claimed that the British had deliberately plotted *Canadien* deaths. Suspicion and hatred were mutual. The old cordiality of a merchant class that had intermarried, learned French, and sometimes even converted to Catholicism was not inherited. British governors, assailed by hostile *patriote* politicians in the Assembly, also worried about the growth of a rancorous, bitter "English party" in Montreal. Elections frequently led to riots, bloodshed, and military intervention. Violent language from journalists like Adam Thom and military drill by young men in the Doric Legion spurred Papineau's followers to respond with fresh extremism in language and tactics.

In 1837, the clash came. Three years earlier, Papineau had listed every imaginable Lower Canadian grievance in his "Ninety-Two Resolutions" and sent the document to London. The Assembly, he promised, would let the colony stagnate until Britain acted. In 1837, Lord John Russell's Whig government sent its reply: his "Ten Resolutions" instructed the governor to reject the Assembly's demand for executive power, and ordered him to give hard-pressed officials their back pay and to govern the colony with or without an elected Assembly.

It was a bad year to provoke a political conflict. While the colony had marked time, tensions had risen. Endless rains in the summer and autumn of 1837 ruined crops. In the United States, President Andrew Jackson's crusade against the banks led to a commercial collapse that spread to Montreal. South of the city, sodden rallies of *habitants* gathered to hear Papineau, cheering his outrage but ignoring his unexpected appeals for prudence and patience. Papineau's indecision was beginning to show, just as the avalanche of anger he had helped to build was beginning to move. Wolfred Nelson, a wartime surgeon, began drilling volunteers at Saint-Dénis.

In Montreal, both *patriotes* and the English drilled. When the governor banned the Doric Legion, it reorganized under another title. Suddenly there were clashes: a violent riot threatened Papineau's house. Only the arrival of British troops saved it. Fearing arrest, Papineau fled to the countryside. The cautious, peace-seeking Lord Gosford resigned as governor; Sir John Colborne, one of the British army's ablest officers, succeeded him.

Given time and a united leadership, the *patriotes* of 1837 might have been a formidable force. At Saint-Dénis on November 23, Nelson's men defeated two hundred British regulars. Young George-Étienne Cartier shared in that victory, but Papineau had fled Saint-Dénis for Saint-Hyacinthe and then slipped across the border to Vermont. Other *patriotes*, like Louis-Hippolyte LaFontaine, hurried to Quebec City to seek peace. Colborne gave the rebels no more time to drill or debate. Beaten at Saint-Dénis, the British troops mounted a swift counterattack on the rebel centres on the Richelieu River. After the winter freeze-up, Colborne sent his men north from Montreal to crush rebels at Saint-Eustache. While his troops fought, his ill-disciplined irregulars looted the countryside, leaving *habitants'* homes blazing behind them. Colborne would be remembered in the historical mythology of French Canada as "*Vieux Brûlot*," the Old Firebrand.

Long after the futility and self-interest of Louis-Joseph Papineau and the *patriotes* had been forgiven, the bitter memory of fire and sword would remain. As in 1760, the *Canadiens* had been defeated. The bitterness of a second conquest engulfed the Lower Canadian leaders, leaving them paralysed and despairing. Would others find strength and ingenuity to survive?

ENGLISH CANADIANS | 4

nglish-speaking people in Lower and Upper Canada had a different memory of their history – sometimes several different memories. Their Canada dated from John Cabot's discovery of his "New Founde Lande" in 1497. The French were the hereditary enemy, conquered in 1759 when James Wolfe led his soldiers up the narrow, ill-guarded Anse au Foulon to occupy the Plains of Abraham.

All memories are selective. Most English Canadians forgot those New Englanders, ransomed from Indian captors, who sometimes adapted so fully to life in New France that they refused to go home. Men from Wolfe's army, most of them Scots, stayed, married, and assimilated, becoming ancestors of such French-speaking Quebec premiers as J.G. Ross and Daniel Johnson. The English also forgot one deft calculation that had helped persuade French diplomats to abandon New France. With no threat from Quebec, the French had reasoned, the American colonists would fight each other. Within fifteen years of the capitulation at Montreal, Britain and her American colonies were indeed at war.

Within a decade of the Quebec Act of 1774, the British had absorbed their worst defeat in two centuries.

The end of the American Revolutionary War in 1783 left Britain with the cold, unprofitable remnants of the continent. Perhaps something might be made of them. After all, Montreal still sat astride the only route to the heart of America. The vast interior of the continent had changed hands too often for anyone to assume that a treaty in 1783 would be the last word. Preferring profits to politics, most of the American merchants at Montreal had remained loyal. British garrisons and their Indian allies would hold the interior forts until the claims of dispossessed Loyalists were satisfied. That might be a long time.

For the moment, the top priority was to cope with the columns of refugees pouring into the province of Quebec. Tools, rations, and livestock were as necessary as land. Bewildered officials, wrestling with problems of wilderness logistics, were cursed as hard-hearted or corrupt. In the wake of the war, ten thousand Loyalists struggled to build homes and farms in the forests along the upper St. Lawrence or below the Niagara Escarpment. Iroquois of the Six Nations, forced into exile as allies of the British, located their own pockets of settlement along Lake Ontario and up the Grand River. Pennsylvania Germans, bound by language and culture as well as loyalty, drove and floated their big Conestoga wagons even further up the valleys of the Grand, the Speed, and the Eramosa rivers.

History is traditionally preoccupied with politics, ideas, and movements. But in the 1790s, and perhaps in any age, these were luxuries only a few could enjoy. For pioneers in a harsh and unfamiliar land, survival was a preoccupation, to be achieved only through relentless, back-breaking labour. The forest was the enemy. Huge first-growth trees resisted the puny axes and saws of settlers struggling to clear fields or merely to break through the overhanging gloom to the sun. The forest accentuated loneliness. Loneliness reduced pioneers to an unsmiling grimness. Women often faced life and even the terrors of childbirth without even a neighbour to help. A single careless blow with an axe could cripple a man or leave him to die in the stench and agony of gangrene. The dark side of pioneer life was only partly veiled by hard drinking or the frantic revelry of barn-raisings, "bees," and militia reviews. Methodist circuit riders, with their fervid camp meetings and personal messages of prayer and redemption, made their denomination the dominant force in frontier religion.

Yet ideals and politics mattered because they gave shape to the thousands of individual struggles for survival. Newcomers they might be, but the king's "old subjects" from below the border had strong views about the political society they wanted. When they turned from their grinding tasks, they could count on outspoken leaders to state their case. Sir John Johnson, superintendent of Indian affairs in New York, became a leading Loyalist in the Canadas. It was he who led the campaign to split the colony to help guarantee an elected Assembly for at least Upper Canadians. William Smith, the former chief justice of New York and now of Quebec, argued for a federation of all the British North American colonies, a precursor for the eventual idea of Confederation in 1867.

The British response was both conservative and generous. The Constitutional Act of 1791 created the two Canadas sought by Johnson and provided them both with a governor, an appointed executive and legislative councils, and an elected Assembly. In the dreams of Colonel John Simcoe, such institutions could turn Upper Canada into "the very image and transcript" of English society. Since taxes had provoked the American Revolution, government in the Canadas would be financed by reserving a seventh of all land for the Crown. Another seventh would finance an established Protestant clergy. Though proposals for a titled aristocracy in the Canadas were abandoned, legislative councillors were granted up to six thousand acres. Wasn't a secure landed gentry the keystone of the English constitution?

If Champlain was the founder of New France, Upper Canada was almost as much the creation of John Simcoe. A successful commander of Loyalist troops, Upper Canada's first lieutenant-governor wanted to reverse the verdict of the American Revolution. With incredible optimism, Colonel Simcoe imagined that he could make a raw, backwoods colony so attractive that Americans would repent their disloyalty and renew their allegiance. His energy matched his ambition. Survey parties vanished into the forest to lay out the gridiron of concession and side roads that still shapes rural Ontario. Soldiers and settlers drove highways of the future through swamp and bush – Yonge Street north from Lake Ontario to Lake Simcoe; Dundas Street west from Yonge Street to Hamilton and to the tiny inland settlement of London. The Kingston Road struggled eastward to the garrison town where Frontenac had once built his fort. Simcoe relocated his capital from Niagara-on-the-Lake to the junction of these roads in malarial lakeside swamps at the muddy little village of York. London, his first choice, had been vetoed as too remote. From his little bungalow, Simcoe dictated letters, dispatches, and instructions, and promoted a flood of proposals for everything from hat-making to a mining industry. His wife, Elizabeth, drew, painted, and wrote letters and diaries in which she left a sometimes sympathetic picture of Upper Canada's first developer.

To prosper, Upper Canada needed far more than the fourteen thousand people who had reached it by 1791. To be a bustling success story, the province must be a haven for all who, Simcoe boldly predicted, would soon weary of the mismanagement and corruption of the American republic. Unmoved by warnings and protests by Loyalists, Simcoe summoned any of His Majesty's late subjects to renew their allegiance in return for excellent free land. People came. Allegiance was a small matter on the frontier; land was everything. Upper Canada's lower peninsula, between Lake Erie and Lake Huron, was directly in the path of the American frontier surge. Simcoe's critics sneered at "late Loyalists," but a steady flow of ox-teams, with their over-loaded wagons, poured into the colony. By 1811, almost ninety thousand people had settled in Upper Canada; distinctions between early and late Loyalists had been worn down by the common pioneering experience.

By then, however, Simcoe had been gone for fifteen years. He was not even knighted for his services. His successors were lesser men, reluctant exiles in a colonial backwater of long winters and steaming, mosquito-ridden summers. Most of Simcoe's vision left with him, but the people still came, for by now even the colony's tiny elite had realized that their huge land grants were almost worthless without the pressure of settle-ment. A fertile tract grew in value if surrounded by prospering farms. Meanwhile, the elite planned to live respectably in town, on the salary and profits of government office.

If Upper Canada seemed a backwater to British officials, it was the front line in British-American relations. South of the Great Lakes, the British clung to their old trading posts, holding out for compensation for the Loyalists and incidentally encour-aging the Indians to resist the advance of American settlers. In 1791, a small American army was destroyed by the Indians. Even though they had warned the Americans of the danger, the British were blamed. Britain's government saw the folly of another war with the United States, especially when the French Revolution was blazing on their doorstep. In 1794, Whitehall conceded the futility of waiting for Loyalist compensation and withdrew from the frontier forts, abandoning their Indian allies to the tide of American settlement. The result, at the Battle of Fallen Timbers in 1794, was a decisive defeat of the great chief Tecumseh and his warriors.

Other factors heightened Anglo-American hostility. In the European war that dragged (with brief intervals) from 1793 to 1815, neutrals found little sympathy. Even the Swiss and the Swedes became involved. British and French alike boarded American ships to seize cargo and seamen. War profits helped the ships' owners to adjust, but Americans boiled at each insult to their young flag. Bitterness grew as one moved west, to mingle with outrage at alleged British backing of the Indians. In the 1812 elections, the western States sent angry "warhawks" to Congress, demanding that President James Madison declare war and promising swift and easy conquest of Canada. "I verily believe," boasted young Henry Clay of Kentucky, "that the militia of Kentucky are alone competent to place Montreal and Upper Canada at your feet." In June 1812, Madison delivered his message: there would be a second War of Independence.

People christened it the War of 1812 and shrouded it with myths. On paper, Clay was right. Seven and a half million Americans could overwhelm half a million British subjects, a fifth of them "late Loyalists." With only fifteen hundred British regulars to defend Upper Canada, Major-General Isaac Brock concluded that unless he won some rapid victories, he would get no help from his legislature and very little from local magistrates and militia colonels. Backed by Indian allies such as Tecumseh and his Shawnee warriors, Brock seized the initiative. A handful of regulars and Indians captured the American fort at Michilimackinac, dominating the Middle West for the rest of the war. As state militias debated whether to cross the border and generals left over from the Revolutionary War trembled for their scalps, Brock and Tecumseh captured an entire army at Detroit. At Queenston Heights, in the final battle of 1812,

Brock fell dead, but his furious redcoats and a revived Upper Canadian militia hurled the American invaders back across the Niagara River.

That one year, 1812, gave Upper Canada most of the patriotic myths it would ever own, from Brock's heroic leadership to the gallantry of the militia (which, for the most part, had waited until the regulars and the Indians determined the outcome). The war continued for two more years of hard-fought victories, painful setbacks, and murderous devastation of frontier communities. The Americans would remember the war for a series of ship-to-ship victories, ignoring the campaigns that ravaged the Upper Canadian landscape. In fact, the Americans had lost the ocean war by 1814 because of the British naval blockade, while their strength and resources grew steadily in the inland campaigns. In 1813, American control of Lake Erie allowed raiding parties to ravage Upper Canada from Sandwich to Norfolk. In 1814, American shipwrights were outbuilding the British dockyard at Kingston. Once the Americans won Lake Ontario, Upper Canada would be indefensible.

Instead, British negotiators ended the war even before its last – and almost bloodiest – battle was fought at New Orleans. The war changed no boundaries, brought no reparations, avenged no wrongs. A Canadian hope that somehow the old fur-trading hinterland might be restored was forlorn. Upper Canadians seeking compensation for burned-out farms and slaughtered livestock would get no reparations from the American perpetrators. Instead, they must look to Britain. Exhausted after a generation of war, the British would not be generous.

English Canadians absorbed proud and bitter memories. In Lower Canada, they felt a pleasing, if temporary, sense of solidarity with the French Canadians. Upper Canadians could be proud of Queenston, the murderous battles of Stoney Creek and Lundy's Lane, and the legend of Laura Secord driving her cow through the American lines to warn Lieutenant James FitzGibbon of an enemy attack. Even more significant was the role of those who had stood loyal and unafraid in the early days of disloyalty and confusion. Archdeacon John Strachan, a Scottish convert to Anglicanism, had faced American invaders with the same stubborn convictions he would expend on Methodists and unbelievers. John Beverley Robinson had shown valour in battle and unshrinking determination as prosecutor at the Ancaster assizes. Robinson's efforts sent eight late-Loyalist traitors to the gallows and confirmed him, though he was barely out of his teens, as Upper Canada's attorney general. The War of 1812 gave the colony's elite credentials of loyalism. If there was a Family Compact in Upper Canada, it was really an unspoken alliance of those who had led and organized the colony in its most threatened years. They had run great risks; they expected the rewards.

After 1815, the colony struggled to rebuild from wartime wreckage and to adapt an economy no longer fed by huge British military spending. Upper Canada's leaders cancelled Simcoe's old welcome to Americans. By insisting on war, the American warhawks helped cancel a process that would probably have led to peaceful absorption of the colony into the United States. Upper Canada would not be American, though at a cost. A flow of superbly qualified American frontiersmen now passed south of the Great Lakes, making the New York and Ohio shorelines flourish with farms, cities, and industries. Upper Canada stagnated. Certainly immigrants came to the colony after 1815, lured by promises of land and opportunity, but they came from a Britain where there were now "too many spoons for the broth." Very few had the skills or the capital to transform wilderness into crude but productive farms. In time, the "late Loyalists," with their mixed allegiance, would be submerged in a tide of English, Irish, and Scottish settlers, but Upper Canadian landowners could still grumble that abstract principles had hurt their profits. The post-war colony was full of grumblers. In part, this was because a generation of relentless labour had paid off. Pre-war settlers had won the leisure to observe the Upper Canadian scene. With a franchise broader than most Britons would enjoy until 1832, there were few barriers to political participation for prosperous farmers or tradesmen. Newspapers were few and costly, and their proprietors depended on government advertising, but they also fed an appetite for gossip and controversy. A red-wigged tempestuous newcomer, William Lyon Mackenzie, helped fill the need. An honest man with a huge bump of self-righteousness, Mackenzie travelled the backwoods and filled his *Colonial Advocate* with the grievances he uncovered, together with serialized novels, moral tracts, helpful hints, and the reports of curiosities that he loved to collect.

The grievances were many, and most grew out of jealousy of the greener fields on the American side of the lakes. Upper Canada was a backwater, short of bridges, roads, and other public works vital to a pioneer society. By American standards, officials were grossly overpaid. Land policies, which left vacant the tracts of crown and clergy land, lengthened the weary trek of farmers to markets. Corruption was an easy cry. In a province that was Methodist if it was anything, how dare Archdeacon Strachan claim to the British government that Upper Canada was Anglican? There was really no mystery: Strachan wanted the clergy reserve revenues for his own denomination. In young Egerton Ryerson, the Methodist dissenters found an eloquent and fearless champion.

The history of Upper Canada has been dominated by one-sided versions of its political struggles. Historians have been captivated by the persuasive venom of Mackenzie's editorials; they have treated the slogans of reformers as though they were factually true. Upper Canada's leaders were probably as honest and conscientious as the times allowed; their fault was a conviction that they must manage everything in the colony, including successive lieutenant-governors. Like most elites, they saw their own best interests and those of the community as much the same. They succumbed to the dangerous error of treating critics, from Robert Gourlay to Robert Baldwin, as mortal enemies.

Whatever Mackenzie might claim, the colony needed the Bank of Upper Canada; but did the bank need to be switched, by legislative chicanery, from Kingston to York? The elite also backed William Hamilton Merritt's Welland Canal with its own funds, but, when the project ran beyond their means, they had no hesitation in using Upper Canada's credit. It was a shrewd stroke to invite British investors to create the Canada Company as an agency to market the crown and clergy reserves and then, by agreement, to force the company to develop the huge Huron Tract between Guelph and Goderich. Was it wise, though, to impose Strachan's son-in-law as the company's Canadian manager?

Oligarchies are seldom self-critical. Upper Canada's leaders could sometimes seem petty and vindictive in their use of power, though they did not defy the law. When sons of York's elite threw Mackenzie's press into the harbour, a court ordered prompt and generous compensation. Mackenzie's own speeches and editorials proved to contemporaries that free speech prevailed, even to an unhealthy degree, in Upper Canada. Leading reformers like Dr. William Baldwin and his eloquent son, Robert, found the excitable editor an embarrassment, but Mackenzie's loyal following of farmers and small-town tradesmen was valuable to the loose reform coalition. Unlike Papineau's *patriotes* in Lower Canada, who commanded a one-sided majority in the Assembly, the reformers and the Tory oligarchy in Upper Canada each commanded only a knot of supporters. Other members floated with the wishes and needs of their frontier constituents, stern against corruption but eager to bargain their vote for a badly needed bridge. In any case, the Assembly could be ignored by legislative and executive councillors who believed themselves appointed for life.

That conviction was suddenly challenged. After more than half a century of Toryism, Britain's Whigs came to power in 1830. In the excited mood, would Radicals be far behind? The turmoil was exaggerated. The new men were as wealthy and almost as cautious as the old. The great Reform Bill of 1832 gave Britons a narrower franchise than Canadians had enjoyed since 1791. Whig aristocrats at the colonial office differed little from their predecessors, though they were a little more willing to listen to professed "Reformers" from the colonies and to give less credence to claims of "Family Compacts" and "Château Clique" Tories. When John Beverley Robinson grumbled that Mackenzie had received a hearing in London for his absurd charges, the indiscretion cost him his post as Attorney General. In 1836, when the Whigs chose a successor to the valiant Sir John Colborne, some Upper Canadians erected banners welcoming their new lieutenant-governor as "A Proven Reformer."

Sir Francis Bond Head certainly had radical ideas. No previous governor had worried about Upper Canada's depleting resources or about the land and hunting rights of the Indians, marginalized and neglected now that their military role had faded. Unlike Colborne, who listened to the oligarchy, Bond Head listened mainly to himself. He appointed Reformers like Baldwin to his executive and then dismissed them when they insisted on their own policies. Bond Head is remembered as a figure of fun who conducted official audiences with his short legs stuck out rigidly in front of him. He was also the would-be dictator who took the field in the 1836 Assembly elections, raised the loyalty cry, and won enough votes to drive most of the Reformers, including Mackenzie, from their seats.

Most sensible Reformers licked their wounds and bided their time. Assembly elections in Upper Canada swung regularly from Tory to Reform; settlers voted alternately for public works or political fireworks. There were also some differences in 1836. The post-1815 flood of British settlers had begun to have political weight. Some signs were ugly. Reformers complained that Tory bullies had attacked their voters at London – although that did not prevent a Reform victory. Orangemen, the Protestant extremists who had been banned in Ireland, surfaced in the eastern districts of Upper Canada to back Bond Head's loyalty call. They were dangerous allies.

William Lyon Mackenzie found defeat intolerable. In 1834, he had enjoyed a brief taste of power as the first mayor of a newly incorporated city of Toronto – the old York. A long visit to the United States convinced him that only republican institutions would give Upper Canada the cheap, honest government its yeoman-farmers needed. To Mackenzie, defeat in 1836 was not an electoral mishap but an act of tyranny enforced by Sir Francis and a corrupt oligarchy. From the analysis came the only possible remedy: revolution.

As in Lower Canada, the times encouraged revolutionary language. Angry American-born farmers in the townships north and west of Toronto heeded Andrew Jackson's populist style in Washington. As in Lower Canada, economic depression descended on Upper Canada, aggravated by Bond Head's insistence that banks and business houses keep their doors open and pay off panic-stricken creditors even if it meant ruin. It was no secret in Toronto that both Canadas faced rebellion, but Bond Head proudly sent every soldier he could find to reinforce the British garrison in Lower Canada.

When Mackenzie shared his plans for proclaiming an Upper Canadian republic, most Reformers were aghast. Robert Baldwin drew away. Others judged that Mackenzie's threat, however foolish, might frighten the governor into concessions. Dr. John Rolph, a veteran Reform politician Mackenzie had designated as president of his provisional government, sought influence with both sides. In the rural townships, simpler men believed in "Little Mac," read his hurriedly printed manifesto, and heeded his call: "Up then, brave Canadians. Get ready your rifles and make short work of it."

The work was short. On December 4, 1837, unaware that Papineau's rebellion had already collapsed, a few hundred men began to gather at Montgomery's Tavern on Yonge Street, a few miles north of Toronto. It was a demoralizing prospect, with rain and wind, and Mackenzie himself in a state of rage and indecision. In Toronto, it was no better. Old Colonel James FitzGibbon, Laura Secord's confidant of 1813, pleaded with Bond Head to abandon his complacency. News of the rebel gathering turned complacency into panic. Thanks to FitzGibbon and a tough young Tory from Hamilton, Allan MacNab, the governor's allies rallied. At dawn on December 7, untrained militia marched up Yonge Street behind bagpipes and bands to meet the frightened, ill-armed rebels. In a few minutes, the battle was over.

Mackenzie fled, sheltered by men and women who risked everything for his safety, until he reached the United States. Militia and Indians patrolled every road, checked every barn, and sent sad little groups of prisoners to face jail, trials, and transportation to Britain's penal colonies. There can seldom have been a rebellion that found fewer supporters at the time or more admirers afterwards.

The Rebellion of 1837 never had a chance of success in Upper Canada. Mackenzie had tried to reverse the election of 1836 and the rejection of the United States in 1812. The absurd little battle north of Toronto led to repression far beyond anything seen in Lower Canada in 1837–38. Two of Mackenzie's lieutenants died on the gallows; ninety-two people were sent to penal colonies.

Hundreds of prosperous but resentful settlers left for the United States. Mackenzie's biographer, William Kilbourn, argued that the rebellion cleared the air. Some of the violence and unreasoning invective went out of Upper Canadian politics. A fresh start was possible, and many old players were gone.

UNITED CANADAS | 5

The 1837 rebellions were the first formative experiences for Cartier, John A. Macdonald, and many of the politicians who launched Confederation thirty years later. In the lower provinces, Confederation with the Canadas revived old fears of the turbulence and disloyalty of 1837. In fact, the rebellions ended an era. They could assume a romantic aura because the old antagonisms died so quickly. Within a decade, Papineau and Mackenzie returned to communities where their luckless followers had been hanged. They were now political relics. Their old friends and enemies were too busy making money and finding political compromises to respond to the two old men.

In 1837 Britain had been euphoric at the accession of the young Queen Victoria. The Canadian rebellions had come as a shocking embarrassment. A shaky Whig regime sought to silence at least some critics by dispatching Lord Durham, "Radical Jack," to solve the Canadian problem. As governor-in-chief and Lord High Commissioner, Durham's power extended to all of British North America. Unfortunately, it did not reach as far as Bermuda, though it was there that, in his first act, he sent his eight leading *patriote* prisoners, liberating the rest. It was wise clemency, but Durham's English enemies crowed that he had exceeded his jurisdiction. After a bare four months, an ailing, exasperated Durham quit. Two years later, after years of chronic ill-health, he was dead.

Durham's four summer months in Canada made his reputation. A man of his firm liberal convictions needed only minutes to challenge the judgements of his military predecessors. The commercial dreams of Montreal merchants and Robert Baldwin's political frustrations made sense to Durham; the claims of French Canadians or the Upper Canadian oligarchy did not. Durham did not have to talk to people to reach conclusions obvious to any intelligent European liberal. "There can hardly be conceived a nationality more destitute of all that can invigorate and elevate a people," Durham reported of the *Canadiens*. They had no history, no literature, and, accordingly, no future. He spent only ten days in Upper Canada, one of them with Robert Baldwin, others devoted to convivial attempts to improve relations with Americans at Niagara Falls. The journey sufficed to convince Durham that there was indeed a "Family Compact" to be dispossessed.

Both judgements were highly dubious, but they lay at the heart of Durham's analysis. So did two more-solid facts. The Montrealers were right: Canada was an economic unit and the split beyond Longueuil had done great economic harm. Baldwin was right too: colonial self-government was a farce if the governor's officials and advisers could ignore the elected Assembly. Constitutional experts insisted that sovereignty could never be split. This, Durham insisted, was nonsense. There were powers vital to an imperial role – foreign affairs, for example, or control of crown lands – that Britain must continue to exercise through its governors. There were many more powers that the colonists could be left to manage.

The Canadas must be reunited, Durham insisted, both for economic reasons and to assist in the inevitable assimilation of the French. In a single Assembly, numbers would give them a small majority, but the tide of immigration promised that it would not be for long. In subjects of colonial interest, the executive council must depend on the Assembly for support. No more than in Britain should a colonial administration continue without the confidence of the elected chamber. The Canadas also needed municipal governments so that the Assembly would no longer ring with controversies better settled at the local parish pump.

In time, Durham's report would be much admired. When it first appeared, it was cordially abused. Then, as often happens, large parts were implemented, and small but significant features were ignored. The Act of Union of 1840 created the United Provinces of Canada. The large debt of Upper Canada was merged with the modest debt of Lower Canada. English would be the language of government and legislature, but even the temporary risk of an Assembly dominated by former *patriotes* was avoided. Each of the old colonies would have forty seats. Nor was Durham's notion of "responsible government" to be entertained. Governors general would choose their advisers and manage the Assembly as best they could.

Throughout 1838, rebel exiles and their warm-hearted American hosts plotted feverishly. Secret societies called Hunters, or *Chasseurs*, proliferated. The border became an armed camp; the internal conflict of 1837 became, for many Canadians, a patriotic struggle against American invasion. Hours after Durham's departure, a new *patriote* army crossed the border south of Montreal. Within a week, Colborne's men had crushed the invaders, but leniency in Lower Canada was given no second chance. Twelve *patriotes* were executed and fifty-eight Lower Canadians were sent to the Australian penal colonies.

In Upper Canada, a drawn-out border conflict and its uncompromising repression discredited Mackenzie and his Tory enemies alike. When Lord Sydenham, the veteran politician chosen to manage the awkward new Union, summoned his first Assembly at Kingston in 1841, Robert Baldwin's moderate Reformers won an easy ascendancy. In Lower Canada, the mood was utterly different. Their rebellion crushed, leading *Canadiens* gave way to despair. Yet life went on and the new game would have to be played. Durham's verdict might be appealed. The young François-Xavier Garneau had set out to defy Durham's judgement that French Canadians had no history by writing it in massive detail. Étienne Parent, editor of *Le Canadien*, argued, like Bédard before him, that the British constitution could still safeguard French-Canadian survival. Forget Durham's errors, Parent urged, go to the Assembly and fight for his idea of responsible government.

The suggestion was adopted, without much acknowledgement, by the ablest colonial politician of the 1840s. Louis-Hippolyte LaFontaine was a plump Montreal lawyer with a fancied likeness to Napoleon and a comparably authoritarian personality. He had split from Papineau in 1837, suffered a brief but beneficial martyrdom in prison, and now was prepared to teach the *Canadiens* how to survive in the new regime. The principles, most of them announced in his address to the voters of Terrebonne in 1841, were clear enough; winning support took a little longer. French Canadians must forget the divisions that had separated the anti-clerical Papineau from the Church and middle-class leaders from *habitants*. Clergy and people must form a tight alliance, of faith and nationality. Next, they must be pragmatic and progressive in order to build an alliance with the Upper Canadian Reformers. Together, they must dominate the new Assembly, and in time they would win the constitutional struggle.

The essence of Canadian political history in the 1840s is the slow completion of LaFontaine's strategy. LaFontaine's alliance with the Reformers was sealed when, defeated in Terrebonne, he accepted Baldwin's invitation to campaign for an Assembly seat in Mackenzie's old territory north of Toronto. Later, LaFontaine returned the favour for a defeated Baldwin. Together, their supporters almost dominated the Assembly.

A succession of governors did what they could. Sir Charles Metcalfe, Sydenham's successor, was in constant pain from a fatal cancer, but he did better than most. He waged the 1844 election campaign virtually as his own party leader, using arguments against patronage and its corruption that a Whiggish breed of Canadian constitutional historians later preferred to ignore. At stake in responsible government, he insisted, was the determination of Baldwin and LaFontaine to distribute offices and public works as spoils to their followers. Metcalfe was perfectly right. High-sounding arguments about British parliamentary institutions and vice-regal tyranny camouflaged the fact that colonial politicians wanted to reward followers and punish opponents in a very American fashion. LaFontaine was right, too, when he argued that it was wiser to sprinkle appointments, commissions, and salaries among the frustrated professionals of Lower Canada than to let them plot new *patriote* uprisings.

Britain did more for the Canadas than send a new constitution and a succession of able but unhealthy governors to enforce it. Durham had also underlined the desperate need for public works on the St. Lawrence rapids, so long delayed by Lower Canada's political impasse. In the 1820s, Britain had spent far more than it wanted to on fortresses and the Rideau Canal in

the event of a repetition of the War of 1812. Now, more grudgingly, it guaranteed huge loans for public works. The colonial
economy, lagging as usual behind an American recovery,
spurted forward.

Hardship in the 1830s had helped drive emigrants from
Britain; prosperity in the 1840s now attracted them to Canada.
The appeal had to be strong. Big, leaky timber ships from
Quebec crammed their "'tween-decks" with steerage passengers, doubling the owners' revenues at a high cost in human
misery. Despite the new quarantine station at Grosse Île, cholera
again came up the river. So did the old-country quarrels of
Orange and Green, of Connaught-men and Cork. Canadians
still complained that better-qualified, more prosperous immigrants usually had plans to continue to the United States. But
immigration filled the newer counties of Canada West (Upper
Canada), and the population rose at twice the rate of growth in
Canada East (Lower Canada). For the first time, many immigrants came without the means or prospect of acquiring land.
Driven out by poverty, overcrowding, and then by the terrible
potato famine of the 1840s, the Irish formed the first waves of
that huge, anonymous army of labourers who dug the canals
and would build the railways, the mines, and the cities of a
developing Canada.

Prosperity and then famine in the 1840s had a revolutionary
impact on British colonial policy. In intellectual circles, the
radical ideas of Adam Smith, Thomas Malthus, and Jeremy
Bentham had long since undermined old convictions about
the necessity of maintaining a self-sufficient empire. Surely, as the
greatest manufacturer and trader in the world, Britain should
be the greatest foe of all constraints against free trade? Buying
timber or wheat in the cheapest market, rather than from
Canada or New Brunswick, would not only benefit Britain, it
would also remove a hidden tax from the poor.

The Canadas were a good illustration of why the new free-trade ideas made sense. Huge spending on defence and the continuing cost of a garrison only aggravated the Americans and brought no return to Britain. The Rebellions of 1837 surely proved that British colonial policies had failed. Prosperity in the early 1840s showed that protection was not needed. The Irish famines were aggravated by tariff barriers to cheap food. The complex system that had protected the markets of English landowners and colonial farmers alike crumbled.

Ideas take time to ferment; nothing happens overnight. By the 1820s, Canadian timber and wheat merchants had had to compete harder in the British market, yet it was difficult for colonials to see that arrangements they took for granted would ever fundamentally change. Whig or Tory, British politics seemed so immovable. Prosperity is also an anaesthetic, and in the 1840s everything was booming. In 1841, twelve thousand tons of shipping cleared the port of Quebec; in 1846, the total reached forty thousand tons. Joseph Masson died the following May in Montreal, the wealthiest merchant in Canada and a reminder that *Canadiens* still could prosper in trade, especially with qualities of self-confidence, ingenuity, and ruthlessness that are rare in any culture. Even the Catholic Church invested in canal companies, steamships, banks, and the first little portage railways.

A visitor to Toronto in 1842 marvelled at its energy: "All is in a whirl and a fizz and one must be in fashion; everything and everybody seems to go by steam." There was money for education too. Appointed chief superintendent of schools for Upper Canada, Egerton Ryerson had moved from defending Methodist rights to building a public system of "non-discriminational schools." For the rest of his life, he would bully, prod, and inspire the cause of public schools. Strachan's dream of an Anglican monopoly of higher education crumbled as Presbyterians and

Methodists used prosperous times to launch their own colleges. In Montreal, Bishop Ignace Bourget brought back the Jesuits and revived a dream as old as Champlain: the conversion of an entire continent. French Canadians became bishops as far away as Oregon and as close as Toronto. Bourget, too, was an educator.

Disasters are rarely predicted and seldom come singly. Montreal had lavished hope and capital on its new canal system as the great route to the Atlantic, not only from Canada West but also from the central United States. Irish canallers built locks to pass the Lachine and Soulanges rapids, dredged a way across the Niagara Peninsula, and cleared a way from Montreal to Detroit. No sooner had they finished than the Americans dropped their duties and enticed traffic down the Erie Canal from Buffalo to the Hudson River. Wheat exports through Montreal dropped from 3.9 million bushels in 1847 to 2.2 million in 1848. While the Irish famine of the 1840s dumped shiploads of penniless, starving people in Canadian ports, the new British commitment to free trade wiped out Canada's only real export market. Then Americans seized the Oregon territory on the remote Pacific coast and demanded that the boundary be set at 54°40', vowing war if they did not get their way. British territory would be shut off from the Pacific.

With all this going on, it seemed almost irrelevant that Whitehall finally allowed the latest governor general, Lord Elgin, to concede the principle of responsible government to a LaFontaine-Baldwin ministry after its election success in 1848, or that he opened the ensuing legislative sessions with a speech in both English and French. By now, the Canadian Parliament had moved from Kingston to a splendid new building in Montreal – a suitable gesture to the commercial (and largely English-speaking) metropolis of the United Provinces.

In the circumstances, with Montreal merchants facing utter ruin and thousands of people unemployed at the busiest season,

LaFontaine and Baldwin showed a surprising lack of tact. The first test of their new power was a Rebellion Losses Bill for Lower Canada, designed to bury forever the bitterness of 1837. Innocents and *patriotes* alike would be recompensed for the depredations of *"Vieux Brûlot,"* Sir John Colborne, and his Montreal militiamen.

English Montrealers were furious. The bill was a provocation to cap their economic woes. On April 25, 1849, they stoned Lord Elgin as he returned from giving the bill his assent. Next, a mob pillaged and burned the new parliament buildings. Some business leaders went further. If Britain had abandoned them, why not seek annexation with the United States? Among the names on the angry manifesto were Alexander Tilloch Galt, William Molson, John Redpath, and a future prime minister, John Abbott. Louis-Joseph Papineau's name was there too. So were those of his ardent new admirers, whose ribbons and banners of revolutionary red gave them the name of *rouges.*

Even as crowds raged through Montreal, the annexationists had their answer. In 1849 there were huge finds of gold in California, fuelling a continental economic boom that would last, with sharp breaks, into the early 1870s. Despite its deepening conflict over states' rights and slavery, the United States surged with prosperity. When Canadian merchants stopped complaining long enough to check their ledgers, they found that their British orders had not dried up after all, and Americans were becoming buyers of Canadian wheat and timber as well as fish from the lower colonies. In 1854, Lord Elgin went to Washington to resolve disputes about trade and fisheries. He returned with a ten-year Reciprocity Treaty that virtually wiped out the boundary as a factor in the trade of natural products. That August, the U.S. Congress ratified the arrangement. American critics complained that Elgin's proposals "floated through on champagne." Southern slaveholders voted for the treaty only after Elgin promised that it would keep the colonies British. They wanted no more "free soil" states.

Their radicalism long since exhausted, LaFontaine and Baldwin soon retired. Their work seemed complete. Canada had a framework of government, education, and municipalities. George-Étienne Cartier had ordered work on a modernized civil code for Canada East that would see the gentle extinction of seigneurialism. In ten years, the *Canadiens* had taken a constitution designed to destroy them and made it work for them. Indeed, they now rather liked the Act of Union. If it had been unfair in 1840 to give each province equal representation, it had gradually become fair now that Canada East had only 1,111,566 people to Canada West's 1,396,091.

The old issues were gone and so were the old alliances. Of course, some people were always exasperated by compromises. Youthful *rouges* from the old *patriote* strongholds of the Richelieu valley stirred with nationalist passion and a nervous anti-clericalism. It seemed impossible that they could ever make common cause with the austere Protestant farmers in the "great western peninsula" of Canada West, with their anger at privilege, patronage, and public spending. "Clear Grits," they called themselves, "pure sand and not a particle of dirt." In the 1850s, though, a big, craggy-faced Scot named George Brown, who had created the Toronto *Globe* and who never questioned his own wisdom, took the Grits in hand. He purged them of Americanism and indiscipline. Above all, Brown reminded them, Protestant English Canadians must show as much solidarity as the Catholic French, or their own religion and rights might be forfeit.

Those who held power had outgrown such preoccupations. LaFontaine's men, re-mustered by Cartier, now called themselves *bleus*, to contrast with *rouges*. They were, appropriately, cool realists from a province that had learned pragmatism. There were Baldwinites, too, like the cunning Francis Hincks, but more weight lay with younger Tories, heirs of the Family Compact and Metcalfe's 1844 campaign. Their leaders were old Sir Allan MacNab from Hamilton, Bond Head's adviser and champion in 1837, and a gawky young lawyer from Kingston, John A. Macdonald. Both men were also pragmatists. "Railways are my politics now," MacNab blandly confessed. The title of their party, the Liberal-Conservatives, welcomed anyone who wanted a share in power.

MacNab's politics were timely. By the 1850s, the railway boom had crossed the Atlantic. Mayors, bankers, and nimble speculators pestered the legislature for charters, planned routes, and interviewed contractors. Francis Hincks went to London to negotiate a line to Halifax with representatives from the lower provinces. Angry Maritimers felt cheated when the Canadians pulled out. Torontonians had even better reason to cry foul when the same Francis Hincks was caught with their mayor plotting an ingenious stock swindle at the cost of their own Northern Railway. Hincks dropped out of sight. Railway promotion was irresistibly corrupting.

In 1850, Canada had about 55 miles (88.5 km) of track. Four years later, Sir Allan MacNab's Great Western Railway covered 254 miles (408.6 km) from Niagara to Windsor. Hinck's London visit had not been wasted. The great British contracting firm of Peto, Brassey, Jackson & Betts persuaded itself that a vast trunk railway from Portland, Maine, passing through Canada to the American Middle West, would become enormously profitable. No one seems to have warned them about rivers, labour costs, politicians, or the effect of Canadian winters on track, locomotives, and rolling stock. By 1861, the line was complete to Sarnia; however, the company's largely British shareholders had to recognize that the Grand Trunk was not only effectively bankrupt, but that the system would never pay a penny unless even more money was poured into it. To demonstrate their imperial vision,

Grand Trunk interests bought control of the Hudson's Bay Company and fantasized about the profits to be made from a real trunk railway across the continent. Meanwhile the company had to find a scheme to keep conductors from "deadheading" passengers for free trips, determine the cheapest way to get tracks standardized to the North American gauge, and learn how to adapt British railway technology to Canada's winters.

Booms end and love affairs cool. By the late 1850s, both fates befell railways in Canada. Politicians who had shared in the "great barbecue" were suddenly suspect. LaFontaine and Baldwin had established a pattern of double-headed ministries as a makeshift for their un-United Province. George-Étienne Cartier and John A. Macdonald emerged as their heirs. Cartier saw no crime in being simultaneously Attorney General and the well-paid lawyer for the Grand Trunk Railway. Indignation over railway corruption united George Brown and the party he preferred to call "Reformers" with Antoine-Aimé Dorion's *rouges*. An Assembly with a large number of "shaky fellows," "loose fish," and "waiters-on-providence" (as Macdonald scornfully called independents) meant that no unpopular government was safe for long.

After Montreal's violent behaviour in 1849, the province's capital alternated (on a costly three-year cycle) between Quebec and Toronto. A firm choice of a capital had to be made. Tactfully, the choice was left to Queen Victoria, guided by pleasant little watercolours done by officers of the Royal Engineers. Photography might have been more honest. The queen chose Bytown, a small, ugly lumber town on the Ottawa River. Not even monarchists accepted the choice, and the Cartier-Macdonald government fell; Brown and Dorion had a chance to govern. Two days later, when the Assembly members had recovered their composure, the *rouge*-Reform alliance was defeated and Cartier and Macdonald resumed power. This "double shuffle" left Brown fuming on the sidelines.

The Upper Canadian Reformers had issues the *rouges* could not share. Late in 1852, after Upper Canadians had drifted home from the long legislative session at Quebec City, the French members voted to allow Catholic public schools in an overwhelmingly Protestant Canada West. Brown and his followers were outraged at such sectarian meddling; they held firmly to the doctrine that separated church and state. With Brown's inspiration, still more grievances were developed against the Lower Canadians. By the 1850s, Canada West's share of the population had become a large and growing majority. The equality of representation imposed by the Act of Union in 1840 had become anathema in Canada West. Brown demanded representation by population. His supporters shortened the slogan to "Rep by Pop," and exploited an easily understood injustice. By the 1860s, "Rep by Pop" had taken hold as a popular cause in Canada West, and support for Macdonald's Liberal-Conservatives diminished at each election. The slogan pitted English against French and, since religious prejudices outweighed race, Protestant against Catholic.

Orange riots in the towns of Canada West were matched by Catholic violence when two apostate priests, Alessandro Gavazzi and Charles Chiniquy, insisted on evangelizing in Montreal and Quebec for Protestantism. With no efficient police forces to control mobs and the British garrison reduced by the need to send troops to the Crimea and India, the province reluctantly organized a five-thousand-man "volunteer militia." The forebear of Canada's armed forces found its primary role as a riot police.

The thought of sectarian conflict might have been farther from people's minds if the example of violence had not been so near at hand. Canadians formed the largest group of immigrants to the United States; hundreds of thousands of *Canadiens* trekked to the New England cotton mills, easing the poverty and overpopulation of Canada East, while farmers and labourers in Canada West ignored the border when seeking work. All kept their relatives aware of American events. Meanwhile, the American slavery issue was brought to Canada West by hundreds of black fugitives, helped into British territory by the men and women of the Underground Railroad. Blacks in Canada experienced plenty of racial discrimination, but their presence was a reminder of the "irrepressible conflict" tearing the United States apart. When it came, in April 1861, the American Civil War divided Canadians as well. Both sides also recognized that the American crisis could easily develop into a threat to Canada.

To most Canadians, defence and foreign policy were British responsibilities. Even Canada's tiny volunteer militia had been left to languish after a few years of enthusiasm. Suddenly, war was imminent. President Lincoln's secretary of state, W.H. Seward, publicly claimed that war with Britain might rally the divided states. Others proposed that annexing Canada could compensate for the departed Confederacy. When an American warship removed Confederate delegates from a British mail steamer, Britain had a solid reason to go to war. In an instant, the British forgot their colonial indifference. Ignoring the cost, thousands of British troops were dispatched to Canada to forestall an American invasion.

The troops were still there in 1862 when the legislature rejected a modest defence program largely as a pretext to defeat the corrupt, tired Cartier-Macdonald government. The beneficiary was John Sandfield Macdonald, a Catholic reformer from Cornwall who disliked Brown. With his partner, Louis Sicotte, a disaffected *bleu*, Sandfield Macdonald believed that "double majorities" of French and English members worked perfectly well. In Britain, the defeat of the Militia Bill produced outrage. The patriotic mood of 1861 that accepted war for Canada if necessary curdled into fury at the foolish and ungrateful colonials. Moreover, as the huge military potential of the United States was mobilized for the Civil War, British strategists came to the cold realization that they could never repeat the victories of the War of 1812. In 1864, a trusted staff officer confirmed that, without a massive effort no British government could afford, the Canadas were indefensible.

That was a secret no colonist was allowed to know, but it lent urgency to the British determination that something must be done about the North American colonies. It was a determination shared by a number of influential private investors in the Grand Trunk Railway. In Canada, too, there was a growing sense that a more profound constitutional change was necessary. Sandfield Macdonald and his closest allies, Luther Holton and the *rouge* A.A. Dorion, had no real policies beyond cost-cutting. Plans for an Intercolonial Railway – a year-round connection to the lower provinces and the ocean – were on hold. So was expansion westward to the Red River colony and the Northwest. In 1863, the American Civil War reached its climax. After Gettysburg, the North could be certain of victory, and no one knew what dangers that might bring to Canada.

By 1864, everything seemed necessary and nothing seemed possible. The two Canadas were trapped in their own histories and by their own geographies. On March 21, its support flaking away, Sandfield Macdonald's government resigned. There had been deadlock; now there was nothing.

6 | LOWER PROVINCES

Beyond the mouth of the St. Lawrence lay four proudly self-reliant British colonies. Native people had lived in the region at least six thousand years before Leif Ericsson's followers attempted a short-lived settlement at L'Anse aux Meadows in Newfoundland. Whether or not John Cabot's *Matthew* entered Bonavista harbour in 1497, his crew was certainly not the first to see Newfoundland. Basque, Portuguese, French, and English fishermen had gone ashore to dry their catch on long racks, or "flakes." The next stage was obvious: developing colonies of fishermen on this distant shore would give them a six-week head start before rival fleets could arrive from Europe. Early attempts at settlement convinced the English that Newfoundland, with its harsh climate and thin soil, could never support serious agriculture. People came anyway, ignoring laws and periodic attempts at deportation, somehow surviving the hardships. Mass starvation remained a hazard of Newfoundland life as late as the 1820s. The jutting peninsula further south initially seemed to be almost as inhospitable.

In later years, on the rare occasions when Maritimers thought about what they insisted on calling "Upper Canada," they frequently deplored the incessant squabbles of French and English, Catholic and Protestant. Yet their own region had the same troublesome diversity, and the same propensity to quarrel with neighbours and subjugate them if they could. Indeed, this existed within each colony. But there was a distinction few people in either region fully appreciated. The Canadians were forced together in their lives and their quarrels by the long, undivided avenue of the St. Lawrence and the Great Lakes. Each of the lower colonies developed as a ring of shoreline settlements. People depended on themselves and their chosen neighbours. If they sought space, they could look out to sea. In all but Prince Edward Island, most of the interior was a rocky, inhospitable wilderness. Very few river valleys – the Saint John, the Miramichi, the St. Croix – beckoned farmers and timber merchants inland. Between the shore and the forest, the more favoured regions offered a chance to farm. Towns and cities developed around harbours. There was timber for ships and housing and export, but for generations, the only real wealth of the region came from the sea.

Acadians were mostly the heirs of the French who had stayed behind when Champlain chose to move from Port Royal to the St. Lawrence. Tossed, for a few turbulent years, between French adventurers and New England pirates, the Acadians were then left to themselves for a century. They learned to dike the rich bottomland of the Minas Basin against the Fundy tides. In 1713, when the Treaty of Utrecht transferred Acadia to the British, perhaps sixteen hundred Acadians were included. It seemed to make no difference to them.

Unhappily for the Acadians, war outpaced fishing and subsistence farming as an industry for the region. The French settlers and the friendly Mi'kmaq and Abenaki Indians had provided a passive flank defence for New France. After 1720, they were supplemented at the far corner of Île Royale by the huge new French fortress of Louisbourg. For all its strength, a British naval squadron and New England militia took the fortress in 1745, only to see it returned to the French by English diplomats. As the French hurried to repair the damage, the British countered by developing the huge natural harbour of Halifax. With its forts, its dockyard, and its garrison mentality, Halifax became a city that subsisted on government and thrived on war. Having ignored the Acadians, both sides now demanded their loyalty. Old loyalties favoured the French, but neither Quebec nor Louisbourg sent protection. Instead, backed by the harsh rules of war, British troops rounded up thousands of Acadians in 1755 and sent them south to be scattered among the Thirteen Colonies. In 1758, with Louisbourg taken again, more Acadians were expelled.

The dispersal was neither complete nor permanent. Many Acadians fled into the woods; others returned when the war was over, to find their farms sold to American speculators. The returning Acadians moved on to Île Saint-Jean and Île Royale – renamed respectively by their English conquerors Prince Edward Island and Cape Breton Island. Others went to the Saint John River valley and later to the North Shore. The French government, which prudently limited its North American commitments to fishing rights on Newfoundland's French Shore, sent Acadians to help populate the tiny islands of St. Pierre and Miquelon, all that remained of Champlain's great colonizing venture.

Like the Acadians, the American settlers who took their place and who spread themselves along the southern and western shores of Nova Scotia largely ignored the self-important little government of merchants and officials at Halifax. They sent home grim corrections to the glowing propaganda that had enticed them to "Nova Scarcity," but, while New Englanders' minds turned to revolution, Nova Scotia's Yankees turned their few leisure thoughts and moments to the "New Light" movement, a passionate religious revival. With a British fleet and garrison at Halifax, the few sparks of revolt in the 1770s were swiftly extinguished. Alarming though they seemed to Halifax Anglicans, the missionaries of the "New Awakening" sought revolutions in morals, not governments. Merchants in Halifax and other ports made too much money from the war to feel rebellious.

The Revolution came to Nova Scotia anyway. Loyalists first arrived in shiploads from Boston in 1776. Tens of thousands more came after the British had abandoned New York in 1783. It was a flood of bitter, defeated exiles, who had suffered much and lost everything for the Crown. The thirty thousand who came to Nova Scotia were not like the toughened farmers who went to Upper Canada. Thousands of once-wealthy Loyalists landed at Shelburne, where a large townsite with specially segregated districts for servants and for blacks had been laid out to welcome them. Promptly, they set to work planning a city hall, street names, and where to house the little fire engine donated by George III. Unfortunately, no labourers appeared to build their houses and not even the toughest frontiersmen could have tilled the rocks and swamps beyond the town. Poorer and wiser, most Loyalists moved on.

At Halifax, Governor John Parr and his council lost patience with "New York office-grabbers." The answer, as in the Canadas but for different reasons, was separation. In 1784 New Brunswick and, for good measure, Cape Breton, became separate colonies. The leading Loyalists were delighted. In New Brunswick, they would build a society that would become "the most gentleman-like on earth." Whole regiments, under their officers, would settle on grants up the Saint John River, with colonels and captains receiving much larger grants to support their social status. Fredericton, safe from American attack up the river, would be a little gem of a capital. In a verdant paradise, Tory values would thrive.

Reality was different. The first fleet reached Saint John on May 18, 1783, to find bare rocks, swamps, and an endless vista of burned-over forest. As the ships departed, one woman felt such a terrible loneliness that "although I had not shed a tear through all the war, I sat down in the damp moss with my baby and cried aloud." A second fleet, with thirty-five hundred people, arrived at the end of 1785 with no time to do more than pitch tents or erect crude huts before winter descended. Brave men simply lay down on the frozen earth and died.

Many Loyalists left. Others accepted the ruin of their dreams and made the best of it. When the huge trees of the Saint John River valley were cleared, the soil was good enough for farming, and the timber slowly formed the basis of a major industry. Saint John grew slowly as a commercial centre, gradually justifying the premature charter that made it the first city in British North America. Behind the genteel Loyalist myth was a hard-grubbing, impoverished existence, mocking the memories of cultivated life in New York or Boston. More than a few Loyalists took their chances and slipped back to the United States, making links that others would later reinforce.

New Brunswick was a victim of émigré illusions. Cape Breton was the little colony almost everyone but its Highland settlers forgot. Both were spared the casual disaster inflicted on Prince Edward Island. In a display of capitalist greed blatant even for the time, English speculators fastened on the island as soon as it was transferred from France in 1763. Sixty-seven "proprietors" drew lots for sixty-seven equal townships of twenty thousand acres, on which they promised to pay quit-rents, develop the fishery, and establish a hundred Protestant settlers within the decade. Only one of them, Samuel Holland, kept his promise. Two others made a feeble attempt. The rest simply waited for squatters to occupy the land and then sent agents to collect the rent. As a result, what was potentially the richest Maritime colony never grew up. By dint of keeping the ear of the British government in London, the proprietors could milk the settlers and do nothing in return. Settlers had no incentive to improve the land or even their own homes. They were even reluctant to build schools or churches. Every political issue seemed to focus on the distant "grantees" and on the officials who always enforced the proprietors' rights and condoned their broken promises.

Loyalist leaders in the Atlantic colonies had concocted a grandiose economic role for their new home. The rich business of supplying food to Britain's slave islands in the Caribbean would be barred to the rebel Americans and switched to the loyal provinces. As rebel Americans looked on, rich cargoes of food and timber would travel south in Nova Scotia and New Brunswick ships. West Indies rum and sugar would move east across the Atlantic. It was absurd. Only because of the squatter-farmers of Prince Edward Island could the Maritimes feed themselves, much less the West Indies. In any case, Britain was determined to make friends, not enemies, of the king's late subjects, the Americans.

The salvation of the Atlantic regions came with war. The struggle with Revolutionary France that began in 1793 and ended with Napoleon's final defeat in 1815 transformed the economy of each of the lower provinces. The naval weakness of Revolutionary France guaranteed near immunity to the ships and ports of the colonies, but wartime fleets and garrisons meant customers who paid in gold. French victories in Europe, and French alliances which closed European ports to British trade, led to a search for substitution. When Baltic ports would no longer supply the Royal Navy's timber and spars, the forests of North America provided admittedly inferior substitutes. Merchants shifted their operations to Saint John and the mouth of the Miramichi. In Newfoundland, peacetime arguments against allowing local settlement and fishing collapsed. In 1809, the huge, unexplored mass of Labrador had been transferred to Newfoundland as a recognition that the island colony now mattered. By war's end, St. John's had become the capital of the island's fishing industry, and in 1817 the first resident governor arrived.

The war was a spur to shipbuilding in every major port of the region. Even minor harbours set up stocks to build schooners for the rich wartime cargoes. There was another more risky but vastly more profitable trade in "privateering," a form of licensed piracy on enemy merchant ships. For many Halifax merchants, including young Samuel Cunard, privateering became the foundation of huge shipping fortunes.

The War of 1812 was a bonanza on top of good fortune. While Upper Canada fought for its existence, New Brunswickers lived in peace with their American neighbours. Furious speeches about seamen's rights and taming British pride had largely been Yankee bluster. Humiliation, felt the New Englanders, was a small price to pay for the huge profits they could draw from wartime trade. By declaring war, President Madison had destroyed the most lucrative mercantile era the northeastern states could remember. They might cheer the victories of the new American frigates, but they would not fight the war. British colonists had no such inhibitions. Battalions from Newfoundland and New Brunswick fought in the defence of Upper Canada. Privateers found new and richer prey. In the final months of the war, British troops brushed aside feeble resistance to occupy much of Maine. Intercepted American customs revenue helped endow Halifax's Dalhousie University.

Whatever many a Maritimer might secretly wish, war could not last forever! Peace brought economic collapse. In Halifax and Saint John, firms went bankrupt by the hundred. The shacks and shanties of St. John's vanished in a huge fire in 1816, and during the following winter, ships brought pathetic appeals for food to fend off imminent starvation. Methodist missionaries, newly arrived in Newfoundland, tactlessly chose the moment to blame Catholics for the region's terrible predicament. Religious riots aggravated the misery.

Yet the prosperous years had left their mark. Halifax's Province House stood as the finest public building in British North America, and an Education Act in 1811 had pioneered secondary education in Nova Scotia. Cheap labour by French and American prisoners had built streets and fine houses. Even Prince Edward Island had found the first few leaders to resist the grantees. A Scottish philanthropist, Lord Selkirk, had given the island an influential voice in London as well as a few hundred Highland settlers. Shipping and the timber trade might be sluggish in the wake of the war, but access to a protected British market lasted for thirty more years. Then, as in the Canadas, American markets would be sought.

In the language of development, the war years had given the lower provinces as good a chance for economic takeoff as they would ever have. Memories of a golden age of Maritime prosperity belonged to only a few. The lives of Maritime farmers, seamen, loggers, and fishermen were brutally hard, dangerous, and financially precarious. Shipping records show a terrible toll of lives in vessels that were helpless in a winter storm on a windward shore. Lighthouses were rare and life-saving nonexistent. Romantic images of lumber camps and the spring log drives overlook the reality of bad food, dangerous work, and a record of disease, crippling injury, and early death. In the colonial assemblies, employers were in control, whether they spoke as Tories or Reformers. The first unions in British North America appeared among Halifax and Saint John longshoremen during the War of 1812. Afterwards, the appearance at regular intervals of laws banning them suggest that at least feeble workers' organizations persisted.

By the 1850s, workers in Saint John had enough confidence to announce their wage rates in newspaper advertisements, and civic officials welcomed union floats and marchers in the city's periodic processions. The reason was simple. The flood of immigration largely bypassed the Atlantic colonies, adding only a healthy quota of Irish to the region's population. Workers were scarce enough to command a price, and merchants and mill owners were prosperous enough to pay it.

Workers with bargaining power because of skills or local scarcity were the exception. Coastal fishermen, particularly in Newfoundland, had no such advantages. Most of them were hopelessly in debt to fish merchants, who supplied their needs and kept them dependent. The transfer of the merchants from Bristol to Newfoundland brought few benefits, beyond providing St. John's with a small middle class and the beginnings of a cultural and social life that the people of the bays and outports would rarely glimpse. A pattern of debt and deference developed in Newfoundland, with even more serious social consequences than the antagonism of proprietors and tenants in Prince Edward Island.

All of the colonies had assemblies, even Cape Breton until it returned to Nova Scotia in 1820. Everywhere, cosy local oligarchies monopolized power, resembling Upper Canada's Family Compact in all but its energy and creativity. Political opposition was much slower to develop, perhaps because of the tradition of expecting little from government. Farmers, the obvious critics of urban elites, remained few and scattered.

Assemblies were like unambitious town councils, willing to share out modest public works and then adjourn. Would-be reformers seemed easy to isolate as "troublemakers." In Newfoundland, a short-lived experiment in parties degenerated into such a bitter Catholic-Protestant conflict that, by common consent in the 1840s, the Assembly was suspended for six years. When it revived, the old divisions remained, but Catholics proclaimed themselves Liberals and Reformers, while the Protestant communities along the north coast described themselves as Conservatives. In New Brunswick, there were no real parties at all until the 1850s, when the issue of prohibiting liquor finally split the colony. Prohibitionists, or "smashers," rallied behind a young Saint John druggist named Samuel Leonard Tilley. His opponents, the "rummies," preferred to consider themselves Conservatives.

Nova Scotians could be disdainful of such crude and primitive politics. Largest and wealthiest of the colonies, Nova Scotia's economy diversified from fishing, farming, and shipbuilding to mining and a little manufacturing. The province slowly outgrew its self-perpetuating merchant elite and perhaps even its parade of stuffy soldier-governors. Thomas McCulloch's Pictou Academy gave early notice that brains and ability could be found outside Halifax. In 1835, a young Haligonian journalist, Joseph Howe, made himself a hero of the hinterland, first by denouncing the Halifax oligarchy, and then by winning acquittal when he was tried for libel.

Like Mackenzie in Upper Canada, Howe was the angry spokesman for Nova Scotia reform, but he was no rebel. His pride combined with an almost mystical faith in Britain and her constitution. Howe denounced the 1837 risings not only for delaying Nova Scotia's constitutional progress but for their disloyalty. He would carry vestiges of a mistrust of the Canadas for a very long time. Through the 1840s, Nova Scotia Reformers articulated and then urged Lord Durham's idea of responsible government. In 1846, new instructions to the governor, Sir John Harvey, made the change. It was done, boasted Howe, "without the shedding of a drop of blood . . . the breaking of a pane of glass." On February 2, 1848, James Uniacke, Howe, and the Reformers took power. Cautiously, and in their own time, the other lower provinces followed suit. In New Brunswick, local politicians themselves delayed party government until 1856. Even then, they were moved more by embarrassment at being last than by real party differences.

Constitutional change came slowly because societies in the lower provinces were smaller and less deeply divided by intractable issues. Ambitious men like Howe combined immense pride and devotion to their communities with an acute yearning for new worlds to conquer. "Boys, brag of your country," he told Nova Scotians. "When I'm abroad, I brag of everything that Nova Scotia is, has or can produce; and when they beat me at everything else, I turn around on them and say: 'How high does your tide rise?'" Yet Howe *wanted* to be abroad, and he pestered the British shamelessly for appointments. Howe promoted railways and promised listeners that in their lifetime they would hear train whistles in the distant Rocky Mountains. Like growing numbers of Canadians, some Maritimers had a vision that reached across British North America. Others, and Howe was among these too, dreamed of an imperial federation in which Nova Scotia might someday be an equal partner with England and Scotland.

Behind the dreams came nagging practical worries. Free trade had frightened the Maritimes as badly as the Canadas, and the ten-year Reciprocity Agreement with the United States, signed in 1854, was vital for the region's fish and timber trade. If the American market should vanish, could the Upper Canadians ever provide a substitute? There was an urgent need for a connecting railway through British territory. It was easy to blame Hincks and the Canadians for the earlier failure, but the real problem remained the route through New Brunswick. Military considerations insisted that it follow the line of meagre little Acadian settlements along the north shore; New Brunswick politicians insisted that it come down the Maine border, along the Saint John River valley, to Fredericton and Saint John, where most of their voters lived. The province had no middle route.

By the 1860s, the maritime colonies faced tough choices. It was less conservatism than a sense of dangerous, uncontrollable choices that hung over the Confederation debate in the Maritimes.

7 | THE GREAT NORTHWEST

People immigrating to Canada have had an awkward
tendency to assume that nothing much worthwhile
has happened before their arrival. Champlain pre-
sumed that Indians would be honoured to transform themselves into good Catholics and subjects of his king. Loyalists,
in both Nova Scotia and Quebec, insisted that these colonies
should be readjusted to meet their desires. The British immigrants who poured into Canada after 1815 felt obliged to
correct the obvious "Americanism" of Upper Canadians. Later
waves of immigration have felt equal freedom to make over
the country in their own image and to denounce opposition as
intolerant and old-fashioned.

The Canadian Northwest has been a particular victim of such
assumptions. The amiable Canadian assumption that the West is
somehow "new" and the North is newer still ignores the fact that
these regions have probably known human habitation longer
than any other part of the continent. The two hundred thousand
Indians who met the Europeans in the 1600s were heirs to millennia of North American experience that probably began in the

far Northwest. The ways of the Indian (and the amazing Inuit north of the subarctic treeline) were very old indeed.

The long native heritage was at least as valuable to the early European invaders as any technology they brought from Europe. The light birchbark canoes of the Algonquin covered distances at a speed that astonished the first explorers, and their snow-shoes made travel possible in the winter. The concoction of buffalo meat, fat, berries, and accidental hair the Indians called pemmican might seem nauseous to Europeans, but it was the only food nourishing and light enough to carry travellers across the Great Plains. Native people, from the tough, adaptable Naskapi to the sophisticated Haida of the Queen Charlottes, were the real ancestors of settlement in the new continent. Only their lack of formal records and writing barred them, by pure convention, from having a "history."

By 1861, the Indians who remained in the sixth of Canada covered by the United Provinces and the Atlantic colonies had been bullied and enticed into the life pattern devised by Sir William Johnson, the first British superintendent of Indians. Johnson devised the treaties of surrender and the land reserves that shaped Indian policy in both Canada and the United States for two centuries. As a means of easing consciences and remov-ing Indians, treaties and reserves were a success; as a basis for equality between Europeans and native people or as fair com-pensation, Johnson's system was a failure. Unfortunately, no one then or later offered acceptable alternatives.

Beyond the limits of the settled colonies, there was no Indian policy at all and no need for it. In five-sixths of British North America, whites and native people lived in what, theoretically, was a simple market relationship of willing sellers and willing buyers. Europeans had manufactured goods; Indians had furs. Simplicity was deceptive. Both sides brought bitter national, commercial, and private rivalries to the transactions. As the

Iroquois had shown, there was nothing primitive in the Indians' understanding of competition, middlemen, or the benefits of playing one tribe of white men against another. From the European side, too, there was nothing simple about a trade that depended on the vagaries of fashion, conducted a thousand or more miles from the nearest seaport among complex and therefore unpredictable people.

Whatever criticisms might be made of the beaver's habits and intellect, there were excellent reasons for adopting the hard-working rodent as a Canadian symbol. Instinct and common sense would have pulled traders and explorers southward in America; the beaver pulled them north. The best pelts came from the colder regions. Diplomacy, not furs, pushed the French into their southward venture into the Ohio valley in the 1740s. So far as commerce, not aggrandizement, was their goal, traders had every reason to stay north of the Great Lakes and well above the invisible line that a later age would identify as the forty-ninth parallel. If the British wanted to share the continent with an expansive United States, the beaver's natural preferences kept Canadians away from the American juggernaut.

That was why the trading rivalry that mattered most in North America was not between French, Dutch, and English traders. In the 1660s, Pierre Radisson and the Sieur de Groseillers showed the English where real profits could be made, and the "Governor and Company of Adventurers of England Trading into Hudson's Bay" acted. There was literally almost nothing on the European maps to explain what Charles II meant by "Rupert's Land" in the Hudson's Bay Company charter of 1670. When clerks wrote about lands draining into Hudson and James bays, they were describing the vastest empire any private corporation ever controlled.

English posts, perched at the mouths of the Moose, the Albany, the Churchill, and the other rivers draining into the bay, transformed the fur trade. English trade goods were by no means superior to most that the French could offer, and their methods were cautious to the point of timidity. The Indians had to make their own toilsome way across the barren "starving country," but the Company's ships could come direct from England, cutting off a thousand miles of portages and transshipments, and getting closer to the best furs than any Montreal-based French trader.

The French had to fight back. In brilliant campaigns, three of them led by a Canadian-born sailor, Pierre le Moyne d'Iberville, the Hudson's Bay Company posts were captured and destroyed. By 1713 only one remained. Then, for reasons of European diplomacy, they were restored. In the years of quasi-peace, the French tried other tactics, planting their own posts upriver from the English, proclaiming alliances and issuing licences to men such as La Vérendrye and his sons, who would probe as far as Lake Winnipeg in search of new business. The tactics worked, though the Indians were shrewd enough to share part of their trade with the English. The Crees, new middlemen in the northern trade, understood even better than the Iroquois the benefits of competition.

After 1760, France was gone, but her complex, aggressive trading system of forts, depots, and highly organized canoe brigades was inherited by the Scottish and New England merchants who followed the British armies into Montreal. The *bourgeois*, or boss, might now speak another language, but *voyageurs* still gathered in the spring to make their marks on the careful, notarized contracts and then to set off in their heavily laden *canots de maître*. They were small, tough men who could paddle twenty hours a day, measuring distances by the time it took to smoke a pipe of tobacco. At Grand Portage they met the smaller canoes of the wintering partners, as far away again from the distant posts. As they transferred their loads and dickered over the trade goods that custom allowed each *voyageur*, the "pork-eaters" from Montreal wondered whether the freedom and adventures of their western counterparts outweighed the hardships and long winters. The men of the upper country, the *pays d'en haut*, were different. Many took Indian wives, vital intermediaries in the trade, cementing in fact and custom the trading alliances of white and native. In time, their wives would be mothers of a new mixed-blood people. Their sons and daughters would grow up divided between Indian ways and the Scots-Presbyterian or *Canadien*-Catholic heritage of a trader or *voyageur* father. The French-speaking would be Métis; the English-speaking "country born," or "half-breeds."

Nothing in 1760 had ended the rivalry of the Hudson's Bay Company and the "peddlers from Quebec." Indeed, the "peddlers" themselves were in ruinous and sometimes murderous competition. Outsiders rarely understood how costly and risky the trade was. It took four or five years of packing, storage, and transportation before goods ordered in England would actually be paid for. Traders carried an impossible load of debt, and even a small disaster could mean ruin. Business logic dictated the only possible solution, a cartel. A first small experiment in 1770 led within seventeen years to the fully grown North West Company. Systematically its few rivals were included or wiped out. The last to go was the short-lived XY Company, formed by traders driven from the southwest by the Americans.

It was the "Nor'westers," the wintering partners, and their servants who learned from the Indians how to live in the West and how to find their way along its rivers and lakes. A rough American, Peter Pond, reached Lake Athabaska in 1778. Alexander Mackenzie, seeking a way over the mountain barrier, first followed the river that would bear his name in 1789. He called it "River of Disappointment" after it had led him to the ice floes of the Arctic Ocean, but he persisted. With better navigational instruments and after terrible dangers, he marked his name on a rock near the Dean Channel on July 22, 1793: the first white man to travel overland to the Pacific Ocean. Others followed; between them, Simon Fraser and David Thompson confirmed the shape of the great rivers and mountain ranges of the Pacific slope. Their purpose, almost always, was business.

The North West Company waged a desperate, Montreal-based struggle to fend off Americans like John Jacob Astor from the south and the Hudson's Bay Company from the north. The HBC responded, abandoning its old policy of waiting for trade. "The sleep by the frozen sea," as scornful critics termed the Company's policy, had to end. The benefits of cheapness (and of leaving the Indians undisturbed) no longer weighed in the ledger. In 1774, Samuel Hearne, having explored on his own as far as the Coppermine River and the Arctic Ocean, went inland to build an HBC post at Cumberland House. Other posts soon followed. Rival posts competed with all the cunning and occasional violence their traders could devise or approve.

By 1811, the Hudson's Bay Company had a new strategy. For years, those few veterans of the trade who loved the country or who would not abandon their Indian wives had settled in the relatively sheltered valley of the Red River. Their "half-breed" and Métis offspring had settled there too, the former turning to farming, the latter to the more adventurous but indispensable life of the buffalo hunt. The huge animals supplied every need of prairie life, including the basis of the Nor'westers' pemmican. In their rivalry with the hated HBC, Nor'westers assured the Métis that, through their mothers' blood, they were the true and only inheritors of the land. Young people, growing up proud in the lore of two cultures, took pleasure in seeing themselves as a "New Nation" with the semi-military structure of the buffalo hunt as their first cultural institution. Leaders like Cuthbert Grant gave the Métis a sense of power. In law, of course, the Charter of 1670 was clear – the Red River valley was part of

Rupert's Land. Having settled destitute Scottish Highlanders in Prince Edward Island and Upper Canada, the philanthropic Lord Selkirk now sought a big block of Hudson's Bay Company stock and proposed to settle still more of his people on its highly recommended Red River land.

In 1811, the company gave Selkirk 106,000 acres at the forks of the Red and the Assiniboine rivers. To every imaginable pioneering misery, from frost and floods to grasshoppers, Selkirk's settlers added an extra calamity: the utter hostility of the Nor'westers and their Métis allies. Nor'westers saw no mystery in the Hudson's Bay Company's motive in planting a colony across their main route to the West and on top of their most basic food supply. Led by Cuthbert Grant and encouraged by the "New Nation" claim that the land was theirs, the Métis harassed the unhappy Highlanders and trampled their crops. At Seven Oaks in 1816, Grant and his Métis shot down twenty-one men from the colony and mutilated some of the corpses. The remaining settlers found a miserable refuge at the far end of Lake Winnipeg.

Selkirk took swift vengeance. Collecting Swiss mercenaries, disbanded after the War of 1812, he headed west. At Fort William, now the Nor'westers' trans-shipment base, he seized prisoners and trading goods. Then he sent his men on to restore the colony. Nervous settlers returned to the Red River, and both Métis and Scots seem to have come to a surprisingly smooth reconciliation. The whole dispute entered the courts, which, unfortunately for Selkirk, were held in the distinctly pro-Nor'wester atmosphere of the Canadas. By the time he had finished with judges, lawyers, and charges of false imprisonment, both the philanthropist's fortune and his health had withered away.

Judicial victory over Selkirk could not save the North West Company. Dissident partners plotted to join the rival company as the explorer, Sir Alexander Mackenzie, had urged years earlier. As ever, the logic of monopoly was inescapable. In 1821, the Hudson's Bay Company absorbed its competitor, cut the long link with Montreal, and secured a twenty-one-year licence for its monopoly from the British government. The Nor'westers, with their reputations for audacity, endurance, and the wild drinking of their Beaver Club, joined their old rival or applied their capital to other commercial dreams in Montreal. Many of them sank into obscure poverty.

In the West, a short, stout Scot named George Simpson emerged as "the little emperor" of the Hudson's Bay domain. By 1839, he had cut out most of the competing posts, reduced costs, and firmly suppressed any costly schemes for settlement or administration. He also established his headquarters in Montreal, though his strict supervision hardly slackened. In 1841, teams of paddlers took him from Fort Churchill on Hudson Bay to Astoria at the mouth of Columbia in only eighty-four days.

Astoria was part of the Pacific domain Simon Fraser and David Thompson had won for the Nor'westers from John Jacob Astor. Politically, its status was controversial. Britain and Spain had drifted close to war in 1790 over the ownership of Nootka Sound, but a firm Captain George Vancouver had made the Spanish accept a diplomatic withdrawal. The War of 1812 had proved a great setback for Americans like Astor, but the tide of history was on their side. In 1818, Britain and the United States agreed to joint occupation of the distant Pacific coast, and, in 1839, the Hudson's Bay Company settled a potential threat from the Russians in Alaska by trading them food supplies for a post.

Sensible Company officials knew that they held the coast on borrowed time. American missionaries had entered the Oregon territory, traders had followed, and troops to protect them were not far behind. So were settlers, pouring through the mountain passes into the rich valleys beyond. Company officials hurried to harvest furs. In 1846, Oregon passed to the United States. The whole coast would have followed as American politicians and editors cried for "Fifty-four-forty or fight." But the Hudson's Bay Company opened a new fort at the tip of Vancouver Island, and British diplomats held firm behind a weak hand. They insisted that the forty-ninth parallel, the international boundary along the Great Plains, be extended over the mountains and pushed across the Juan de Fuca Strait. (Even then, no one knew that San Juan Island straddled the line, and another war scare would occur in 1860 before the Americans won that prize.)

All things considered, British North Americans were lucky in their boundary settlement. As usual, they were utterly unprepared for war, and in 1846, Americans really were in a fighting mood; instead, they went off and fought the unfortunate Mexicans. As for the Hudson's Bay Company, it had suffered a serious blow. The Company's prestige depended on an air of permanency, summed up by the rude version of the letters on its flag – "Here Before Christ." Canadians and imperial-minded Britons awoke at last to the realization that a trading company was a very feeble steward for desirable territory. Britain's new free-trade ideology was utterly out of sympathy with government-licensed monopolies. Still, actually doing something would be troublesome too, and the Company got a second chance. In return for promising serious colonization within five years, it was given Vancouver Island to manage as a crown colony.

Even if the Company could have changed its ways, it had no time to do so. In 1849 every mobile colonist set off for the gold fields of California. A few retired officials, two tiny parties from the Red River, and some tourists were all that the Company could muster by 1851 when a hardened veteran of the Company service,

James Douglas, became governor. People seemed to have forgotten about British Columbia until suddenly, in 1858, the colony had its own gold rush. Thousands of miners, prospectors, and hangers-on poured up the Fraser valley and on to new discoveries in the Cariboo. The moment demanded a tough old autocrat, and Douglas rose to the occasion in the full knowledge that he faced another Oregon. A separate mainland colony was proclaimed. A smart detachment of Royal Engineers arrived, not as a garrison but as road builders and as discreet backup for an extraordinary one-man embodiment of British justice, Matthew Baillie Begbie. It would take months before the colonial secretary in London could review his sentence, Judge Begbie informed one convicted murderer, "but you will not be interested in what he decided, for you are to be hanged Monday morning." The goldfields were unusually peaceful.

By 1866, both the gold and the rush were gone, leaving two tiny colonies, two capitals (at Victoria and New Westminster), and one large debt – for roads built through the mountains did not come cheap. With much grumbling, the colonies were reunited, the Company relinquished its power (in 1867), and in 1868 the capital was restored to Victoria. The nearby British naval base at Esquimalt provided some reassurance and a source of gunboats for frequent expeditions to overawe coastal Indians.

The Company had prided itself on maintaining good relations with Indians – mainly just by leaving them alone. Growing numbers of missionaries found a humanitarian audience in mid-Victorian Britain for their allegations of Company neglect or sharp practice. A tiny British garrison in Red River, sent ostensibly for the Oregon crisis, was needed to maintain dwindling Company authority. Neither the troops nor the military pensioners who replaced them were much use as police.

In 1849, Guillaume Sayer appeared at the Red River court to be found guilty of breaking the Hudson's Bay Company's monopoly. Since he brought several hundred fellow Métis with him, the judge prudently decided that no punishment was in order. The high-wheeled Red River carts would be free to screech and squeal their way south to St. Paul as they pleased. The Métis had become formidable. In 1851, as their women and children sheltered behind the carts and helped load their rifles, eighty buffalo hunters slaughtered attacking Sioux at the battle of Grand Côteau. The Sayer case and Grand Côteau became triumphant national symbols for the "New Nation."

The Company itself collected its supplies from St. Paul. Steamboat and railway connections were far better than the old route from the Bay. Old links with Canada revived. So did Canadian interest. The Company had deliberately encouraged a belief that the prairies were a sub-Arctic wasteland, and the harsh experience of the Selkirk settlers had confirmed the image. French-Canadian missionaries to the Métis, mindful of the Jesuit *Rélations* and the blessings of martyrdom, exaggerated their sufferings. The Grit farmers of Upper Canada were unimpressed. Like their American cousins, they looked on the frontier as a heritage for their sons, and they had not the slightest respect for the Hudson's Bay Company. When, in 1857, the British Parliament appointed a Select Committee to review the Company's licence renewal, George Brown and his Reformers made sure that Canada was strongly represented.

Precise information on the area was still scarce. In 1857–58, two expeditions, one British and the other Canadian, set out to report on prospects for western settlement. For the British, John Palliser concluded that the wooded parklands of the Red, Assiniboine, and North Saskatchewan river valleys were suitable for agriculture, but the treeless prairie to the south was too arid ever to be farmed. Henry Youle Hind, a professor of chemistry at the University of Toronto, delighted his Canadian sponsors by reporting rapturously on prospects for the entire region.

Strong supporting evidence came opportunely from Lorin Blodgett, an American, who showed that lines of identical temperatures ran northwest and southwest, not along latitudes. Farming *was* possible. Suddenly, a new design for British North America became exciting economically.

PART II

A MARI USQUE AD MARE

I | CONFEDERATION

In a virtually continent-wide coincidence, almost all British North Americans in the 1860s were obliged to take thought for their future. Railway-building showed how to break the barriers of distance and climate, but at a cost no single colony could afford. Railways also brought foreign investors to the region. Their perspective was broader, if no less self-interested, than that of local people and their politicians.

However parochial they were, most British North Americans recognized the power of the United States. In 1847 the Americans had absorbed Texas and California with unnerving speed. In the 1850s the Fraser and Cariboo gold rushes might well have provided a pretext to add British Columbia to the American Union. South of the tiny Red River Colony, Minnesota had become a state: its politicians made no secret of their annexationist intentions. From 1861 to 1865, Americans were preoccupied with their Civil War, but, as the Montreal-Irish orator D'Arcy McGee warned, war was an appetite that grew with feeding. Even after four years of fighting and half a million dead, the military strength of the United States seemed to keep on growing. If Washington wanted a pretext to turn northward, one would not be hard to find.

Captivated by the South's romantic image, some young Canadians had helped Confederates use Canadian bases to plot their attacks. Some Southerners launched a murderous raid on St. Albans, Vermont, in 1864, escaped to Canada, and went free. The furious Americans promptly closed their borders, imposed the use of passports, and announced that the cherished Reciprocity Agreement would end in 1866. Here was yet another reason for the British colonies to look to each other, if only as substitute markets.

North American union was no new idea. As early as 1783, a British staff officer had urged it. In 1785, the Loyalist chief justice of Quebec, William Smith, devised a scheme for a central legislature. A colonial union was one of many ideas that cascaded through William Lyon Mackenzie's mind. Lord Durham had promoted the notion when he summoned lieutenant-governors and their councils to meet him in 1838. James W. Johnston, Howe's opponent in Nova Scotia, had been so impressed with Durham's idea that he promoted union during the 1850s. So had British governors like Lord Elgin and his able successor, Sir Edward Head. Why not? The colonies were all British – Canada East no less than the others – and they all lived in the shadow of the largest, if not necessarily the happiest, federal union in the world.

If the military and economic threat from the United States was the firmest prod in making the British colonies consider closer union, the breakdown of American federalism was also a useful warning. The real issue in the Civil War, as contemporaries understood matters, was not slavery but states' rights. The South's "peculiar institution" had led to secession in 1861, but it was the claim of state sovereignty that allowed the Confederacy to raise armies and paralysed the will of the rest of the nation. Federalism might seem a logical answer to the problems of the United Provinces or even of British North America as a whole, but the experience of the best-known example was not reassuring.

Still, the experiment had to be considered. When the Reformers of Canada West had met in convention in 1859, impatient to press representation by population, George Brown persuaded them to consider some form of federalism as a possible compromise. A year earlier, the one-time annexationist and voice of Montreal business, Alexander Tilloch Galt, switched from the Reformers to Macdonald and Cartier on condition that they take up the notion of a British North American federation. Unimpressed by constitutional novelties, Cartier and Macdonald had to do something to retain a valuable new partner.

By the spring of 1864, colonial union was no longer a novelty but an opportunity. If Macdonald could not stem the tide of votes to Reform and "Rep by Pop," his career would end. Cartier now foresaw a political battle his *Canadiens* could not win. Two years of feeble double-majority government had proved to all but John Sandfield Macdonald that a double majority, drawn from each of the United Provinces, was ineffective. Sandfield Macdonald's bitter rival, George Brown, saw his chance. Between 1861 and 1864, Canadians had experienced two elections, four governments, and three very dangerous years. Outsiders knew that Brown and the Tory leader, John A. Macdonald, were mortal enemies. The bibulous opportunist and the self-righteous autocrat hated each other. They might also use each other.

On June 14, a short-lived Macdonald-Cartier government was defeated. In the confusion, George Brown rose to announce he would enter any coalition pledged to find a way out of the constitutional impasse. An ecstatic but tiny French-Canadian *bleu* practically clambered up the massive Brown to embrace him. The House cheered. Under the titular leadership of Sir Étienne-Paschal Taché, a veteran of the War of 1812, the Great Coalition was announced on June 30. The report of a legislature committee, chaired by Brown through much of the 1864 session, provided ready-made constitutional policies. Where could they be presented? Then came news that leaders of three of Britain's Atlantic colonies would meet at Charlottetown on September 1. At once the Canadians asked for and received an invitation.

Maritime union, the original Charlottetown topic, was at least as old an idea as British North American federalism, just as obvious, and just as impossible. Union was a perennial favourite of British lieutenant-governors like John Manners Sutton and Arthur Gordon in New Brunswick. How better might they advance the region (and their own careers)? Nova Scotians fancied the idea, but only because they would obviously dominate the union. In New Brunswick, it took all of Gordon's charm to interest Premier Leonard Tilley. With Prince Edward Island's known hostility, only by holding the Maritime Union Conference in Charlottetown could supporters be sure that the Island's leaders would show up. Indeed, only the unexpected inquiry from the Canadas ensured that the Conference happened at all.

The Charlottetown Conference became an unexpected triumph for the Canadians. Since the Maritimers had nothing much to discuss, they cheerfully agreed to hear their visitors. Well-briefed and rehearsed, Macdonald, Cartier, Brown, and Galt each spoke brilliantly in his field of expertise. Lavish entertainment ashore and on the Canadians' ship, the *Queen Victoria*, made the first week of September pass like a dream. Next, the Canadians and their hosts moved on to Halifax and then to Saint John, with more speeches, banquets, and toasts, and an agreement that all would meet at Quebec on October 10.

The Quebec meeting was longer, tougher, and much more specific. It almost began with tragedy when the *Queen Victoria*, sent to collect delegates, wives, and marriageable daughters, nearly foundered in a storm. At Quebec, Newfoundland was also represented. So was Britain. Colonel W.F.D. Jervois, who believed Canada to be indefensible, obediently went to Quebec to tell delegates how a modest military effort could keep the colonies safe. Details of discussion at the closed meetings are sparse and one-sided, taken largely from minutes kept by Hewitt Bernard, Macdonald's secretary, and from the letters sent home by George Brown to his young wife. Again, the Canadians were the best prepared, and almost all the seventy-two resolutions adopted between October 10 and 28 were their work.

The speed and good humour of the meetings concealed real differences. Macdonald made no secret of his preference for a single legislative union. Federalism, he insisted, had been discredited by the American experience. To a large degree, he had his way. Confederation, as it emerged from Quebec, gave the central government infinitely greater powers than Washington then exercised. In the division of responsibilities, the future Section 91 not only gave the central power a healthy list of tasks to ensure "peace, order and good government" but also left any "residual" or unspecified powers to the centre. Provincial responsibilities were so modest as to be almost municipal in scope – education, local roads and improvements, and "charitable and eleemosynary institutions." Moreover, provinces would be limited to the meagre revenue from direct taxes, and their laws could be suspended or even disallowed by the central authority. An impressive amount of discussion focused on the proposed upper house of the new federal Parliament; even that debate concentrated on the provincial membership, almost ignoring the fact that the future prime minister would pick all the senators.

Yet Macdonald really did not win. His partner and closest ally, George-Étienne Cartier, insisted on a federal system. On behalf of his French-Canadian colleagues, Cartier argued that the provincial powers, which would be their only bulwark against an even larger Anglo-Saxon majority, would be very real indeed. "Property and civil rights," for example, was a phrase from the old Quebec Act that had guaranteed the *Canadiens'* identity; it must now be a provincial responsibility. Cartier's chief ally would soon be a short, bespectacled Ontario Reformer from Kingston named Oliver Mowat, whose actual contribution to Confederation was federal power to delay or cancel provincial laws. Mowat would change.

At the end of October 1864 the Confederation agreement was set. Many delegates headed on to Montreal, Toronto, and westward to see the vast potential of territory most of them had never visited, and to share the heady excitement of banquet oratory. Both the Canadian coalition and the British, contented midwives for the process, could congratulate themselves on an easy victory. Certainly the coalition government approached the provincial Parliament with confidence. Meeting for the last time at Quebec City, with their speeches recorded and published, members tackled the Confederation issues with energy and occasional flashes of vision. Many criticisms were predictable. The intercolonial railway demanded by Nova Scotia would be too costly; financial terms for the lower provinces were too generous.

French Canadians obviously had much to lose. Cartier and his deputy, Hector Langevin, did their utmost to keep nervous *bleus* in line, boasting of the powers left for the new province of Quebec and insisting that *Canadiens* would now be masters in their own jurisdiction. A.A. Dorion and the *rouges* condemned the new arrangement as fatal to French Canada and a number of younger *bleus*, Honoré Mercier among them, abandoned their allegiance. Minorities have minorities of their own. Speaking for the English of Canada East, Christopher Dunkin predicted that too many interests – regional, racial, religious, and political – would persist in the new Confederation to allow any new national community to develop. His warnings would be remembered.

Macdonald, Cartier, Brown, and especially the fiery D'Arcy McGee, cajoled and persuaded their supporters and occasionally lifted emotions above mundane criticism. As they spoke, the great Civil War was winding to its end and the threat of the blue-clad Union armies hung over the debate. If the Americans came, talk of local rights, and especially of French-Canadian survival, would be academic. Everyone knew it. The vote was decisive. Members from Canada West voted 54-8 for Confederation; from Canada East the margin was 37-25, though the French-speaking majority was only four. The next business, a $2 million loan for fortifications, passed swiftly, and the leading ministers left at once for London to pursue both matters with the British.

Confederation passed, though more painfully than its architects in Canada had expected. It was another story in the lower provinces. The euphoria of September 1864 vanished by November when the delegates came home. It was obvious almost at once that neither island colony would join. Prince Edward Island delegates had opposed "Rep by Pop" at Quebec and had lost. Was that a foretaste of Confederation majorities? Times were good; the little island would manage on its own. It could even afford its own railway without going on bended knee to Canada. Newfoundland too would turn its back. St. John's, where political and business power met, was closer to London than to the newly designated capital of Ottawa. Its merchant elite had no plans to share its power. Hard times had justified sending delegates to Quebec, but fish prices were climbing again, prosperity bred confidence, and the Water Street merchants of St. John's spread the word: Confederation meant conscription and Canadian taxes. In the 1869 election, the pro-Confederates lost.

In Nova Scotia, James Johnston and Charles Tupper had brought the Conservatives to power in 1864, so at least time was on their side. Opinion was not. Joseph Howe had left politics in 1863. He had squandered some of his influence by anti-Catholic bigotry, but his power was immense. At times Howe had backed a North American union, but his real dream remained an imperial federation with Britain. Early in 1865, Howe acted. The pro-Confederation editor of the Halifax *Chronicle* was fired. Soon, the paper's columns carried "The Botheration Letters," brilliant invective against Confederation and its sponsors. The author was anonymous, but every Nova Scotian knew the voice of Joseph Howe. Tupper, premier since 1864, could feel his support slipping.

Across the Bay of Fundy, matters were even worse. Tilley did not have time. His anti-liquor Liberals had held office for a decade, accumulating splits and enemies. An election was due and Governor Gordon insisted that it be held before the legislature could endorse the Quebec Resolution. Anti-Confederates were ready. Tilley, they said, had sold New Brunswickers for eighty cents a head – the $200,000 the Quebec proposals would pay the colony for its customs revenues. By the end of March 1865, Tilley was out and his old enemy, Albert J. Smith, was in.

Without the two island colonies, Confederation could go forward; without New Brunswick to link Nova Scotia to central Canada, it was dead. Somehow, the idea must be resuscitated. The British finally decided to help. A pro-Confederate governor arrived in Nova Scotia and Arthur Gordon in New Brunswick got orders to help Tilley if he could. In London, Canadians received a guarantee for their fortification loan and a vague but seemingly valuable pledge that, if they took their own defence seriously, "the Imperial Government fully acknowledged the reciprocal obligation of defending every portion of the Empire with all the resources at its command." That was an answer to Maritimers who insisted that Confederation would tie them to a defenceless interior.

Unknowingly, the Americans helped as well. The termination of reciprocity with its accompanying fishing agreements in 1866 hurt the lower provinces as much as Canada. Albert Smith had boasted that he could get a better deal from Washington than from any Confederate politician. He returned empty-handed and humiliated. His support began to crumble. The huge American armies had disbanded with impressive speed after the Civil War, but they left a bitter residue. In the cities of the North, the Fenian Brotherhood pledged to liberate Ireland from English rule and recruited widely among the Union's Irish soldiers. By enlisting hardened veterans with ready access to arms and American sympathy, the Fenians planned to form an army to conquer Canada and hold her hostage for Ireland's freedom. It was a wild scheme, growing ever wilder in the reports sent by informers and secret agents to British and Canadian authorities. Thousands marched, applauded fiery speeches, and went home; the patriots and unemployed who might act numbered only in the hundreds. In response, British troops and Canadian militia trained, planned, and occupied frontier posts. Border towns buzzed with rumours and false alarms.

Suddenly, the rumours came true. On May 31, 1866, sixteen hundred Fenians scrambled ashore at Fort Erie. By June 3, they had all fled or been captured, but not before they had defeated two small forces of Canadian militia. At Pigeon Hill, just over the Vermont border, another eighteen hundred Fenians camped for a day before American authorities seized their leaders and supplies. The most fatuous but also the most significant incursion ended a month earlier when Fenians, clustered on the Maine border, had tried to raid Campobello Island. For New

Brunswick, it was traumatic. Not even in the comic-opera Aroostook War in the 1840s, when a contested boundary with Maine had finally been settled, had the colony felt so threatened. A few hundred ill-led, demoralized Fenians suddenly made a union with Canada appear sensible. As Smith's support faded, the lieutenant-governor discreetly used his power to force a new election. Funds from Montreal reinforced the cause of Confederation. This time Tilley was triumphant.

Both Tilley and Tupper avoided asking their legislatures to endorse the Quebec Resolutions. Instead, they sought a mandate to negotiate still better terms in Britain. The hint was hardly needed. The Canadians had manoeuvring room, and the British were now almost beside themselves with eagerness. The reasons were unflattering. British investors feared for their money in the hands of any individual colonies. Some of them had major investment plans, from expanding the Grand Trunk to building a transcontinental railway line. Politically, the doctrines of free trade and imperial separation had reached their height. "I cannot shut my eyes to the fact that they want to get rid of us," an unhappy Galt reported from London in 1865. "They have a servile fear of the United States and would rather give us up than defend us, or incur the risk of war with that country." Confederation would legitimate the unloading of British North America.

When delegates from Canada, Nova Scotia, and New Brunswick met in London at the Westminster Palace Hotel, the mood of the Quebec Conference revived. Tilley and Tupper secured better financial terms, and the educational rights of religious (though not linguistic) minorities were improved. The Intercolonial Railway, merely discussed before, became a legal obligation. In their own draft, the Canadians, monarchists to the core, had proposed that their creation be termed "the Kingdom of Canada." After the British warned that American sensibilities might be aroused, a devoutly Christian Leonard Tilley offered both an alternative and a national motto by thumbing his Bible to Psalms 72:8: "He shall have dominion also from sea to sea, and from the river until the ends of the earth."

Without particular ceremony or sense of occasion, the British Parliament passed the act as Canadians had designed it, correcting a word or phrase here or there as legislative draftsmen advised, but giving the colonials, for the first time, a constitution that was as homemade as it could be. One lapse went unnoticed: nowhere did the British North America Act, 1867, explain how the colonists would share in its future amendment.

Long after, lawyers and historians would debate what the Fathers of Confederation had really meant by all their torrents of words between 1864 and 1867. Were the Quebec Resolutions a treaty, inviolable by the participating provinces? Macdonald and Cartier certainly said so to fend off would-be amenders in their Canadian Parliament, but they altered many terms when they got to London in 1866, and they would unilaterally amend them later. Was the BNA Act a compact, either among the three original colonies, or among the two founding nations of French and English, or, even more far-fetched, among all current and future provinces? Such a notion would become fashionable in the 1880s, supported by the painstaking accumulation of random quotations. As a historical interpretation of what happened in the 1860s, the compact theory is absurd. Before Confederation, and long after, sensible Canadians have understood that peace, order, and good government in their country depended on the reasonable long-run harmony of French and English. That notion was not embodied in the British North America Act; it was left for ensuing generations to rediscover or neglect at their peril.

NATION-BUILDING | 2

Confederation had been a means to many ends. By 1867, one purpose mattered more than the others: the bid to establish a transcontinental nation. Sir John A. Macdonald, newly knighted and invited to be the Dominion's first prime minister, would never forget that goal.

First he must form a government. The big gothic-style buildings at Ottawa and the timid bureaucrats of the United Provinces would form the foundation. Few officials would leave the lower provinces. As for the new governments of Ontario and Quebec, they started from scratch. Forming a cabinet was harder. In the Canadas, ministers had represented interests as well as departments. That continued, but it was now so much more complex. Quebec, for example, must have four ministers: one for English Protestants and the others to balance the rivalry of Montreal, with two ministers, and Quebec City. There was no room for the brilliant D'Arcy McGee: he would have to wait. Nine months later, still a mere MP, McGee lay dead in the Ottawa slush, the victim of a Fenian bullet.

In November 1867, Macdonald was ready to face elections. The outcome reflected the Confederation debate. In Nova Scotia, only Tupper survived the anti-Confederate tide. New Brunswick split narrowly for Tilley. Quebec went solidly for Cartier's *bleus*. In Ontario, where George Brown had worked since 1865 for a Reform sweep, the *Globe* publisher lost his own seat. Sir John A. Macdonald was exultant. In Ontario, Macdonald invited Sandfield Macdonald to head a "patent combination," a coalition of Tories and old Reformers. Again Brown was worsted. Pierre Chauveau, the education reformer and *bleu*, became Quebec's premier. In Ottawa the Dominion's first Parliament pitted 108 government supporters against a mixed bag of 72 *rouges*, Reformers, and Maritime anti-Confederates.

Safe in power, Macdonald had much to do. Joseph Howe's campaign to repeal confederation made no headway in Britain, but Nova Scotia's bitterness could not be allowed to fester. By 1869, Howe had accepted as "better terms" a richer subsidy than the original eighty cents a head and, despite inevitable cries of treason, joined Macdonald's cabinet. After her 1869 election, Newfoundland would wait for eighty more years. (In 1895, Canada had another chance – but balked at the cost of $4 million in financial aid. A generation of Newfoundlanders concluded that Canadians were mean-minded folk.) Prince Edward Island was different. The fatal lure of railways soon left the tiny colony $3 million in debt. Anxious island politicians turned to Ottawa and got terms they could not refuse: complete transfer of the provincial debt, and hard cash to buy out the notorious "proprietors." By 1873, the island was a province.

A more nerve-wracking issue for Macdonald was safeguarding the West. The Americans were moving. In 1867, they bought Alaska from the Russians for $7.2 million and they sent a consul to the Red River. Canada saw that legal haggling with the Hudson's Bay Company must end. In 1868, Cartier and a former Ontario Grit, William McDougall, went to London, paid $1.5 million for title to Rupert's Land, and guaranteed that a twentieth of the land in the fertile belt would remain with the old Company. Formal transfer would come "at a date to be determined." Meanwhile, Canada would send survey crews and a road-building gang to link the Red River settlement with Lake Superior.

It really was too good to be true. McDougall, a long-time campaigner for the Northwest as an outlet for Ontario farmers' sons, was named governor. An appointed council and a small police force would keep the peace and suppress American troublemakers. Warnings from Catholic missionaries and Hudson's Bay officials were discounted. A perennial optimist, Cartier knew that all would be well. McDougall was confident of dependable information from Canadians at the Red River.

Both men were wrong. The Canadians, with their knowing-newcomer arrogance, were detested. Company authority, shrinking since the Sayer case in 1849, collapsed under the strain of the unpopular land transfer. English-speaking settlers might accept their fate; the Métis would not. Their disciplined hunting organization made them a force. Their old belief that as the "New Nation" they had inherited the land gave them a unifying cause. Fearful of an influx of Protestant farmers, Catholic priests encouraged Métis militants. Still, without young Louis Riel, Métis resistance might have been mere grumbling. The ambitious son of a respected father, Riel had gone to Montreal for a classical education. He found no vocation for the Church or the law and drifted home, qualified for no career but politics. The man and the moment met. Riel's guidance turned a national council of the Métis into the real authority in the Red River.

McDougall helped the Métis too. As the would-be governor approached, the Métis formed a committee, mustered their forces, and seized Fort Garry, the Hudson's Bay Company's main base. Rather than wait for the Company to hand over its territory, McDougall crossed the border. Métis guards promptly expelled him. On December 1, the frustrated official stepped a few feet over the boundary line, proclaimed Canadian sovereignty, fluttered a Union Jack in the icy wind, and retreated to his hotel room to pen a proclamation commanding all loyal Canadians at the Red River to support his authority. The few Canadians who did so promptly found themselves in the ice-cold cells of Fort Garry. Louis Riel finally had a case for proclaiming his provisional government: no other power existed in the colony.

In Ottawa, Macdonald was aghast. By his folly, McDougall had displayed Canada's impotence to Americans and Métis alike. If annexationists wanted a pretext to interfere, they would have a long winter before Canada could do anything. A steady stream of intermediaries, from old Joseph Howe to Donald A. Smith, Hudson's Bay Company commissioner in Montreal, set out for the Red River. Riel met most of them with threats and legitimate suspicion. Though he lacked western experience, Smith was by far the ablest. He patiently manoeuvred Riel and the varied factions in the colony into stating their demands, choosing delegates, and dispatching them to Ottawa. Riel's ambitions, after all, were not bizarre: he wanted Red River to be a province like the others. If the French could become Canadians, so could the Métis.

Unfortunately for Donald Smith, Riel, and many other people, the patriotic Canadians in the Red River knew nothing of Macdonald's strategy. Their loyalty and injured pride demanded more heroic action against the man McDougall had designated as a rebel. A new and even more bungled assault was mounted in February 1870; again Métis horsemen captured the perpetrators. This time, the mood was different. Riel felt his authority challenged. Dissuaded by Smith and the community from executing a Canadian leader, Charles Boulton, he chose smaller fry. Thomas Scott, a big, combative Ontarian, had been savagely beaten for insulting his guards. Now, after a Métis court martial, he was taken out on March 4, 1870, and shot. "We must make Canada respect us," Riel told Smith in justification.

It was a major blunder. Scott was a blemished martyr. Since he had led a strike for unpaid wages and was an Orangeman, many historians have agreed with Riel that Scott must have been a man of bad character. No one should be shot on such evidence. Contemporaries considered his death a murder. Scott's killing stoked the fires of Ontario Protestantism. Brown, the *Globe*, and the Grits had an issue the smallest mind could understand: Macdonald was bargaining with a murderous rebel. Initially dismayed by the killing, Quebec listened to the Ontario furor and decided that Riel must be forgiven. Riel's friends in Montreal decided that the Métis were guardians of a part of the French-Canadian patrimony, though most Québécois preferred to admire it from a distance.

Macdonald kept his eye on his purpose. Red River delegates were escorted past Ontario law officers, their desires were met, and they returned triumphant with virtually all they had sought: the colony would become a small province of Manitoba (extending west to Portage la Prairie and north to the lakes). The duality of French and English, Catholic and Protestant, as it had existed in 1870, was secure forever. There would even be an upper and a lower house in the provincial legislature, and, best of all, Ottawa would pay the bills. Only one desire was unsatisfied: an amnesty. It had been promised and expected, but that was before Scott died.

To confirm the transfer from British sovereignty to Canadian rule, a joint Anglo-Canadian military expedition would show the flag to Americans, Indians, and the disaffected. Moved by land hunger, curiosity, and vengeful patriotism, young Ontarians flocked to join up; young *Canadiens* did not. The Red River Expedition of 1870 was a logistic triumph, navigating the old *voyageur* route from Port Arthur to Fort Garry without losing a man. It was also a political misfortune, introducing the young Dominion to the West as a punitive authority. A small garrison remained in Manitoba until 1877. Prudently, Riel fled before the approaching troops. A stabler and more robust personality might well, like Mackenzie and Papineau, have resumed a conventional political career, most probably in the Conservative ranks. Riel remained a hero to the Métis, but, by killing Scott, he robbed himself of immediate recognition as the founder of Manitoba.

The Red River Colony was only a part of the West. In contrast, drawing British Columbia into Confederation proved deceptively simple. After the gold ran out, the miners departed, leaving behind a largely British and Canadian elite of officials, ranchers, and professionals, and a very large debt. The colony's leaders would have preferred the status quo; some merchants eagerly agitated for annexation with the United States. However, the editor of the Victoria *British Colonist* (a Nova Scotian named William Smith who renamed himself Amor De Cosmos) insisted that Canada be approached. A new British governor agreed, and, in the summer of 1870, two delegates made their laborious way to Ottawa via San Francisco. Macdonald was away, spending a restful summer in Charlottetown, but Cartier was on the job and eager to make a coup. British Columbia needed money: for purposes of subsidy, Ottawa would pretend that it had sixty thousand people instead of twenty-eight thousand. (No one even considered the colony's Indians – a loosely estimated eighty-two thousand!) The delegates hoped for a wagon road across the Rockies, but Cartier remembered the old Grand Trunk dream – British Columbia would have a full transcontinental railway within a decade of joining Confederation. It was an offer British Columbia could not possibly refuse. By July 20, 1871, it was a province.

Between British Columbia and the Red River lay what an officially sponsored traveller, Captain William Butler, called "The Great Lone Land," peopled by Indians, a few Métis, and even fewer white trappers, traders, and missionaries. Herds of buffalo, the basis of life for most of the inhabitants, headed relentlessly towards extinction. Repeating rifles and an American slaughter policy, designed to starve the warlike Sioux Indians, annually decimated the herds, though this was not easily apparent in Ottawa or even Fort Garry.

Canada wanted its West but it could not afford Indian wars. Her officials set out to negotiate a system of Indian treaties and surrenders, with reserves, payments, medals, and a "medicine chest." The goal was to clear land for settlers at minimum cost, but Ottawa could not stop there. The establishment of American whisky traders at Fort Whoop-up on Canadian territory and the savage slaughter of an Indian party in the Cypress Hills were early warnings of trouble. The mounted police force planned for the Red River was revived. Policemen traditionally wore blue, but scarlet tunics would leave no doubt that a different sovereignty prevailed above the forty-ninth parallel. The North West Mounted Police was Macdonald's fondest creation. Canadians would later pretend that they were uniquely devoted to law and order. In fact, peace and good order in the remote territories were needed to deny American cavalry or vigilantes any pretext for invading Canadian soil.

That soil would also have to support a railway. Cartier's pledge was about as troubling to his colleagues as MacDougall's folly had been in 1869. A three-thousand-mile railway from Montreal to the Pacific was a huge undertaking, especially at a time when Ottawa was pouring money into the Intercolonial

Railway. The Pacific line would have to be a private venture, financed, if possible, by huge western land grants. Fortunately, two rival syndicates were bidding for the contract. Senator David Macpherson in Toronto was Macdonald's old friend, but he was a lobbyist for the Grand Trunk, and no vote-conscious government would dare help that greedy and unloved company. In Montreal, the ruthless shipping magnate Sir Hugh Allan formed a rival group secretly backed by American railroad interests. Allan had money and he used it, buying up newspapers, young lawyers, even priests, to pressure Cartier and the entire Tory government.

With his national achievements and prosperity, Macdonald should have been impregnable. He was not. The Riel affair had turned both Ontario and Quebec against him. At the end of 1871, Ontario Liberals used Riel and the Red River to batter Sandfield Macdonald into defeat. Conservative Catholics in Quebec concluded that the Church should resume the kind of political leadership it had exerted after the 1837–38 rebellions. The pragmatic and corruptible *bleus* must be disciplined; the anticlerical *rouges* must be destroyed. In New Brunswick, a new provincial government belatedly introduced a tax-supported nondenominational public school system, consciously rejecting the Ontario example of dual public and Catholic schools. French and Catholic protests led nowhere. In Ottawa, the Conservatives refused to disallow the New Brunswick act, insisting that central governments must not interfere in provincial jurisdictions. It was an argument as important to Quebec as to any province, but furious Catholics and *Canadiens* were not appeased. In 1871, Quebec's ultramontane bishops approved a "Catholic Program" and commanded faithful voters to support candidates who endorsed it. It was a weapon primarily against *rouges*, but it was also designed to split the *bleus* and to shatter the convenient alliance that LaFontaine had forged in the 1840s. The Macdonald government was adrift in a sea of troubles.

By 1871, the British had claimed their price for Confederation: liberation from North American entanglements. Eager to save money and worried by the new power of Germany in Europe, William Gladstone's Liberal government brought many colonial garrisons home. Troops in Canada stayed just long enough to join the Red River Expedition and to fend off the last Fenian attacks on Quebec. By the fall of 1871, red-coated regulars remained only at Halifax. A few hundred Canadian gunners, hurriedly recruited to guard abandoned forts at Quebec and Kingston, were no substitute for the British garrisons, and no one replaced the $6 million a year they contributed to the Canadian economy.

The British decision made military sense. As Colonel Jervois had concluded in 1864, Canada was indefensible against American assault. It also made diplomatic sense for Canada to clean the slate of Anglo-American grievances. The list was long, ranging from Britain's responsibility for Confederate commerce raiders to American negligence in the Fenian raids. Long before the delegates met in Washington in 1871, with Sir John A. Macdonald a reluctant participant, the scenario was predictable. Americans would bluster and threaten; the British would retreat. Canadian claims against the United States would be traded against American claims on Britain. So it happened. From fishing rights to hard cash, Canadian expectations scattered in the wind when the Treaty of Washington was signed. Exasperated by his supercilious fellow British delegates, Macdonald had to accept their argument that lasting peace with the Americans was an inestimable benefit. The problem was that voters would not estimate it either.

Re-election in 1872 became a desperate struggle, to be waged by every trick in the book. To the despair of its chief engineer, Sandford Fleming, the Intercolonial became a vast funnel, pouring contracts and patronage into the Maritimes. In Ontario, where George Brown had had his striking printers arrested, labour votes were garnered by a law legalizing unions. An even tougher law against most strike activities reassured employers. It was not enough. Everywhere, government candidates faced trouble. Ontario farmers were furious that Macdonald had not rescued reciprocity in Washington. Quebec *bleus* split on the Catholic Program. "Confederation is only yet in the gristle," a worried Macdonald wrote to a friend, "and it will require five years more before it hardens into bone." It was the kind of argument that usually precedes questionable expedients. Cartier had turned to Sir Hugh Allan for cash and, as the campaign intensified, Macdonald followed. "I must have another ten thousand," he wired the magnate's solicitor in August 1872. "Will be the last time of asking. Do not fail me."

Macdonald won – narrowly – with 104 seats to 96, but there were too many "loose fish" on both sides to be certain. In Montreal, Cartier lost his seat. Without Manitoba and a solid British Columbia, now eager for the railway, there would have been no victory. Sir Hugh would have his reward. For a million acres of land no official had ever seen and a list of other conditions, the government handed Allan a railway charter – on condition that his American partners be cut out. The old rogue agreed. The partners did not. Had they not fed most of the money to Allan for the election? A secret raid on the office of Allan's solicitor delivered a bag of evidence to the opposition, including Macdonald's desperate message. Had $162,000 or even $350,000 been poured into the campaign? When even the prime minister earned only $8000 a year, either sum was enormous. The conclusion was obvious. "The Government got the money," explained Edward Blake, Ontario's Liberal premier, "and Sir Hugh Allan got the Charter."

Brown, Blake, Alexander Mackenzie, and other Ontario Liberals had always insisted that Macdonald was crooked as well as tricky. At last they had proof. Committees, a royal commission, and procedural delays could not stop the "loose fish" from swimming to safety. Among them was Donald Smith, the successful negotiator of Red River. Fuelled by discreet glasses of gin, Macdonald offered a superb defence on November 3, but fatigue and alcohol sent him to bed for two days. By the time he revived on November 5, his government had collapsed. Members simply switched sides.

As certainly as anything in politics, Macdonald's political career was finished. His party might well follow him into oblivion. The Liberals would inherit his achievements – if they could form a government. The obvious leaders – Blake, Brown – refused to serve. Grim, honest Alexander Mackenzie, an immigrant stonemason who had made good in Sarnia, became Canada's second prime minister. His task was to unite the rival factions that had sat in opposition. On only one thing could they and the country agree: wickedness must be condemned. Constituency elections at the time were spaced over weeks. Voters publicly declared their choice. Starting with safe Liberal seats to show the trend, Mackenzie emerged with 138 of the 206 seats. The Conservatives kept a mere 67, almost half of them in Quebec. Manitoba sent a solitary independent. He took the oath, signed his name, Louis Riel, and fled to Hull for safety.

In opposition, Liberals had denounced every nation-building policy, from better terms for Nova Scotia to the great railway. It had been easy for Macdonald to persuade supporters, including the latest governor general, Lord Dufferin, that Confederation was unsafe in Liberal hands. Yet Mackenzie had backed the project and he backed it still. The change of government brought rational, overdue reforms. Electoral corruption would surely be harder if voters used a secret ballot and if general elections occurred on the same day, not at the government's convenience. The Supreme Court, promised in the

British North America Act, was created to please nationalists – and promptly undermined by allowing appeals of its judgements to continue to the Judicial Committee of the Privy Council in London. At Kingston, Mackenzie opened a tiny Royal Military College to train not simply officers but the engineers that a young country needed.

Yet governments inherit far more than they create. By 1876, the Intercolonial was completed to Halifax. Mackenzie's efforts to prune waste came too late to straighten the wandering tracks or curb political appointment of employees. The ICR became a beloved example for enemies of public enterprise. When Mackenzie cancelled the Allan contract and announced that the promised Pacific railway would be built by the government in slow stages, British Columbians claimed betrayal and threatened secession. Mackenzie's critics promised another dose of corruption. What they got was painful progress from the Lakehead to the thriving little town of Winnipeg.

Progress was slow for an unexpected reason: Canada was suddenly deep in an economic depression. The post-Confederation years had been an Indian summer of prosperity, continuing two decades of almost unbroken growth. Regions and industries suffered occasionally but recovery soon followed. Even the loss of reciprocity in 1866 seemed relatively painless. Good times had made Confederation easier to promote. Assuming colonial debts, building railways, and improving transfer payments from Ottawa seemed a good idea when revenues grew even faster than spending, from $14 million in 1867 to $25 million in 1874. The first signs of trouble became visible in 1873, when banks failed in distant Vienna. Trade and credit suddenly contracted. By 1874, the danger signs were so obvious that businessmen and politicians changed the subject. By 1875, the economic slump was unmistakable.

As usual, some individuals and communities escaped with no more than worries and a few prospered so mightily that some economic historians would later deny that a depression had occurred. Contemporaries knew better. Revenues, based on import duties, fell drastically. Innocent of theories of counter-cyclical financing, Mackenzie's government set a public example of cost-cutting and, with deep regret (for free trade was Liberal gospel in Canada as well as Britain), raised tariff rates to 17.5 per cent. George Brown went to Washington on Mackenzie's behalf, and negotiated and actually won a new reciprocity treaty, only to see it trampled to death by protectionists in the United States Senate. No wonder there was no money for British Columbia's railway. In a grudging compromise, extorted by British mediators, Ottawa agreed to spend $2 million a year and complete the line by 1890.

The economic crisis, with its thousands of hungry unemployed, spread to every part of Canada. By grim coincidence, the timber and shipping industries that had built the prosperity of the Maritimes and the St. Lawrence region entered a crisis. The age of "wooden ships and iron men" was passing. Iron hulls and steam engines replaced the wooden sailing ships that had drifted down the ways in Saint John, Quebec, and a score of other Canadian ports. Nova Scotia's coal mines and a primitive iron industry could not hope to compete with British yards. Prudent merchants could shift their capital to new investments; seamen and shipyard workers simply had to move away. At Quebec and Montreal, *Canadien* shipbuilders waged violent battles for the jobs of Irish longshoremen. In Saint John, long, hopeless strikes brought the city's proud labour unions to the edge of extinction. In 1877, a disastrous fire left thirteen thousand homeless. It was a common enough catastrophe, but it was almost more than the beleaguered New Brunswick city could endure.

Labour violence shifted easily to the old issues of sect and race. In 1875, Toronto police fought bloody battles to protect

Catholic marchers from Protestant mobs. In Montreal, thousands of militia mobilized to back a ban on Orange processions. After the Liberal victory in 1874, Catholic Programmists no longer divided their fire between *rouges* and *bleus*. Bishop Bourget and his supporters now waged virtual holy war on the Liberals, provincial and federal, Catholic or secular. Clergy, thundering from their pulpits, had no trouble reminding the faithful that Heaven was blue and Hell was red. In 1877, the young Wilfrid Laurier was defeated in a brutal by-election in his native Drummond-Arthabaska. Weeks later, he won a seat in Quebec-East. Quebec City's Archbishop Elzéar-Alexandre Taschereau had an old hatred for Bourget and the Jesuits and a discreet affection for conservative young Liberals. Nothing was ever quite as monolithic in French Canada as it seemed.

Wilfrid Laurier would have a future. The frail, handsome lawyer insisted that he was the heir of Englishmen like Gladstone and Bright, not of European anti-Catholic liberals. Yet, for Liberals as a whole, that Gladstonian free-trade heritage brought political paralysis. Despite conventional wisdom, the depression was slow to lift. Sir Richard Cartwright, the big, bewhiskered, blustering ex-Tory who served as Mackenzie's minister of finance, had a convert's fanaticism. Free trade was his new gospel, and he would not abandon it, whatever the arguments offered by powerful deputations of businessmen and manufacturers. Even if Americans sent tariffs soaring, they were wrong and free trade was right. A wealth of conventional wisdom sustained him. So did his prime minister.

Sir John A. Macdonald thought differently. He had somehow survived his own despair, a near-defeat in Kingston, and inevitable party disaffection. Perhaps it was simply his durable, unquenchable charm. "When fortune empties her chamberpot on your head," he told a friend in 1875, "smile, and say 'we are going to have a summer shower.'" The shower had ended.

Memories of the Pacific scandal were buried now by the misery and hopelessness of a depression and exasperation at a government seemingly unwilling to do anything to help. Tariffs were not a heresy to Macdonald – nothing was if it won votes. Surely manufacturers, fed up with American dumping of goods over the 17.5 per cent tariff barrier, had a point. They also promised more financial support than Hugh Allan had ever mustered. Two summers of political picnics across Ontario in 1876 and 1877 told Macdonald what people wanted and how to put his case.

Once again, the old man assured them, he would be the nation-builder. He urged not "protection," but a "National Policy," a "judicious readjustment of the Tariff," to "benefit the agricultural, the mining, the manufacturing and other interests of the Dominion." Meanwhile Mackenzie was utterly confident. There might be local setbacks, but huge meetings cheered him and the rightness of his policies. Macdonald's sly scheme to tax 95 per cent of Canadians for the benefit of 5 per cent would surely destroy the Conservative party.

On September 17, 1878, for the first time in their history, Canadians voted on the same day, and they destroyed Mackenzie. The 1874 election was more than reversed, with 142 Conservatives to only 64 Liberals. When the last figures trickled in, 52.5 per cent of voters favoured the Tories and 46.3 per cent supported Liberal candidates. The voters preferred "Macdonald drunk to Mackenzie sober"; warm humanity to dry integrity. At sixty-three, Sir John A. Macdonald could resume his work.

3 | NATIONAL POLICY

I n only a decade, the Dominion had met most of the goals of Confederation. Seven provinces and the huge North-West Territories ran from one ocean to the other. In 1880, when the British transferred their claims to the Arctic islands to Ottawa, Canadians heard of a third ocean few had considered in 1867. In Canada, the French-English stalemate was over. Even under the Liberals, Macdonald's policy of strong central government had largely prevailed. Most people blamed politicians, not Confederation, for the bad times of the 1870s.

Now Macdonald was free to implement his "National Policy" and retire triumphant. Most Canadians knew it as the "NP," as comforting and vague as any good political slogan. Sir Leonard Tilley would manage the details of the new tariff, and the corridors outside his office echoed with business deputations. More powerful capitalists met discreetly with Macdonald in a comfortable Toronto hotel room that the *Globe* promptly christened "the Red Chamber." The NP forged a new alliance of business and government, and so long as Liberals raged at protection, capitalists would cling to the Tories as though their economic lives depended on it.

On March 14, 1879, Tilley finally announced the new tariffs. Amid the inevitable grumbling one thing was clear: from textiles to farm machinery, Canadian manufacturers could depend on a secure national market. Making that market grow was the next priority. The recipe was simple. By filling the empty Northwest with settlers, a flood of natural products could pour eastward to pay for a returning flow of manufactured goods. The Pacific railway must be hurried not simply to reassure British Columbians but to serve the government's prime economic strategy. Pay-as-you-go, Mackenzie-style, was too slow to suit anyone.

The most promising private developer was a Montreal-based syndicate that had bought out a bankrupt railway running from St. Paul, Minnesota, north to Winnipeg. At its head was the respectable George Stephen of the Bank of Montreal, but there were also fuzzy links with Jim Hill, promoter of the Northern Pacific Railroad. And Stephen's major partner was the man who had deserted Macdonald in 1873, the ubiquitous Donald A. Smith. Sir John A. hardly hesitated; grudges were not his style. For $25 million in cash, 25 million acres along the line, a twenty-year monopoly, and permanent exemption from local taxes on its property, Stephen's syndicate would build the line. The new railway would create a huge corporation whose fortunes would be bound to the Conservative party.

Liberals thundered at the prodigality of the terms and the lack of guarantees. Their outrage only aligned Macdonald and business more closely. There were other enemies too. Officials of the Grand Trunk warned British investors against the new Canadian Pacific Railway Company. Experts warned that the CPR plan to build along the northern shore of Lake Superior was impossible. The experts were wrong. The impossible simply took longer and cost a lot more than CPR promoters had planned. A formidable American engineer, William Cornelius Van Horne, managed the construction and galvanized the huge labour gangs. To cut off the Northern Pacific from future Canadian business, the company abandoned Sandford Fleming's original northerly route through the Yellowhead Pass and headed straight west across the prairie, through the Palliser Triangle. Experts snorted that the CPR would never sell the arid land. They were kept ignorant of a more frightening risk. As Van Horne's crews raced westwards across the flat prairie, and Andrew Onderdonk's Chinese labourers struggled eastwards through the Coast Mountains, surveyors had yet to discover a pass through the difficult Selkirk Range. Only in August 1882 could they report that a way had finally been found.

In the mood of that year, Canadians might have forgiven such colossal risk-taking. With the new decade, a little prosperity had returned and the adventure of nation-building was again in style. Led now by the high-principled but ponderous Edward Blake, Liberals offered crushing condemnation of each Macdonald policy. Blake's "voluble virtue" could not bury a suspicion that, back in office, Liberals would either do the same as the Tories or nothing at all. Meanwhile, Macdonald's MPs claimed credit for each new factory and job. There were many of them.

A little-noticed victim of the National Policy was Canada's merchant fleet, the fourth largest in the world in 1867. Ottawa worried about railways, manufacturers, and farmers; shipping policy was limited to tight-fisted efforts to make coastal navigation a little safer. The Maritime region's powerful representatives – Charles Tupper, John Thompson, and William Fielding – failed to crusade for the kind of laws that Britain had used to foster a merchant marine. In the 1870s and 1880s Canadian shipping grew impressively in vessel size and efficiency; "Down East" skippers and crews won high reputations. It made no difference. Falling shipping rates persuaded owners to put their money elsewhere. A great industry was dying and few Canadians even mourned its passing.

Instead, new fortunes grew in the Maritimes. Manufacturers often complained that they got no protection from "Upper Canada"; in fact, they prospered. Factories sprouted in towns like Moncton and Amherst along the line of the Intercolonial. Coal from Pictou and Cape Breton promised to fuel the new Canadian industrial revolution. Growth was fastest, of course, where markets already were largest – in southern Quebec and Ontario. Railways confirmed the favourites – Montreal, Toronto, Hamilton – but they also fostered smaller cities where cheap labour could be drawn from oversized farm families. The flow of *Canadiens* to New England mills was diverted to Scugog, Magog, Valleyfield, and other new textile towns.

In time, Canadians learned to condemn the new factories and the squalid houses and narrow streets that grew up around them. Economic principles as well as political friendships deterred governments from meddling with long hours, unsafe machinery, and harsh factory discipline. Factory safety laws, adopted by Ontario and Quebec by 1887, were ill-enforced deterrents against employing women and children. The few trade unions organized skilled workers in construction jobs, the railways, and old crafts like printing. The Knights of Labor, a radical and idealistic working-class movement, swept into Canada from the United States in the 1880s and won short-lived political influence for workers in Ontario and Quebec. The Knights left a residue of radical ideas and leaders, but it was virtually dead by the end of the 1880s.

Middle-class humanitarians did as much as unions to ease some of the worst consequences of urban and industrial growth in the wake of the National Policy. Defending the sanctity of the family from drunkenness, prostitution, and bad sanitation gave the wives and daughters of the middle class their first reason to demand a political voice to fight vice, whisky and high infant mortality. Dr. Emily Stowe, Canada's first woman doctor, mustered a coalition of reforming forces in the 1880s to launch her campaign for women's suffrage. Women, clergy, and an emerging medical profession forced city councils to create more efficient police forces, recruit health inspectors, and develop water and sewage systems. Private investors discovered that monopoly franchises to provide streetcars, electricity, and telephone service were highly profitable. One-sided contracts depended on easygoing self-interest among urban politicians. In 1886, reform mayors in both Montreal and Toronto waged short-lived crusades against assorted municipal evils, from pit privies to prostitution. The squalid, corrupt state of contemporary American cities such as Chicago or Philadelphia spurred a short-lived Canadian righteousness.

Early in the 1880s, most Canadians were too pleased with themselves to be critical. Benjamin Disraeli had taught British Conservatives that imperialism could win working-class votes. Canadians too were "British" and shared vicariously in the thrill of distant wars. They were flattered when Queen Victoria spared her fourth daughter, Princess Louise, to accompany her husband the Marquis of Lorne to what Disraeli affably described as "one of our great vice-royalties." But their pleasure was spiced with a determination to show a sturdy indifference to snobbish affectation. As head of the Clan Campbell, Lorne was shocked when Canadian Campbells proved reluctant to doff their caps to their feudal chief. In 1881, the Marquis of Lorne, as Canada's new governor general, launched the Royal Society of Canada to honour the Dominion's scientific and literary achievements. The *Globe* dismissed it as "a mutual admiration society for nincompoops." More comfortable with intellectual distinction, *Canadiens* rejoiced when their poet, Louis Fréchette, won the French Academy's Prix Montyon in 1880. In the same year, as part of festivities to entice *Canadiens* home from New England, Montreal's Calixa Lavallée composed *O Canada*, a future national anthem.

When Macdonald sought re-election in 1882, he faced an easy victory. He took no chances, rigging the boundaries of Ontario constituencies just in case farmers really did deplore the tariff, and supporting Home Rule for Ireland to consolidate his Irish-Catholic support. The British were not amused. Nor did they welcome the creation of a powerful High Commission in London as a quasi-embassy for the Dominion. The British, however, did not vote in Canadian elections, and those who did gave Macdonald 139 seats to Blake's 71. It was hard to quarrel with prosperity.

That prosperity depended on the West. In 1881, a record number of immigrants poured into Canada, and many of them headed for Manitoba. By 1883, the postage-stamp-sized province had filled its best farmland, largely with the sons of Ontario. Winnipeg had grown from a few shacks to a town of ten thousand people – ugly, flat, but dotted with churches and schools and vacant lots that sold for an incredible $750 a running foot. The Marquis of Lorne, travelling west in 1881, dutifully inspected the Mounted Police, two thousand loyal Blackfoot warriors, and the Rockies. An entourage of British newspapermen was properly impressed by the prospects for farming and ranching.

As usual, the bubble burst – in the summer of 1883. Land prices tumbled. Fortunes invested in land along a northerly CPR line vanished when the railway took the southern route. Almost everyone blamed Ottawa. Furious at the fate of their speculations, farmers met to share grievances over freight rates and elevator monopolies and created the first of many prairie protest movements. Métis, who had sold the grants received as part of the 1870 agreement and moved west to the valley of the South Saskatchewan, again saw surveyors and recognized the vanguard of white settlement. The buffalo hunt was gone; the railway and river steamboats threatened their livelihood as teamsters. Métis settlers demanded title to riverfront lots they had staked out. Ottawa hesitated. How could the Métis be discouraged from again selling their land as so many had in Manitoba? Catholic missionaries proposed putting Métis on reserves, but the government refused to treat Métis like Indians.

Indian reserves were not an encouraging model. Perhaps the government had no better solution, once the buffalo were gone, than to form reserves and teach native people to be farmers. Good answers are still hard to find. Certainly no one anticipated the resources or patience necessary to turn nomadic hunters into peasants. Ottawa expected the job to be finished in a generation. When the buffalo vanished in 1879, Ottawa authorized government rations for starving, destitute Indian bands. Food was used as pressure to force the last roving bands to choose reserves and to heed their white farm instructors. After bad times returned in 1883, shrinking federal revenue and official impatience coalesced. To force Indians to tend their herds and their fields, rations were cut. Ottawa discounted police warnings that the Indian reserves seethed with resentment.

Ottawa was not wholly unreasonable, though it was certainly remote. Macdonald, who kept personal control of Indian policy, recognized that; whether it was quick or slow, transition would be painful. It was wiser to strengthen the police than to allow Indians to fantasize about revival of the buffalo. Moreover, as the economic slump returned, the government had immediate worries. By the end of 1883, the CPR floundered toward bankruptcy. The immigrant flow had stopped. Land sales had not provided the promised revenue. The Grand Trunk's warnings to British and European investors had succeeded. In London, Sir Alexander Galt, Canada's new high commissioner, failed to get the British to invest in the CPR or to assist emigration.

Macdonald himself was ready to retire, but so were too many of his trusted contemporaries. Persuaded by his wife to seek the bright lights of London, Sir Charles Tupper followed Galt as High Commissioner. Tilley withdrew to Fredericton as lieutenant-governor. Macdonald's preferred successor, D'Alton McCarthy, a young Irish-born Protestant, needed his Toronto law practice to pay his debts. John Thompson, a solid, sensible Nova Scotian who had served briefly as provincial premier, reluctantly came to Ottawa in 1885. In an age of religious divisions, Protestant bigots found in him a fatal flaw. Born a Baptist, he had converted to his wife's Catholicism to become, in the vicious language of the day, a "pervert." Quebec offered no powerful successor to Cartier, dead from Bright's disease in 1873. Sir Hector Langevin, the portly, dignified guardian of the alliance with the clergy, was, Macdonald curtly admitted, "lath painted to look like steel." Langevin was also tangled in the corruption of his Department of Public Works. His rival was Joseph Chapleau, bold, arrogant, and opportunistic. Chapleau spoke for the old pragmatic *bleu* tradition. He despised the Catholic ultramontanes or *Castors*[*] who mustered so many forces in his fiefdom of Montreal. Neither man could unite Quebec; either would destroy the other if he could.

After early success, Macdonald was adrift on a sea of troubles. The grievances of Indians, Métis, or settlers were lost in the waves. With the unfinished CPR foundering, Macdonald faced a bitter struggle with his own caucus to approve a loan. Resentful

---

[*] The name came from the skunk-like spray of the beaver, not from its industriousness or rich pelt.

that CPR spending had not helped their province much, French-Canadian members refused to vote until Macdonald pledged funds for the ailing, corruptly managed North Shore Railway from Montreal to Quebec City. New Brunswickers bargained their support for a "short line" that would take the CPR from Montreal through Maine to Saint John. In a single year, Canada's national debt rose by 50 per cent. By the winter of 1884–85, the CPR loan was spent, gaps remained north of Lake Superior and in the Rockies, and unpaid employees went on strike. The paycar sat at Montreal, empty.

Macdonald's *deus ex machina* arrived on March 16, 1885, as dramatic news. Police and Métis had clashed at Duck Lake, near Prince Albert. A dozen police and volunteers lay dead in the snow. The rest had fled. The peace and order that were Macdonald's prime goals for protecting and settling the West lay shattered. The young Dominion faced its first national crisis.

Anyone who wanted could read the background. Sheaves of petitions from settlers and Métis, and long, worried reports from police and officials filled government files. One petition was the work of Louis Riel, summoned back from self-imposed exile in Montana by a Métis deputation financed by Prince Albert's white settlers. To them, Riel was the man of 1870 who had forced a distant Ottawa to do his bidding. Fifteen years, some of them in Quebec's terrible Beauport lunatic asylum outside Quebec, had transformed Riel from a young excitable politician to a moody religious visionary, bitter at his own poverty and failure. At times he seemed content to draft petitions for land claims and more elected members in the territorial assembly at Regina or for his own financial claims on the government. "My name is Riel and I want material," he told a local politician. In other moods, he invented *l'Union Métisse de St-Joseph*, dreamed of a Métis empire of the South Saskatchewan, and proposed that Bishop Bourget of Montreal should become the pope of the New World while Riel shared it among the poor of Catholic Europe. Missionaries and Métis grew alarmed at sacrilege. Summoned to join the new movement, Indians listened and kept their own counsel. In Regina, Lieutenant-Governor Edgar Dewdney sent police reinforcements to the district and proposed to go north later in the spring to negotiate face-to-face.

Riel did not wait. On March 18 he seized power, arresting clergy, local officials, and any who disagreed with him. Next day, he proclaimed his new provisional government, a theocratic regime he called the "Exovedate." Prayer became his preoccupation during the weeks he expected to wait while the distant government sent negotiators, as it had in 1870. At Duck Lake, he had hoped to capture the police as hostages. The bloodshed appalled him, and he allowed the survivors to escape. At the Cut Knife and Frog Lake reserves, young Cree warriors took the police defeat as a signal for war. Two whites died near Battleford and nine more at Frog Lake, two of them Catholic missionaries. Across the Northwest, panic-stricken white settlers wired Ottawa for troops and weapons, and crowded into police forts.

Though caught by surprise, the government had no intention of negotiating. Instead, it improvised brilliantly. A CPR promise that it would somehow get troops and equipment over its unfinished track was argument enough for a further loan. Within a month, an army of five thousand regulars, militia, and local volunteers had spread across the Northwest. Major General Fred Middleton, the British officer commanding the militia, was old and pompous, but he was also able, clear-headed, and an expert in the kind of mobile warfare the 1885 campaign demanded. On May 12, two months after Riel proclaimed his Exovedate, Middleton had survived two setbacks and captured Riel's stronghold at Batoche. A few days later, Riel himself surrendered. Though Indians had fought more successfully than Riel's divided followers, their resistance collapsed with the fall of Batoche.

The 1885 rebellion is a thicket of self-serving myths. The CPR pretended that it had saved the Northwest from Riel. In fact Riel saved the CPR from ruin. Canadian troops could just as easily have passed through the United States; some did. The Americans were eager to help stop a dangerous threat north of their border. The corporation that made a difference was the Hudson's Bay Company. Without its transport and supplies, Middleton could hardly have stirred beyond the CPR track. Middleton's subordinates resented him, but he set out sooner and marched faster than the experts advised, split his forces only at Ottawa's insistence, and did all he could to save his raw troops from surprise or heavy casualties. In both purposes, he succeeded. Middleton's greatest ally was Louis Riel. Having launched his Métis and Indian followers in open revolt, Riel retreated into mysticism, inhibiting every intelligent effort at self-defence. A Half-Breed Claims Commission, established before the outbreak, settled Métis land claims, but Riel's failure removed pressure to reassess Indian policy or the future of the people he led. The rebellion of 1885 proved disastrous to Indians and Métis alike.

Riel's egoism was unquenched. At Regina, where he was allowed to use the police commissioner's office, he wrote to Macdonald to ask for a state trial in Ottawa. Once acquitted, he would like to be premier of Manitoba. Macdonald had other plans. Those who had plotted the outbreak would be punished as a warning to anyone else who might fish in troubled waters. Investigation found no widespread conspiracy, only Riel. He was tried at Regina for high treason. Lawyers dispatched by the Quebec *rouges* tried to prove that Riel was insane, but when Riel spoke on his own behalf, he was rational and persuasive. Only one verdict was possible, but a western jury understood Riel's grievances well enough to add their own plea for mercy. The judge condemned him to hang.

A later generation, using a colloquial definition of "treason," may insist that Riel never betrayed anyone. This is undoubtedly true. However, the language of law and that of popular parlance sometimes differ. No one had denied that he had "levied war upon Her Majesty," and it is worth remembering that it was for this kind of treason that he was condemned. Egomania, folly, and religious eccentricity had nothing to do with the law.

Riel's sentence split Canadian opinion. For partisan reasons, Liberals blamed Macdonald for the outbreak, not the Métis. Ontarians assumed that the law would now take its course, as it had not in 1870. *Canadiens* were as shocked by the rebellion as anyone and even more horrified by the murder of missionaries, but by summer they had shifted ground. Riel became the pathetic madman, alone in his Regina cell. French Canadians had refused to join the flood of western settlement, but the Métis remained their proxies and their grievances were real enough. Joseph Israël Tarte, a veteran *bleu* organizer, warned: "At the moment when the corpse of Riel falls through the trap and twists in convulsions of agony, at that moment an abyss will be dug that will separate Quebec from English-speaking Canada." The decision rested with Macdonald, and it had been made long before controversy broke out. Few politicians had more contempt for public opinion – "mere newspapers," he called it – or for the Orange Lodge. Macdonald was a patient man, and if Quebec colleagues insisted on allowing appeals or on more medical examinations of Riel's sanity, he would wait. Finally his three French-speaking Quebec ministers gave their consent. On November 16, 1885, Riel was hanged.

"Old Tomorrow" had learned that political fires sooner or later die down. Macdonald was partly right. The fires would die, but not soon. On November 22, huge crowds packed

Montreal's Champ de Mars. "If I had been on the banks of the Saskatchewan," shouted Wilfrid Laurier, "I too would have shouldered my musket." Even more heard Honoré Mercier, the former *bleu*, now Quebec Liberal leader. The Riel crisis made him leader of the Parti National, a strange new alliance of *Castors* and *rouges*. "Riel, our brother, is dead," cried Mercier, "victim of his devotion to the cause of the Métis, of whom he was the leader, victim of fanaticism and treason – of the fanaticism of Sir John and some of his friends, of the treason of three of our people who sold their brother to keep their portfolios." In Ottawa, Conservative strategists manoeuvred to control the damage. On a key vote, condemning the government, sixteen French Canadians abandoned the government, but twenty-three English-speaking Liberals deserted Edward Blake's party.

In much of Canada, the scars of the Northwest Rebellion soon vanished. In the West, settlers were too busy struggling with homesteads and an alarming new drought cycle to care very much. The notion of a Protestant Ontario ravening for Riel's blood is an ugly myth perpetuated by lazy historians. Violent editorials from the Orange *Sentinel* or the radical Toronto *News* should be set against major Liberal papers which condemned Macdonald as much as Riel for the tragedy. Blake's defence of Riel in 1886 and his insistence on Laurier as his successor in 1887 were two of the decisive steps in determining the future of the Liberal party. They were acts of a party whose electorate was mostly Ontarian.

POLITICAL REVOLUTION | 4

By now the elements of Macdonald's National Policy were in place. On November 7, 1885, a white-bearded Donald Smith pounded home the last iron spike of the CPR. Passengers could soon travel the three thousand miles from Montreal to Burrard Inlet in a week. On the way, they would pass the world's largest nickel deposit, accidentally discovered by CPR survey crews near Sudbury. Settlers, coming west on the CPR's colonist cars, would find land offices ready to help them locate and "prove up" their quarter-section grants in the vast checkerboard pattern the surveyors had laid on the prairie. At Indian Head, a government experimental farm began to wrestle with the problems of prairie agriculture. In the East, Macdonald's 1882 victory had convinced even timid investors that protective tariffs would last. New factories opened and old ones expanded, despite the return of hard times.

In Parliament, newspaper editorials, and countless country stores, the merits of the "NP" were endlessly debated. So was Riel's execution. Symbolically as important as the CPR in opening the West for peaceful white settlement, Riel's death handed Quebec to Honoré Mercier. By the end of 1887, the CPR's monopoly clause also undermined John Norquay's Conservatives in Manitoba. In British Columbia, the choice of Vancouver as CPR terminus had infuriated both Victoria and New Westminster. Onderdonk's Chinese encouraged employers to seek cheap labour from Canton for the province's mines and forest industry. White workers found a solid economic basis for their racial prejudices. The result was a durable, radical labour movement, toe-to-toe with British Columbia's wealthiest entrepreneurs.

Eastern workers might owe their jobs to National Policy tariffs, but they had little else in common with their bosses. Commentators warned that Canada would soon see the labour violence of the United States or the class warfare of Europe. A royal commission on the relations of capital and labour, designed to glorify the achievements of the National Policy, collected testimony of employer tyranny and greed. Rather than suggest significant reforms, the commission was content to scold. "To obtain a very large percentage of work with the smallest possible outlay of wages," a commissioner concluded, "appears to be the one fixed and dominant idea."

Farmers were even more resentful than workers. No policy could have protected them from a cycle of drought, poor yields, and low world prices, but the NP included nothing specific to please them. Western settlers complained that CPR freight rates and policies reflected all the evils of monopoly. Farmers everywhere condemned a tariff that forced them to pay more for their balers, binders, and hay rakes and, for that matter, for the boots, ribbons, and corsets their wives wanted for their Sunday best. In the 1870s, joining farm organizations like the Grange had helped make some farmers non-partisan but class-conscious. Now the Grange was supplanted by the militant

Patrons of Industry. The American-based organization soon had thousands of members across Ontario and the West, denouncing tariffs, monopolies, and political corruption.

Caught between Mercier and Mowat, with his policies under attack and the country plainly in trouble, Macdonald should have lost the 1887 election. Edward Blake wore out his audiences and himself with carefully documented proof of blunders, failures, and maladministration. In Quebec, the ghost of Riel stalked every *bleu*. It was all in vain. Macdonald emerged victorious with 126 seats to Blake's 89. *Bleus* even won a tiny majority in French Canada. Sick and humiliated, Blake quit.

Every problem remained and some of them grew worse as Canada followed the world deeper into the depression. Macdonald had won because Blake had been too honest to offer any panaceas. For all his denunciations, the Liberal leader could see no fundamental alternative to the NP – except, of course, his own incorruptible management. Others insisted that Canadians had alternatives to both the NP and to the shapeless, corrupt compromises of Macdonald's pluralist politics. Since 1884, when Torontonians had formed a branch of the British-born Imperial Federation League, their rising star had been Macdonald's possible successor, the handsome, eloquent young D'Alton McCarthy. His speeches had a powerful appeal to those English-speaking Canadians who believed that their country would be a simpler, happier place if the battle on the Plains of Abraham had represented a final solution. Quebec's apparent insistence that Riel go free because he was French struck McCarthy's followers as a case in point. McCarthy's cold, logical mind rejected the florid excesses of Orange bigotry; it pierced deeper, to even more dangerous ideas. Nations, he insisted, grew from common experiences and language. Canada must be British or French, Protestant or Catholic. A choice must be made firmly and soon. Ontario audiences agreed.

McCarthy's British-Canadian nationalism was a perfect foil for Mercier. In his own way, McCarthy echoed all of Mercier's criticisms of the *bleus*. As Quebec premier, Mercier was scrupulously fair to his English Protestant minority, but he presented himself, as no *bleu* premier had ever dared, as the outspoken champion of a French, Catholic Quebec. Mercier defied anticlerical opinion by appointing Curé François-Xavier Labelle, an ardent promoter of northern settlement, as deputy minister for colonization. He visited Paris and Rome and returned bedecked with French and papal decorations. Mercier launched railways and public works Quebec could not afford but which it badly wanted.

Above all, Mercier settled the tiresome old Jesuit-estates issue in a way deliberately designed to tease the Equal Righters and to win more French and Catholic votes. For years, the Jesuit-estates issue had only divided Catholics. Confiscated in 1800, after the last Jesuit in Lower Canada died, the rich estates had helped finance both Catholic and Protestant schools. When the Jesuits returned to Canada in 1843, they asked for their land back. Rival Catholic orders had grown used to their share of Jesuit revenues, and the quarrel poisoned Church relations for decades. Mercier's trip to Rome gave him a solution. The Jesuits would get their lands back. Protestants were happy with $60,000 in compensation, and $400,000 more in public funds would be shared among Catholics, with the pope as final arbiter of the distribution.

Mercier knew perfectly well that any reference to the pope and Jesuits would arouse Protestant militants, and they rose to the bait. Across Ontario and in English-speaking Quebec, protest meetings denounced papal meddling, appealed for "equal rights for all," and demanded that Ottawa disallow the Jesuit Estates Act. Horrified at the bigotry and appalled at the political folly of followers like McCarthy who had joined the campaign,

Macdonald refused. By a vote of 188 to 13, Parliament agreed with the prime minister. Across the country, new equal-rights associations hailed the dissenters as the "Noble Thirteen." In a ragbag of Liberals and Tories, D'Alton McCarthy shone as a leader. By preferring his principles over ambition, McCarthy had become a dangerous man in Canadian politics.

Manitoba's John Norquay had been defeated by a lacklustre Liberal named Thomas Greenway. Within two years, Greenway's government was mired in failure and minor scandal. During the summer of 1889, McCarthy visited the West, drawing throngs to the parks and picnic grounds of raw prairie towns. Two decades of immigration had transformed the Red River Colony into a little Ontario. Crowds cheered themselves hoarse at McCarthy's assault on separate schools and French. Westerners, he claimed, had the power "to make this a British country in fact as in name." Bereft of policy, Greenway Liberals heard the cheers and took the hint. In 1890, a new law gave the little province its first "national school" system, nondenominational, English-speaking, and publicly financed. Greenway won a new and bigger majority. The guarantees that missionaries and Métis had inserted in the Manitoba Act of 1870 vanished under majority assault. Under that act, it was now up to Ottawa to provide remedies.

Between them, Mercier and McCarthy had severely damaged the *bleu*-Tory alliance that had held power since 1854. In Manitoba, McCarthy's views had been seized on by Liberals. This was acutely embarrassing to the party's new federal leader. On retiring, Blake had insisted that Wilfrid Laurier become his successor. The young Quebec politician hesitated: he had neither the health nor the private wealth for the job. Worse, in the mood of the times, could a French-speaking Catholic ever be accepted by the Grit strongholds of Ontario? Party elders quietly agreed, but perhaps Laurier would do for a while until a real leader was found. The interim leader lasted thirty-two years.

Liberal strategists agreed on one point: Blake had lost in 1887 because he failed to provide the "heroic remedy" Canadians wanted. One was now available. Erastus Wiman, a Canadian expatriate and New York millionaire, and Samuel Ritchie, the American who developed Sudbury's nickel, urged a "Continental Union" of Canada and the United States, with a common tariff wall against the world. If full annexation followed, so be it. Massive Canadian emigration to the United States and the failure of the National Policy had long ago revealed Confederation as a failure. "CU," as the scheme was abbreviated, delighted inveterate free traders like Sir Richard Cartwright. Edward Farrer, the lively journalist who now edited the *Globe*, took up the idea. So did Goldwin Smith, a former Oxford professor who had moved to Toronto, married a rich widow, and appointed himself Canada's resident intellectual. Annexation, Smith believed, was only a logical first step to a transatlantic English-speaking union. Americans would achieve what Canadians had been too timid to accomplish: the full assimilation of French-Canadian Catholics.

For Laurier, annexation was repugnant; even a customs union was too heroic. A compromise version – unrestricted reciprocity – seemed ideal. Customs barriers between the two countries would vanish, but each would set its own tariffs against the world. Economic details never bothered Laurier; it was politics that mattered. Unrestricted reciprocity, or "UR," satisfied party veterans like Cartwright. It gave the Liberals a neat slogan to match "NP." Above all, it captivated Ontario farmers and distracted them from Laurier's race and religion, and his accented, if eloquent, English. Even loyal Canadians still pined for the old Reciprocity Agreement. A flood of emigrants from Ontario as well as Quebec farms had confirmed what visitors reported: the United States was booming while Canada stagnated. Karl Marx's partner, Friedrich Engels, finally found a positive word for capitalism when he visited Canada in 1888. After three days of viewing decayed towns and ruined farmsteads, Engels recognized "how necessary the feverish speculative spirit of the Americans is for the rapid development of a new country." Canadians who agreed could choose between Commercial Union and unrestricted reciprocity.

Did either policy threaten an end to an independent Canada? Did anyone care? By the end of the 1880s, many agreed with Laurier himself: "We have come to a period in the history of this young country when premature dissolution seems to be at hand." In Winnipeg, the *Free Press* warned Newfoundland, bankrupt and contemplating Confederation, to give the Dominion a wide berth. "There are few provinces, if any, in it today that would not rejoice to be out of it." In 1887, J.W. Longley had been attorney general in a Liberal government bent on repealing Nova Scotia's membership in Confederation. Now, as Erastus Wiman's agent, he travelled the United States promoting Continental Union.

Yet envy of the Americans mingled with fear and resentment. In 1890, Canadians had plenty of reason to see the harsh as well as the prosperous side of their neighbours. On both coasts, fisheries agreements had proved costly and painful. In the Bering Sea, American warships seized Canadian sealing vessels in the name of conservation while American sealers went undisturbed. James Blaine, the new secretary of state, had made his name with Irish voters as an enemy of Britain and Canada. In Congress, the new McKinley tariff promised to end Canada's important cross-border grain trade. During speaking tours in 1890, Macdonald found that farmers could talk of little else.

The Old Chieftain's first notion was to outflank Laurier by seeking a modest reciprocity agreement and unveiling it for the 1891 election. Blaine refused to see an official delegation from a mere British colony; then he told a curious congressman that he knew of no Canadian negotiations, and Macdonald's scheme failed. Next Macdonald tried another strategy – bolder, more dangerous, but closer to his heart. Talk of dissolution and annexation and continental union disgusted him. In 1887, he had fought a winter campaign, enduring draughty meeting halls, icy sleigh rides, and long hours in unheated railway cars. At seventy-six he did not want another, but time was not on his side. On February 2, 1891, the old man called the election.

Experts foresaw defeat. Yet, as long as Macdonald lived, the old Conservative alliance would survive. To save the NP, business would fill the party coffers. William Van Horne pledged that every CPR employee was "a circumcised Tory." One issue might again pull weary voters back to the Conservatives: loyalty. A German-Canadian journalist, Louis Kribs, coined a slogan: "The Old Man, the Old Flag, the Old Policy." Across Canada, even in Quebec, Macdonald summoned personal and imperial loyalty. "A British subject I was born, a British subject I will die," he cried. "With my utmost effort, with my latest breath, will I oppose the 'veiled treason' which attempts with sordid means and mercenary proffers to lure our people from their allegiance." Posters, more elaborate than in earlier elections, depicted Laurier and Cartwright negotiating with Americans behind the Old Chieftain's back. Two weeks into the campaign, Macdonald revealed the "treason": printers' proofs of a pamphlet by Ned Farrer arguing not just for annexation but revealing how America could squeeze Canadians into surrender. Since Farrer edited the leading Liberal newspaper, the link to Laurier hardly needed to be made.

Laurier was not helpless. In Quebec, Mercier offered full support. In Ontario, Mowat was staunch and as unquestionably pro-British as Macdonald. Grit farmers liked the Liberal trade policy. So did Quebec farmers, despite warnings from their bishops that annexation might result. On March 5, the great loyalty campaign ended. In Quebec, Laurier took 37 of 65 seats; in Ontario, Macdonald emerged with a mere 4-seat margin. It was the rest of Canada – the "shreds and patches," as Cartwright called them – that settled the outcome: 121 seats for Macdonald, 94 seats for Laurier. The Tory margin came from the CPR-dominated regions and from the Maritimes, where British loyalty mattered.

Three months later, Macdonald was dead. The campaign killed him. He died believing that he had saved the country he had created. Many of Canada's three-quarters of a million voters felt that they knew him, with his huge nose and his flying hair, his wit and his patient cynicism. "You'll never die, John A.," the crowds had shouted. Now he was suddenly gone, without an obvious successor. Would the young Dominion die with him? His contemporaries and later generations regretted that the undoubted first Father of Confederation never provided uplifting moral lessons for the young. In fact, Macdonald had shown how to manage Canada, with infinite patience and cunning, by bold vision and an infinity of small compromises, and by remembering that every enemy might someday be needed as a friend.

"A week is a long time in politics," said a later British prime minister. Macdonald knew it well. By 1891, Riel, equal rights, and Jesuit estates barely mattered. The election was over before the 1891 census revealed evidence of depopulation. By then prosperity seemed to be returning. Britain absorbed the wheat excluded by the McKinley tariff and asked for more. A mining boom began in the Kootenay region of British Columbia, and a new railway through the Crowsnest Pass was projected.

Macdonald's successor was old Sir John Abbott, a venerable senator who had signed the Annexation Manifesto in 1849 and whose ransacked office provided the evidence of Macdonald's corrupt dealing in 1872. A cabinet of tired ministers chose him because he was "not particularly obnoxious to anybody." Abbott might have promoted the ambitious Joseph Chapleau to be his lieutenant, but, he reasoned, he would also have hurt poor old Sir Hector Langevin's feelings. Someone else would do that.

For years, J. Israël Tarte, Quebec Tory organizer and Chapleau's ally, had slowly gathered evidence of corrupt contracts and kickbacks in Langevin's Department of Public Works. Instead of tearing themselves and Laurier apart over their defeat, the Liberals acquired Tarte as a convert and his scandals as ammunition. A veteran Tory MP and a cluster of officials went to jail. Langevin might well have joined them had he not resigned. Liberal rejoicing was premature. Suddenly, amidst the chaotic finances of a bankrupt Baie des Chaleurs Railway, Honoré Mercier's corruption lay exposed. Canadians discovered who had paid for his luxurious trips to Paris and Rome. Quebec's Conservatives swept Mercier's nationalist regime from office and then turned to the unpopular business of restoring Quebec's financial credit. A Mercier for a Langevin: all politicians were tarred with the same brush.

Liberal troubles were not over. In 1891, Blake and Mowat had seen the annexationist implications of Laurier's policy of unrestricted reciprocity. Both men loyally kept silent, but with the election over, Blake explained in an open letter why he had not stood again in West Durham. His message virtually accused his fellow Liberals of plotting treason. To be fair, Blake himself never intended the consequences of his letter. After every general election, the parties laid a host of charges of electoral malpractice. Party managers then met, traded cases, and settled on a few to be fought through the courts and in by-elections. With their coffers bulging, this time the Tories insisted on trying every charge. The penniless Liberals had no means to defend themselves. Blake's West Durham letter cost the Liberals over thirty seats. By 1895, the Tory majority had climbed from thirty-one to sixty-three. To many Liberals, it was proof enough that Laurier's leadership had been a sad mistake. Even without the Old Chieftain, the Tories seemed unbeatable.

Appearances deceived. One small nagging issue slowly tore the government apart: the Manitoba schools. As usual, "Old Tomorrow" had put off the issue. So did Abbott. A strong successor could have made a decision, confident that the inevitable turbulence would have settled before another election. No competent lawyer could doubt Ottawa's duty. As a province, Manitoba could enact its Schools Act, but under the remedial sections of the Manitoba Act, Ottawa was equally obliged to restore the rights of the French and Catholic minority. Majority rights, a compact of founding nations, or Protestant survival were not at issue; only the political will to enforce the law.

By November 1892 Abbott was fed up with politics and quit. His successor seemed inevitable. Rarely had a more decent or honourable man come to Ottawa than Sir John Thompson. His wisdom was apparent in Canada's new Criminal Code and other reforms as minister of justice. Dignified, an able debater, knowledgeable, Thompson never overcame one political affliction, his conversion to Catholicism. As prime minister, he could never rise up and flatten the bigots. He could not promote Chapleau because Tory Orangemen would have protested, so the last great *bleu* left for gilded retirement as lieutenant-governor of Quebec. Thompson was left with extremists; F.A. Angers, an ultramontane *Castor* whom Chapleau despised, and N. Clarke Wallace, past grand master of the Orange Lodge.

For all his wisdom, Thompson was not the man to deal with the Manitoba issue. Instead, he sent it back to the courts for two more years, forcing the Manitoba minorities to wait and showing even the most patient French Canadians that Ottawa would do almost anything to avoid upholding equality of language and religion in the West. Only a month before the judicial committee decided the obvious – that Ottawa had the right to impose remedial legislation – Thompson died suddenly at Windsor Castle while visiting Queen Victoria.

Sir Charles Tupper was now the obvious prime minister, though some cabinet ministers shuddered at the prospect of the bullying "War Horse of the Cumberland." They were saved by an unexpected ally. Lord Aberdeen, a Scottish Liberal, was now governor general, but the formidable Lady Aberdeen was in charge. Like many others, she detested Tupper. Left to herself, she might have summoned Laurier, but her husband compromised. Another decrepit veteran, Senator Mackenzie Bowell, an honest but indecisive Orangeman, followed Thompson. All hope of firm action on Manitoba faded. First Angers and then Wallace left the cabinet.

Once again in a state of gloom after the latest worldwide economic crash in 1893, Canadians diverted themselves with Bowell's fumbling. First, he politely invited Manitoba to mend its ways. The province's able attorney general, Clifford Sifton, waited eight months and said no. In January 1896 seven federal cabinet ministers resigned in a body to force Bowell to quit. First Bowell branded them a "Nest of Traitors"; then he took them back. Nearing the end of its five-year term, Parliament started to debate remedial legislation for the Manitoba minority. To delay proceedings, Laurier's Liberals delivered endless speeches until, on April 24, the eighth parliament expired.

What was Laurier doing? In 1891, he had fumbled his first test; Manitoba Schools seemed even harder. In 1893, the first national Liberal convention met in Ottawa, buried unrestricted reciprocity, and found a compromise. The Manitoba issue was not resolved. Laurier was trapped between the Protestants of Ontario and Manitoba and the threat, brought by the great missionary from the Northwest, Father Albert Lacombe, that Quebec's bishops would rise as one man to support remedial legislation. Canada in the 1890s was aflame with religious conflict. Emotions set blazing by the Equal Rights Association had not gone out. In 1894, a Protestant Protective Association elected fourteen Ontario members against Oliver Mowat. In Quebec, clerics revived the old Holy War against the *rouges*. What could a French-Canadian Catholic with a following in Protestant Canada do?

The answer was that he would do nothing. It was the first evidence that Laurier was Sir John A.'s true disciple. J. Israël Tarte, the ex-*bleu*, was now his closest confidant. In Quebec, where the turncoat had applied his remarkable talents to building a Laurier machine, Tarte made a crucial discovery: ordinary French Canadians knew little and cared less about Manitoba. They did not intend to go there. They did not care much for those who had. On the other hand, with both Macdonald and Mercier gone, and a colourless Conservative government in Quebec City, *Canadiens* yearned for real political leadership. Wilfrid Laurier was the only candidate. Faced with this shrewd analysis, Laurier's course was clear: silence and inaction. It was, after all, the ultimate privilege of an opposition leader. Forced to speak, Laurier recalled the old French fable of the man who had shed his coat for the sun, not the wind. Coercion, he warned, would never work: "If it were in my power, I would try the sunny way." It was a message that Tarte could sell on Laurier's behalf; he believed in it himself. Outside Quebec, Laurier could preach provincial rights. It now seemed a safe doctrine everywhere.

On April 23, the 1896 election campaign began. By prior agreement, only then did Tupper replace Bowell, becoming the fifth prime minister in five years. Everywhere he found division and defection in Tory ranks. Chapleau ignored the party that had ignored him; secretly he sent *bleu* supporters to Laurier. In Ontario, Tory candidates denounced the remedial legislation they had supposedly spent months trying to push through

Parliament; in Quebec, Conservatives proclaimed their devotion to minority rights. Mostly, they counted on the bishops. The bishops met and proclaimed it "a great wrong" to back any candidate who refused to back remedial action. Promptly, all but eight of Laurier's Quebec candidates swore their support for remedial legislation. Only Bourget's disciple, Bishop Louis-François Laflèche of Trois-Rivières, issued his customary denunciation of the Liberals. He was echoed by some Ontario Protestants. A Liberal vote, warned one Methodist preacher, "would stare the voter in the face at Judgement Day and condemn him to eternal perdition."

Despite the air of religious intolerance, clerical threats had surprisingly little effect in 1896. In fact, it was Sir Charles Tupper who was his party's chief asset. The dogged old man bullied his worn-out party machine into action. Though both D'Alton McCarthy and N. Clarke Wallace campaigned as hard for Laurier as they did for themselves, Tupper and the old issues of industry and tariff protection prevented a Tory rout. When the polls closed, Laurier's Liberals had won 118 seats to Tupper's 88. The Patrons of Industry, rustic pioneers for future third parties, elected three members from Ontario.

In an election full of ironies, the greatest was in Manitoba. Only with great difficulty could the two Protestant champions, Sifton and McCarthy, get elected. Manitobans voted 47 per cent for the party favouring remedial legislation, and only 35 per cent for the Liberals.

A political revolution was complete. Canadians in 1896 could not know it, but the Liberals would prove even more durable in office than the Conservatives. Neither period of hegemony was unbroken. Macdonald had lost to Mackenzie; Laurier would lose to Robert Borden. Yet both parties would regain power and cling to it because Macdonald and Laurier each mastered the compromises that made Canada possible.

Like most revolutions, the political upheaval that occurred in Canada between 1886 and 1896 changed symbols, not substance. The Liberals had won and continued to win when they remembered their core of support in Quebec, the expectations of the business community, and the scattered, contradictory grievances of the rest of Canada. Sir John A. Macdonald had found his successor at last.

PART III

"THE CENTURY OF CANADA"

I | FLOURISHING

C anadians would later recognize 1896 as one of the decisive years of their history. At the time, they barely noticed. Of course, politics and the federal election were common preoccupations. On the other hand, Canadians largely ignored a border dispute between Venezuela and British Guiana that almost brought war between Britain and the United States – with Canada as the inevitable battle-ground. Apart from buying a few rifles and machine guns for her ill-equipped militia, the Dominion did nothing. In Britain, the consequences were much more profound, but history seldom shows its significance all at once.

Canadians ignored other vital events of the year. Washington announced the end of homesteading on public lands. Manitoba persuaded William Mackenzie and his burly partner Donald Mann to build a line from Gladstone to Dauphin for $7000 a mile. In August, a man known as "Lying George" Carmack, with two Indian companions, Skookum Jim and Tagish Charlie, found gold near the Klondike River. All three developments were probably as significant for Canada as Laurier's 1896 election victory. So were other events. Gold, pouring out of South African mines by the 1890s, sent prices for food and other natural products climbing. Shipping rates stayed low, continuing the slow strangulation of an old Maritime industry but making it feasible once again to pour wheat into the European market. In 1895, workmen began the first hydroelectric installation at Niagara Falls. After Canadian engineers solved the problem of winter freeze-up, "white coal" would provide a basis for significant industrial growth.

Instead of hope, most Canadians in 1896 shared a durable gloom. In June, the Bank of Commerce reported on a year "of constant anxiety and almost unexampled difficulty in making profits and avoiding losses." Farmers grumbled at the McKinley tariff. Worse would come when the Republicans, as now seemed inevitable, returned to power. A promising cattle trade with Britain ended after severe quarantine regulations were enacted.

Meanwhile, Laurier's victorious Liberals took power. The handover was graceless. Tupper made a post-election bid to cram Tories into every vacant judgeship and Senate seat. The Aberdeens refused to sign the appointments, and the old man resigned in a snarling constitutional fury. Most Canadians were amused that Tupper had forgotten to fill the jobs before voting day, when the patronage might have won him votes or campaign funds.

The new prime minister would make no such errors. Laurier looked frail, but he had grown healthier with age. Voters and even colleagues knew him as an elegant, courtly man, with an aura that inspired love but never familiarity. Laurier had no taste for laborious detail; he could be captivated by ideas and he had the language to captivate others. Some ministers deceived themselves that the prime minister was a charming lightweight, to be used for their purposes. Such men were dismissed with icy ruthlessness and found themselves too isolated for vengeance.

On the low road of politics as on the high, Laurier was a consummate expert.

He showed his skills immediately. The new cabinet was the ablest Canada had yet seen. Nova Scotia's William Fielding, one of three provincial premiers brought to Ottawa, took finance; Cartwright, the unrepentant free-trader, was relegated to trade and commerce. The tariff would be safe with Fielding. Oliver Mowat became minister of justice. Old *rouge* comrades were set aside for Tarte, the link with the *bleus*. He would wield the immense patronage of public works. To settle Manitoba, Laurier adopted more than "sunny ways." To earn his cabinet post, Clifford Sifton had to talk Thomas Greenway into a compromise. Manitoba's minorities could get an education in their own language if they formed classes of ten or more students. Religious instruction would occur at the end of the day. Catholic bishops threatened new holy wars at the inadequacy of the settlement but a papal envoy insisted on restraint. An old, dangerous issue vanished, and some bishops found pleasure in dealing with a French and Catholic prime minister.

Laurier took office with few policies. He simply inherited the old NP. History played into his hands. The National Policy had rested on false assumptions: Canada in the 1880s was not yet an east-west economy. Her products went to Britain, the United States, or stayed home unsold. Immigrants refused to go to Canada's Northwest while good American land remained unsettled. Macdonald's policy flew in the face of facts. Suddenly the facts changed. When American public land was closed in 1896, Canada's prairies became the "Last Best West." Rising world prices and cheap shipping created a world market for the hard spring wheat from Canada. It was Laurier who could claim that "this scientific tariff of ours" safeguarded a booming western market for Canadian manufacturers.

Laurier's good fortune was as much an accident as was

Carmack's discovery of gold. The resulting gold fever drew swarms of prospectors to the Yukon. The Klondike created few durable fortunes and established no permanent industry, and by 1899 the bonanza was over. The gold rush provided a brief but dramatic economic stimulus for British Columbia and Alberta, and it drew a flood of attention to Canada. Photographs of sourdoughs and the Chilkoot Pass did not dispel the Dominion's image of "Our Lady of the Snows"; they did replace Engels's 1888 impression of stagnant decay with a vision of dynamism and wealth, and of law and order firmly enforced by scarlet-coated policemen. As Macdonald's heir, Laurier responded to the Klondike discovery much as the Old Chieftain might have. Mounted police and soldiers were sent to preserve order, not merely for its own sake but to give Americans in nearby Alaska no pretext for intervention. A railway link was considered but abandoned as too costly and slow. Only in 1899, after most of the Yukon's thirty thousand people were thinking of leaving, was a territorial government in place.

It was Canada's good fortune that so many Americans always believed that the northern prairie was as cold as the Yukon. The illusion had discouraged neighbourly covetousness. With no other outlet for the younger sons who had always gone west to homestead, Americans came to Canada to see for themselves. As minister of the interior, Clifford Sifton had the happy role of presiding over their exploration. He did so with flair. Editors and farm leaders joined guided tours. Lush Canadian produce won prizes at agricultural shows. The claims of Red Fife wheat were trumpeted until it was supplanted, in 1903, by an even finer product of the Dominion's experimental farms, Charles Saunders's Marquis. Visitors revelled in Sifton's philosophy. "One of the principal ideas western men have," he boasted, "is that it is right to take anything in sight provided nobody else is ahead of them."

American homesteaders, often with an Ontario ancestor or two, made an easy transition. Most had experience in dryland agriculture and support from a family farm back in Kansas or Minnesota. Sifton was not content to wait. Bales of pamphlets and speakers armed with magic lantern slides set off for the traditional source of immigrants, Britain. Colonization agents waited at Hamburg and Bremen, where European immigrants embarked for America. To populate the Canadian West, Sifton ignored old priorities of race and language. Years later he explained that he had sought "stout, hardy peasants in sheepskin coats," who could endure pioneering hardships and make the prairie prosper. If they were Poles or Germans or Ukrainians, the "national schools" he had won for Manitoba would turn their children into good Canadians.

The newcomers justified Sifton's expectations. The North West Mounted Police, whose systematic patrols and hard-headed welfare programs were as vital to prairie homesteading as railway and land offices, judged "Sifton's sheepskins" with a stern but practical eye and found them acceptable. Others did not pass their test. Keir Hardie, the Scottish socialist, was shocked to find that English labourers were among the least favoured species of settler. Employers loudly complained about their trade union ideas. Meanwhile Canadian labour protested immigration policies that undermined wage rates with floods of cheap labour.

With or without Sifton, the Canadian West's time had come. Between 1896 and 1911, more than a million people poured into the region. Wheat production rose from 29 to 209 million bushels a year. A spiderweb of railway branch lines spread across the prairie, built mainly by homesteaders in need of cash between seeding and harvest time. Ten miles was as far as any settler could haul wheat in a horse-drawn wagon. Wherever rail lines passed, towns could grow. In Sifton's free-enterprise West, land speculators could build extravagant dreams of future metropolises on local pride and cupidity. Sometimes the land speculators struck pay dirt. In 1900, Saskatoon was a general store. In 1902, it was hard to find twenty houses to make it a village. Three years later it was a city. The 1911 census found twelve thousand people, a university, and two transcontinental railways. More ended like Dominion City, a hole on the map.

Prairie settlers had little in common with the self-sufficient backwoodsmen in Upper Canada or the *habitants* of New France. Beyond turf for their first leaky sod hut and a flurry of birds and small animals for the pot, the land provided little but a cash crop. Pioneers were consumers. To build homes, they needed lumber from British Columbia and nails, glass, and furniture from the East. Fuel for the long prairie winter came from coal mines that Sir Alexander Galt's sons had profitably developed in the foothills of the Rockies. It was very much as Sir John A. Macdonald would have predicted, with the infuriating exception that Liberals were in power, taking the political and (in Sifton's case) the personal profits.

In 1897, for example, it was perfectly in the NP tradition that the CPR would receive a handsome subsidy for pushing a line through the Crowsnest Pass to Vancouver. This restored a Canadian presence in a region American mining companies were treating as their own backyard. The CPR gained subsidies, a new region, and an unexpected dividend, the rich Sullivan mine at Trail. In return, the railway agreed to a perpetual freeze on the freight rates for wheat heading east and manufactured goods heading west. In an age of stable prices, the Crowsnest rate seemed like a fair deal.

Meanwhile, in 1898, barely noticed by most Canadians, the Intercolonial Railway finally reached Montreal in its long struggle to become profitable. In its patronage-ridden career, the ICR had served its region as best it could. Unlike the CPR, which thirsted for profits, the ICR needed political friends and found them by cutting its rates. It did so still. Maritime producers got rates as much as 50 per cent lower than in central Canada – and even lower ones could be negotiated. While the Maritime age of wood, wind, and water was ending, a new industrialism had already taken its place. In 1870, New Brunswick's manufacturing income per capita was close to the national average, and it kept on growing. Between 1900 and 1920, manufacturing grew four-fold in Nova Scotia and fivefold in New Brunswick. Two iron and steel complexes developed; so did sugar refining, clothing and shoe factories, and a host of engineering and hardware manufacturers. Thanks to the ICR's rates, even prairie residents used Simms's brushes, ate Ganong's chocolates, and spread Crosby's molasses. The Maritimes grumbled and prospered, a satisfying combination.

At times, Laurier could even improve on Macdonald. Caught between Liberal protectionists and free traders, with a rising chorus of imperialists in Toronto and English-speaking Montreal, a fumbler would have failed. Between them, Fielding and Laurier united disparate forces in their 1897 budget by pro-claiming a unilateral "imperial preference." The reductions hurt few entrenched interests, pleased tariff cutters, and helped Laurier cut an imperial figure when he went to London for Queen Victoria's Diamond Jubilee. British audiences applauded the effusively eloquent French Canadian. His private views were less welcome. Britain's colonial secretary, Joseph Chamberlain, found the newly knighted Sir Wilfrid opposed to British schemes to involve Canada in imperial defence.

This, too, was in the Macdonald tradition. The old man had despised "over-washed Englishmen" and dismissed D'Alton McCarthy's "imperial federation" as nonsense. British overtures for military aid during the 1885 Sudan crisis had been politely rejected. Militia colonels "anxious for excitement or notoriety," Macdonald insisted, did not speak for Canada.

In 1891, when Macdonald had proclaimed "a British subject I was born, a British subject I will die," he meant no more than had Laurier in 1897, when he declared to London audiences, "I am British to the core." Since neither man wanted to be an American, the alternative was to be British. Being English was something else. Some English-speaking Canadians wanted a closer British connection. McCarthy and imperial federationists saw being British as an alternative to being merely Canadian. In the post-1896 prosperity, some Canadians became vastly more positive. In its sensational heyday, British imperialism offered the vulgar conceit of racial superiority. Its American counterpart, triumphant in Cuba and the Philippines in 1898, had a similar appeal. Sprayed by the same effusions, influential Canadians espoused a flattering "imperial nationalism." If, as British and American imperialists insisted, northern races easily dominated those in warmer climates, who were more northerly than Canadians? Soon, Canadians would dominate the British Empire. Meanwhile, in the novels of Gilbert Parker and the Rev. C.W. Gordon (writing as Ralph Connor) they could rejoice in fictional triumphs of physical and moral courage. They could yearn for Canada to be summoned to play a heroic role in the world.

Such notions, fostered by an outspoken English-Canadian elite, were far from universal. Imperialism was as absurd as ever to families with roots deep in Ontario or Maritime soil and their minds preoccupied with economic realities. *Canadiens* remembered Mercier's warning that the imperialists yearned to conscript their sons and send them to perish on the burning Sahara. On public occasions it was still polite to attribute *la survivance* to British justice, but most French Canadians naturally preferred to keep the credit themselves. The clergy might preach a dutiful allegiance, but they could not urge love. Of course, no more than English Canadians did *Canadiens* know or care what their partners in Confederation really felt.

Sir Wilfrid was almost uniquely knowledgeable. Years before, he offered Torontonians his most memorable image of Canadian duality. Describing the waters of the Ottawa River and the Great Lakes, meeting below the island of Montreal, he recalled: "There they run parallel, separate, distinguishable, and yet are one stream, flowing within the same banks." Under Laurier, pure luck had given Liberalism an almost mystical association with prosperity, but Laurier himself committed Liberals to the holy grail of national unity.

Laurier's first test came in 1899, with a crisis in distant South Africa. Two tiny Boer republics had concluded that preservation of their Old Testament lifestyle compelled them to drive the British into the sea. In ordinary times, Britain would have met the challenge alone, but her diplomacy had isolated her from the European powers. If her self-governing colonies voluntarily displayed their solidarity, the approaching war might be deterred; at the very least, Europe would be impressed. Laurier easily gained unanimous parliamentary approval for Britain's opposition to the Boers. Sending a military contingent was another matter. If Britain were in real danger, Canada would respond; the Boers posed no such threat. Of course, Britain was entitled to recruit soldiers in Canada. Alternatively, an outspoken Tory MP and imperialist, Lieutenant-Colonel Sam Hughes, offered to raise thousands of volunteers. Neither arrangement met Britain's need to display imperial solidarity to a hostile world.

Within two weeks of the outbreak of war in October 1899, Laurier's cautious policy collapsed. In Toronto and Montreal, concerted press campaigns by mass-circulation English papers demanded action. Leaks from London and Ottawa about plans for a contingent hinted at government duplicity. Some cabinet ministers demanded an official force. On October 14, Laurier gave in. In fifteen days, a thousand volunteers were recruited, equipped, and dispatched to Cape Town. A second contingent left early in 1900. Donald Smith, now Lord Strathcona, the Canadian high commissioner in London, raised a mounted regiment at his own expense. Though the British paid almost the full cost of the troops in South Africa, the men served under Canadian officers, performed well, and came home with a strong sense of national identity.

The warlike experience might have united Canadians in a new pride, as it did Australians. In fact, it created new divisions. News of a British victory led to street battles between French- and English-speaking university students in Montreal. Ontario Tories insisted that Laurier was controlled by the wicked J. Israël Tarte, and that French Canadians had shown disloyalty in Britain's hour of need. As usual, one extremism called forth its counterpart. Jules-Paul Tardivel, a Kentucky-born convert to ultramontane nationalism, offered readers of *La Vérité* new and more passionate arguments against Canada.

Those were not the arguments of the young MP for Labelle. Papineau's grandson, Henri Bourassa, was a lifelong admirer of Laurier but he was too intelligent, logical, and proud to be anyone's disciple. Sending an official contingent had shocked him, and he forced Parliament to debate the issue. Had Laurier bowed to imperial coercion? Had he set a fearful precedent for future British wars? If so much was necessary against two tiny, remote nations, Bourassa asked, "how many men shall we send, and how many millions shall we expend to fight a first class power or a coalition of powers?" From Laurier came denials that any precedent had been set.

Bourassa was no threat – yet. As the 1900 election approached, it was Ontario that threatened Laurier's majority. In most of

Canada, Tupper's collection of government scandals and mis-judgements faded amidst such unprecedented prosperity. Who cared if the Liberals had stolen Conservative policies: political larceny was no crime. Left to their own devices, Ontario Tories returned to the old racial and religious hatreds. The Liberals made sure that Irish and *Canadien* voters were listening. A phrase of Tupper's, "Laurier is too English for me," was torn out of context and blazoned across Ontario by the Liberals – admittedly to little effect. Tupper won Ontario but little else. Laurier emerged with 133 seats to Tupper's 80. The Tories became what the Liberals had been, a party of outsiders, tied to Ontario's prejudices. His party had "Francophobia on the brain," moaned an Ottawa Tory editor.

Preserving national unity had persuaded a reluctant Laurier to send troops to South Africa. So had a more pragmatic concern: British diplomatic leverage was needed for Canada's final boundary dispute. In 1898, a joint high commission had left two bitter issues of Canadian-American relations unsettled: reciprocity and the Alaska boundary. Until the Klondike discoveries, no one had bothered much about the vague, straggling line down maps of the Alaska Panhandle, or about the 1825 Anglo-Russian treaty that had determined the location of the line. British pressure would surely help the Americans to be reasonable. Nothing was more unlikely. In the full flush of American imperialism, President Teddy Roosevelt was in a bullying mood. Businessmen in Seattle and Tacoma were eager for northern wealth. Three-quarters of a century of neglect had enfeebled a weak Canadian-British case. Britain was grateful for U.S. support in its South African war. Moreover, Britain had long ago determined its North American course: war was not an option. On October 17, 1903, the British delegate, Lord Alverstone, declined to cause "an international calamity" and sided with three partisan American commissioners, leaving two equally partisan

Canadians to cry foul. Roosevelt's view of the Alaska boundary prevailed. Canada lost coastal access to the Yukon.

More fortunate than Macdonald in 1871, Laurier cheerfully blamed the British for the Alaska boundary fiasco. Still, it is hard to see Lord Alverstone's villainy. He had avoided a war for which Canadians were as unprepared as the British and in which they would have suffered vastly more. Economics, not boundaries, already condemned the Yukon to be bypassed for another forty years. That barely mattered. The Boer War had fostered Canadian military nationalism. The Alaska disappointment prodded Canadians to develop diplomatic independence and a new, purely Canadian nationalism. This was now Henri Bourassa's ideal. John Skirving Ewart, a Winnipeg lawyer who had helped defend Riel in 1885 and Manitoba's Catholics in the 1890s, echoed him. In *The Kingdom of Canada* (1908), Ewart argued the disturbing notion that Canada should stand on its own as a sovereign state. "How are we to unify Canada?" he asked, and answered himself, "Make her a nation in name as well as in fact."

Few Canadians echoed Ewart and Bourassa. Only a minority cared about such matters; most of them felt happier with Laurier's vague bid to the British to "call us to your councils," or his insistence that Canada would not be sucked into "the vortex of European militarism." In the wake of South Africa, Joseph Chamberlain had plans to organize military commitments. By taking over British dockyards and fortifications at Halifax and Esquimalt in 1905, Ottawa sought to pre-empt pressures at home or from London for any greater roles in imperial defence.

Imperialism and nationalism were distractions from the main business of Canadians and immigrants alike. Both were eager to get rich. Laurier approved. Earlier he had adopted unrestricted reciprocity to distract attention from divisive issues of race and religion; now the Liberal leader recognized that prosperity and national unity went together. In his first term, Laurier had simply inherited and refined the National Policy. Safely re-elected, he added his own dimension. By 1900 it was obvious that a single transcontinental rail line would not suffice for the expanding West. In 1901, bad management and lack of freight cars kept the CPR from moving more than a third of a bumper crop before freeze-up on Lake Superior. Angry farmers launched the Territorial Grain Growers' Association to protest the blockage and even took the railway to court. Expansion was the answer. "We want all the railways we can get," declared the Manitoba *Free Press*; farmers, promoters, contractors, politicians, and assorted self-interested "boodlers" agreed.

In the West, the CPR had a dangerous competitor in William Mackenzie and Donald Mann's Canadian Northern Railway. Its jerry-built tracks, laid by farmers in the spirit of an old-fashioned barn-raising and equipped with second-hand rolling stock, formed a network north of the CPR line, reaching west to Edmonton and east to Port Arthur, where it competed with the CPR terminus at Fort William. Lake ships had barely ten weeks to rush the western harvest down the lakes and canals to Montreal. In eastern Canada, the Grand Trunk was excluded from the western bonanza. Its new American-born manager, Charles Hays, finally admitted what most people had long suspected: the Portland-to-Chicago route would never pay a dividend. To prosper, his long-suffering shareholders needed a true transcontinental.

One solution was obvious. The Grand Trunk and the Canadian Northern should merge. Laurier even presided over a few meetings. They failed. Confident of prairie backing, Mackenzie and Mann demanded control. Hays disparaged "that little bunch of lines up around Winnipeg" and reminded Liberals of past political services. Laurier might have forced a shotgun marriage, but the visionary and the politician took over. In 1903, Laurier unveiled his policy. Tories might boast of the CPR; Liberals would do even better. Sifton insisted that the West would have 12 million people within a generation. Boldness was justified. A government-built National Transcontinental would start from the Intercolonial headquarters at Moncton, cross the St. Lawrence at Quebec City, and traverse the clay-belt region of northern Quebec and Ontario on the way to Winnipeg. The Grand Trunk would lease the line for ninety-nine years and construct its own Grand Trunk Pacific line to Prince Rupert on the Pacific coast. As for Mackenzie and Mann, they were free to come east whenever they wanted. Canadians gasped. Hardly an interest was untouched, from bankers and contractors to Quebec's clergy and *nationalistes*, guaranteed new space for clay-belt colonization. Only the minister of railways, A.G. Blair, was angry, partly because he had not been consulted, partly because he favoured Mackenzie and Mann. Laurier got rid of him. The opposition protested too – with little more effect. Tupper's heir, a drab, honest Halifax lawyer, Robert Borden, was dismayed by a scheme that loaded taxpayers with nine-tenths of the cost while the Grand Trunk was almost guaranteed its profits. If they had paused to reflect, Canadians might have agreed. Instead, Laurier cheered them on with logic usually found in a school playground: "I am aware that this plan may scare the timid and frighten the irresolute," he admitted, "but I may claim that every man who has in his bosom a stout Canadian heart will welcome it as worthy of this young nation."

Railway development pushed Canadians toward their northern frontier. The National Transcontinental, the Canadian Northern, and the Grant Trunk Pacific cut across the Canadian Shield and the park belt that fringed the prairies. If colonists faced a grim future farming the clay belt, a pulp and paper industry would grow up from the now-accessible forests. So would a mining industry. Its harbinger was the great complex Francis Clergue and American capital built at Sault Ste. Marie.

Ships of his Lake Superior Consolidated Corporation brought iron ore to the mills and smelters Clergue housed in impressive stone buildings. Trains of his Algoma Central Railway hauled in timber and nickel ore. Tourists and promoters marvelled – until 1903 when the grandiose enterprise collapsed. Ontario's Liberal government glumly assumed the debts and persisted in its dreams for what people called "New Ontario." Later that year, as the province's Temiskaming and Northern Ontario Railway pushed north, miners uncovered the richest silver deposits in the world at Cobalt. Other provinces imitated their neighbour in furious mining promotion.

Never in their history had Canadians experienced such a run of prosperity. In 1904, they could re-elect the architect. Only a scheme (dreamed up by A.G. Blair with Mackenzie and Mann money) to buy up Liberal newspapers and turn them Tory briefly troubled the government campaign. Laurier disposed of the plot by threatening exposure. Then he travelled the country with a ringing message. "Let me tell you, my fellow Canadians," the prime minister told an audience packed into Toronto's Massey Hall, "that all the signs point this way, that the twentieth century shall be the century of Canada and of Canadian development. For the next seventy-five years, nay for the next hundred years, Canada shall be the star towards which all men who love progress and freedom shall come."

Torontonians cheered (though they voted Conservative). Even Laurier now accepted that old habit. He had rich compensations. Not since the Pacific Scandal election of 1874 had a party won such a majority: 138 Liberals to only 75 Conservatives. Every Tory in Nova Scotia – including Robert Borden – was beaten.

Prosperity certainly had its rewards.

QUESTIONING | 2

Voters rewarded Laurier as the political designer of their prosperity, though businessmen were the real heroes. This was a novelty. Canadians had never before attributed omniscience or patriotism to their industrial and financial magnates. For the most part, business leaders led decorous, frugal lives, worked long hours, and deferred gratification for the hereafter. They and their families ate much the same monotonous meals as humbler Canadians (though even the lower middle class expected to be served by a maid). They dressed for respectability, not the climate, and suffered without complaint.

The gulf between rich and poor now widened. Aristocratic visitors to Canada marvelled at the vulgarity of the wealthy, not at their seeming scarcity. Huge and sometimes hideous new mansions sprouted in major cities. Elegant automobiles, often costing more than the prime minister's annual salary, stood at the porte cochère. Americans referred to their post–Civil War era of corrupt and speculative wealth as "the Great Barbecue." Laurier presided over the Canadian counterpart. Some of its leading beneficiaries, like Toronto's Henry Pellatt, "helped" Liberal ministers with their investments. In return, business- men expected their desires to be respected. The righteous grum- bled about cartels and the "trusts"; no serious corrective legislation was enacted. British Columbians clamoured against Oriental immigration, but so long as Sir James Dunsmuir, the province's chief mine owner, wanted cheap labour for his coal mines, the Chinese suffered no more than a head tax and a ban on bringing their wives. In Ontario, small businessmen demanded publicly owned hydroelectricity delivered at cost instead of having the power of Niagara Falls left to an avari- cious Toronto-based monopoly. When provincial Liberals backed the private monopoly in 1905, their scandal-ridden government lost power to the Tories. By 1907, Ontario's pub- licly owned hydro system, commanded by the autocratic Adam Beck, demonstrated the blessings of business socialism. In Quebec and Manitoba, hydro developers wisely made peace with business critics.

Business had some reforming instincts. Sir Clifford Sifton, a millionaire as well as a politician, turned the Canadian Commission of Conservation into a powerful if short-lived force for environmental improvements. He opposed power exports to the United States; worried publicly about pollution, drainage, forest fires, and migratory birds; and promoted town planning. Canada's cities, slum-ridden and mortally dangerous to small children, cried out for reform. In 1901, mayors Oliver Howland of Toronto and W.D. Lighthall of Westmount formed the League of Canadian Municipalities with the virtuous goal of eliminating politics and making city government "a business proposition."

Even in prosperity, businessmen grumbled endlessly about unions, free-trade farmers, politicians, and the relentless struggle for "a living profit." The strain of competition, some claimed, led to "dyspepsia of the mind." It also led to a dramatic growth in joint stock ownership to finance the expensive new machinery, and, after 1909, a wave of consolidations and mergers that fully justified the fears of enemies of "trusts" and critics of unearned wealth. Max Aitken, fresh from New Brunswick, earned $1.5 million in common stock for organizing Canada Cement and almost as much for creating the Steel Company of Canada. At thirty-one, Aitken's fortune launched him into British publishing and politics. By thirty-six, he had engineered a change of government.

Admiration for businessmen and the affluence they apparently created was widespread but not universal. Whether or not business methods could reform cities, industries helped to make them grimy, overcrowded, and slum-ridden. Electricity now lighted main streets and the wealthier districts of major cities, but the poles marched past poorer streets without connections. Herbert Ames, a Montreal businessman-reformer, explored and catalogued incomes and living conditions in working-class wards of his city. Officials, clergy, and journalists did much the same work in Toronto, Winnipeg, Halifax, and Vancouver. Perhaps it was a sign of prosperity that anyone cared, though investigation seldom led to substantial action.

The plight of the poor had an old and easy explanation. Men were masters of their fate – though it troubled softer consciences that women and children usually shared a man's misfortune. In the Methodist *Christian Guardian*, the Rev. E.H. Dewart offered a brisk dose of conventional wisdom: "The best anti-poverty society is an association of men who would adopt as their governing principle in life, industry, sobriety, economy and intelligence." In so hard-drinking a society as Canada, sobriety needed extra help. Temperance, transformed slowly into total abstinence and prohibition, had been the single most powerful social reform crusade in nineteenth-century Canada.

Most Protestants and even some Catholics endorsed it like an extra gospel, though it would have been un-Canadian if the French had not differed markedly from the English on the question. A national referendum in 1898 favoured prohibition for Canada, but Laurier politely ignored the vote. Less than half the population bothered to vote and Quebec was stoutly opposed.

Prohibition drew women into political life as defenders of the sacred institution of the family. Rare eccentrics like Toronto's superintendent of schools, James L. Hughes, Tory, Orange, and educational reformer, insisted on the fundamental equality of men and women. So did women who, at the end of Queen Victoria's reign, began to break down barriers to law, medicine, and university education. More common was faith in "maternal feminism," the divinely sanctioned role of women as wives, mothers, and guardians of social convention against those heedless brutes, their husbands. The nurturing role grew as Victorian Canadians came to see their children not as undersized adults but as beings in a key stage of development. Nursing, teaching, perhaps even medicine became logical extensions of the maternal role. So did social reform.

Canadian women usually sought political rights to gain specific goals. The Woman's Christian Temperance Union (founded at Owen Sound in 1874), in conjunction with broader organizations like the Dominion Alliance, attacked liquor. Adelaide Hunter Hoodless crusaded for pasteurization of milk and for university-based training in domestic science. Her Women's Institutes became one of the organizations Canada has given the world. The National Council of Canadian Women, launched in 1893 by the redoubtable Lady Aberdeen, denounced liquor, divorce, prostitution, profiteering, and "the modern cult of self-indulgence and its god, pleasure." Dominated by the wives of the elite, the council insisted that women would do more good by gentle persuasion than by thrusting themselves into the corrupt world of politics. Not all agreed. Emily Stowe, Canada's first woman doctor, pioneered the women's suffrage issue in Toronto in the 1880s. Her daughter, Amelia Stowe-Gullen, continued the crusade, but it was in the new Canadian West that the flame burned most brightly. Winnipeg's Nellie McClung, a novelist and ingenious publicist, burlesqued Manitoba's all-male legislature and its pompous premier, Sir Rodmond Roblin. Cora Hind, a brilliant Winnipeg crop forecaster, and Emily Murphy, later an Alberta judge and a novelist whose best-known work dealt with drug addiction, were powerful allies. So were leaders of the West's agrarian movement. E.A. Partridge of the *Grain Growers' Guide* wondered pointedly why the vote was available to "the lowest imbruted foreign hobo" but not to Canadian women.

Though the National Council grew to 250,000 members – about half as many people as backed Laurier in 1904 – most Canadian women remained collectively silent. So did the mass of Canadian workers. Prosperity was by no means evenly shared. It dribbled slowly across the widening divide between employer and employee. A powerful, if misleading, impression that the wealthy were self-made discouraged egalitarian yearnings. The flood of immigrants, most of whom entered into direct competition with Canadian workers in factories and construction camps, was a practical weapon against employee militancy. Devotion to the protective tariff and foreign investment coincided, in business ideology, with faith in a free labour market and abhorrence of foreign labour agitators. In 1903, Senator James Lougheed of Alberta sponsored a law threatening American union organizers with two years in jail. The bill passed the Senate but the lower house was too busy to debate it.

In 1900, to win over workers, the Liberals created a small Department of Labour. A promising and dependable young graduate student, William Lyon Mackenzie King, grandson of the Upper Canadian rebel, was put in charge. King's duties (carried out by Liberals in the tiny union movement) included collecting the first statistics on employment and the cost of living. In 1900, labour union membership was first counted. Between 1900 and 1911, union membership grew from 20,000 to 120,000 – 8 per cent of the entire labour force, male and female.

Organized labour was a feeble, divided critic of a prosperity that gave most workers little more than a precarious subsistence. From Charlottetown to Vancouver, skilled workers began joining international affiliates of the American Federation of Labor. Ralph Smith, a Liberal and president of the Trades and Labor Congress, tried to kick the internationals out of the organization. Instead, the TLC met at Berlin [Kitchener], Ontario, in 1902 and gave Smith the boot. Employers had to run their own anti-AFL crusade, borrowing familiar American tools – strike-breakers, calls on the militia, and "yellow dog" contracts (solemn oaths extracted from employees never even to consider union membership on pain of fine and dismissal). After 1902, union growth slowed and strikes grew longer and more bitter. A lengthy Alberta coal strike in 1906, just before the coldest winter in western memory, publicized Mackenzie King's talent as a conciliator and led to the Industrial Disputes Investigation Act (IDI Act) of 1907. By publicizing issues and forcing negotiation, the IDI Act was probably more helpful to unions than its critics could admit, but neither King nor business ever conceded that unions had a right to exist or that workers had a right to bargain collectively. Mere recognition was the issue in long, violent, and often unsuccessful strikes. In 1909–10, most of Canada's tiny regular army stood guard over Cape Breton coal mines until starvation forced miners to abandon the international union of their choice.

In Europe and even in the United States, the new century saw the emergence of powerful labour and socialist movements and strong, even violent, challenges to business power. Canada, in contrast, was a backwater for radical and union activity. The doctrinaire Socialist Party of Canada won two seats in the British Columbia legislature in 1902. Municipal voters sometimes elected a socialist. Distance, small numbers, and divisions kept labour from becoming a national force. Skilled workers in craft unions felt no link with the unorganized, unskilled majority. Some unions, like the Western Federation of Miners and, later, the Industrial Workers of the World, tried to organize the migrant army of "bunkhouse men" in construction, logging, and mining camps. Their revolutionary passion made few lasting converts. In Quebec, the clergy did its best to shield *Canadiens* from socialist and materialist influences. *Nationalistes* approved.

Where labour votes were concentrated, workers elected Montreal's Alphonse Verville president of the Trades and Labor Congress. Médéric Martin, a cigar-maker, defeated the former provincial treasurer in 1914 to become mayor of Montreal. In Toronto, Horatio Hocken, an Orange Tory, recalled his leadership of the 1872 printers' strike to win the mayoralty. Hocken built parks, playgrounds, public baths, and a municipal abattoir and cold storage to fight the meat trust. Free milk for slum children cut infant mortality. Toronto workers embraced Tory democracy.

Farmers regained their political influence, too. It was not easy. The Grange and then the Patrons of Industry collapsed in a wreckage of mismanagement and political betrayal. Only the grievances survived – the tariff, rural depopulation, and jarring reminders of lack of respect for the nation's primary producers. Canadian farmers resented "Hey Rube" jokes and taunts. Western farmers felt a heightened sense of exasperation. Eastern farms had diversified enough that no climatic or market disaster was total. The western wheat monoculture in a region of unpredictable and often merciless weather, and the exactions of railways, elevator and milling monopolies, and the Winnipeg Grain Exchange, often reduced many prairie farmers to penury. Rainfall, frost, soil conditions, and pests could not be helped, but once a farmer had hauled his grain ten miles to the one available elevator, he could hardly take it home again. The only answer to arrogant, dishonest elevator agents or to mysterious fluctuations in the commodity markets was political action and co-operation. The message was preached by cautious Liberals like W.R. Motherwell, founder of the Territorial Grain Growers' Association, or by passionate socialists like E.A. Partridge, editor of the *Grain Growers' Guide*. Farmers grasped it. So did politicians. Across the vast West, farmers were the only voters in sight, and, unlike workers, their minds were not easily distracted.

A federal Grains Act in 1900, imposing regulations and inspectors, proved ineffective but instructive. Partridge success-fully promoted a Grain Growers' Grain Company and a reluc-tant Manitoba government coerced the Grain Exchange into granting it a seat. Farmer-owned elevator companies spread across the West. So did farm organizations and subscriptions to the *Grain Growers' Guide*. At least some readers absorbed Partridge's view that the story of the West was "a history of heartless robbery . . . by the big 'vested' interests – so called from the size of their owners' vests."

Another prairie issue was the future of the North-West Territories. By 1897, a long campaign led by a Regina lawyer, Frederick Haultain, won responsible government for the Territories. In 1904, both parties promised provincial status, and in 1905, Laurier was ready to act. By splitting the two new provinces of Alberta and Saskatchewan at the sixtieth meridian, he separated Regina's Haultain, the grand old man of territorial politics, from most of his supporters. Both new provinces elected strong Liberal governments. Federal control of land and resources ensured more free homesteads and a friendly investment climate. A generous financial settlement, soon extended to other provinces as a "final and unalterable" resolution of old fiscal arguments, guaranteed political peace and economic prosperity for the prairies.

There was one small problem. The new provinces assumed that their Ontario-style system of schools would continue. Even Protestants accepted some minority Catholic rights. Privately, however, Laurier had promised Catholic bishops a return to their full equality of 1875. In the draft autonomy bills, he had quietly inserted the appropriate clauses. Astonished and furious, Clifford Sifton resigned. Fielding threatened to follow. Bitter at the "betrayal" by his Protestant colleagues, Laurier compromised. The cabinet conflict became public. Richard Bedford Bennett, Alberta's Tory leader, came east to light the Ontario heather, denouncing Catholic-inspired coercion. Fiercer by far was the anger of Henri Bourassa: by retreating, claimed Bourassa, Laurier had made the West "a land of refuge for the scum of all nations." Armand Lavergne, once Laurier's friend and now Bourassa's chief supporter, went farther. "In constituting the French Canadian . . . the equal in rights and privileges to the Doukhobor or the Galician who had just disembarked," he declared, "we have opened a gulf between eastern and western Canadians which nothing will fill."

French Canadians, of course, had shown little sign of wishing to share the West, and Laurier's leadership was certain proof of their influence on federal matters. Quebec's phenomenal birthrate, its provincial government, an energetic Catholic clergy, and a distinctive culture might have seemed a sufficient guarantee for the French fact in North America. Instead, French Canada in the 1900s experienced an acute crisis of self-confidence, aggravated by Liberal policies and the Laurier prosperity. The West had few attractions for *Canadiens*, but they saw the floods of immigrants hurried through Quebec by Sifton's agents. Many halted in Montreal to create Jewish, Greek, and Italian ghettoes with customs and languages even stranger and more unwelcome than the English and Irish. British Canadians grumbled about foreigners, but they were as certain as Sifton that assimilation would come. French Canadians saw only newcomers who neither understood nor respected the old racial compact and compromises.

Some French Canadians, like Rodolphe Forget, J.D. Rolland, and François Béique, became millionaires in the Laurier business bonanza; but most depended on jobs created by English-speaking employers. Once half-English, Montreal was now filled with rural French Canadians who no longer fled to New England. Were the slums of Quebec's largest city any less alien? As a French tourist complained, one could live for weeks in Montreal without seeing or hearing any language but English. Quebec's government, Liberal since 1897, saw its role as fervent promoter of the private development of natural resources as much as factories. Only if English and American capital expanded the provincial economy could Quebec afford the costly and futile colonization projects favoured by the Church and *nationalistes*.

Bourassa had fled federal politics, turned his fire on the provincial Liberals, and now toyed with a more progressive version of the nationalist program. Errol Bouchette, Quebec's first economist of note, pleaded with Quebeckers to regain control of their own resources and industries, by public ownership if necessary. Opinion leaders recoiled at such socialist heresies. Bourassa recommended control of trusts, Catholic unions for *Canadien* workers, even the municipal reforms urged by Montreal's civic-conscious English-speaking business leaders. But no more than Papineau, his grandfather, could Bourassa free himself from a traditional, rural view of French Canada's future. Colonists tilling the thin soils of northern Quebec could blame their troubles on politicians. The hardships depicted in Louis Hémon's *Maria Chapdelaine* must be endured, and, like Maria, French Canadians must reject the easy life of assimilation to remain true to their traditions. "It is not necessary for us to possess industry and money," declared Jules-Paul Tardivel. "We would no longer be French Canadians but Americans like the others. Our mission is to possess the soil and to spread ideas."

Such notions had limited appeal for hard-headed and hedonistic *Canadiens*. The preaching of clergy and intellectuals should not be confused with public opinion but, at intervals, they connected. Bourassa and his youthful followers increasingly saw Laurier as a sell-out to imperialists, materialists, and exploiters, but ordinary French Canadians had less reason than their English-speaking neighbours to revel in Laurier's economic achievements. Nor were those achievements always apparent.

By 1908, the federal Liberals looked shopworn and dirty. The country had survived a short but sharp recession in 1907, the harbinger of worse to come. Robert Borden, still Tory leader, chose that year to unveil his Halifax Program, a reaffirmation of the National Policy, spiced by calls for public ownership of telephones, telegraphs, and railways, an efficient and reformed civil service, and a ban on election contributions from corporations. Laurier introduced a civil service commission and waited patiently as Tories denounced Borden's proposals as insufferable socialism. As voter bait, the Tories were back to what contemporary Americans christened "muckraking." Admittedly the scandals were rich and redolent, from Sifton's corrupt old Department of the Interior to the supply contracts for the government's Arctic voyages of explorations. The government replied in kind, and the 1908 campaign was as sordid as any Canadian election in history. On election day, the Liberals retained 135 seats to the Conservatives' 85.

In 1908, the Liberal slogan was "let Laurier finish his work." Probably Laurier's work was done. In 1909, Mackenzie King, elected to Parliament in 1908, became minister of a full-fledged Department of Labour. A tiny Department of External Affairs opened over an Ottawa barbershop, to do what Laurier never quite managed: make systematic replies to the relentless flow of British memoranda on diplomacy, shipping, defence, and utter esoterica. Few Canadians noticed, but diplomacy had done better for them since the Alaska dispute. In 1904, the French abandoned their troublesome old landing rights on the Newfoundland coast. Tribunals accepted Canadian views of a controversy over the Bering Sea and the ninety-year-old fisheries disagreement with the Americans. Laurier could have left with his country prosperous and respected. Instead, he looked at his aging colleagues, saw no successor, and carried on.

Some old issues took new shapes. In Europe, Britain had ended her old hostility to France and Russia because an old friend had become a dangerous new threat. Germany's industrial power had given her the world's best army. Now her dockyards delivered enough battleships to challenge the Royal Navy's supremacy. Wealthy British taxpayers, required to finance a modest welfare state as well as a massive expansion of their fleet, threatened rebellion. Britain tried to share its costs with its young dominions. Laurier saw a political trap and found an escape. Launching a small Canadian navy would look helpful, but both control and spending would remain at home. To his delight, the Tories sponsored a navy resolution. Parliament unanimously agreed.

Then Laurier's luck ran out. Within a year both imperialists and Quebec nationalists had denounced the new Naval Service

Act. Laurier had offered a "tin-pot navy," imperialists raged, when Britain needed battleships. In his newly launched newspaper, *Le Devoir*, Henri Bourassa claimed that the navy was a subterfuge for committing Canada to imperial wars and the conscription of young *Canadiens*. Who could distinguish between British and Canadian warships bearing identical White Ensigns? A by-election in rural Quebec in the autumn of 1910 showed *nationalistes* that they had finally found a popular issue.

Laurier was unafraid. He spent that summer in a triumphal visit to the West. He saw with his own eyes vast grain fields and booming cities. The 1907 recession had been a mere hiccup in the process of endless growth. Homesteaders flowed westward in ever greater numbers. With few misgivings, officials sent them to till the Palliser Triangle. Heavy rains in the Triangle in 1910 seemed to confirm their wisdom. Of course, there were discontents. Delegations met the prime minister to repeat old grievances about tariffs, freight rates, and land policies. As ever, Laurier pursed his lips, claimed deep concern, and promised action. That fall, a thousand farmers staged the first "March on Ottawa," coming, like most of their successors, by train and not on foot. Again Laurier promised action.

Thanks to Washington, for once he delivered. By signing the Payne-Aldrich Bill, which sent American tariffs to new heights, President William Taft finally provoked a free-trade revolt in a midterm election year. Dusting off Canadian reciprocity, Taft argued, would please the western states. With astonishing speed, an agreement was signed and dispatched to both Canada and the Congress for approval. In Ottawa, a Tory politician later confessed that his heart sank to his boots. After half a century of trying for reciprocity, Laurier could claim the coup. Then politicians went home to their ridings and got another shock: Canadians were displeased. After years of prosperity and east-west trade, Canadians no longer cared about reciprocity. In fact, for millions of them in business, factories, and transportation, reciprocity was a deadly threat to profits and jobs. In Toronto, eighteen prominent Liberals, led by Clifford Sifton and Sir Edmund Walker of the Bank of Commerce, publicly broke with Laurier. In Montreal, Sir William Van Horne of the CPR brusquely commanded his business associates to "bust the damned thing."

Neither Borden nor Laurier immediately grasped their altered fortunes. Exasperated by a Tory filibuster on the Reciprocity Agreement, Laurier called an election for September 21, 1911. In Quebec, Tory businessmen now funnelled cash to Bourassa and the *nationalistes*, allowing them to veto candidates and manage the Conservative provincial campaign. In return, the *nationalistes* hoped, Bourassa supporters would hold the balance of power. Elsewhere, anti-Americanism and reciprocity were the real issues. The Tories benefited from a flood of money and smooth provincial organizations in Ontario, Manitoba, and British Columbia. As election day approached, Laurier foresaw defeat. Rowdy mobs in Montreal drove him from his platform to seek refuge in a railway car. On September 21, Conservative candidates swept 107 seats outside Quebec, 4 short of a majority. Quebec gave Borden 27 more (mostly from rural counties) for a total of 134. Laurier salvaged only 87. Most of his ministers, Mackenzie King among them, lost.

Bourassa had miscalculated. Robert Borden could manage without his candidates, though some secured minor portfolios. Like Laurier in 1896, Borden sought compromise and moderation. Thomas White, a Liberal defector from Toronto's financial community, became minister of finance; George Eulas Foster, scourge of the Liberals in the opposition years, had to settle, like Cartwright in 1896, for trade and commerce. Reluctantly, Borden accepted Sam Hughes, the favourite of Orangemen and imperialists, as minister of militia, an obscure enough portfolio in normal times. Borden set reforms afoot in the civil service, proposed a commission to set a "scientific" tariff, and launched an investigation of the scandalously mismanaged and overdue National Transcontinental. Manitoba's northern border, a hot issue for three years, moved north to join its western neighbours at the sixtieth parallel, while both Ontario and Quebec expanded to include the vast region around Hudson Bay. Privately, Borden complained that he could have done a great deal more if his colleagues had not wasted so much of their time quarrelling about political favours.

Borden's distaste for patronage was only one difference from Laurier and Macdonald. Another was his view of empire. The Tory-*nationaliste* alliance on the naval question had been based on self-deception. Like old Joseph Howe, but unlike Laurier or Macdonald, Borden believed in a form of imperial federation. Some day, dominions would sit as equals with the mother country, but they would have to earn their places by honourable sacrifice. Such an opportunity had come. After direct consultations with the British admiralty, Borden announced that Canada would send $5 million to buy three dreadnoughts, the largest battleships. His Quebec lieutenant, Frederick Monk, immediately demanded a referendum. Borden refused. Monk resigned. Liberals filibustered, dragging the debate into 1913. Then Borden's brightest recruit, Arthur Meighen, devised a closure motion to cut off debate. This early use of closure encouraged a Liberal-dominated Senate to reject the naval policy and, for good measure, Borden's tariff commission and a federal highways law as well.

The Senate felt empowered because Borden's government was now in deadly trouble. The long era of prosperity was over. By 1912, a worldwide depression was taking hold. Arriving in greater numbers to escape economic woes at home, immigrants joined growing armies of unemployed in Canadian cities. In

1913 and 1914 the prairies suffered the first widespread crop failures in a decade. The ecological folly of farming the drought-prone Palliser Triangle was exposed. Close to completion, the new transcontinental railways found themselves in a desperate credit squeeze. Hardest hit was the Canadian Northern as well as its main financier, Toronto's Bank of Commerce. Having lavished favours on the Liberals, Mackenzie and Mann now had to plead for Tory sympathy. The thirst for political vengeance had to be resisted by an argument as old as the Grand Trunk in the 1850s: railway bankruptcy would destroy Canadian credit with foreign investors.

Beset by problems inherited from Laurier, Borden faced new difficulties created by Ontario Tories. Encouraged by Michael Fallon, Roman Catholic bishop of London, and by resentment at French-Canadian settlement in Ontario's eastern counties, Sir James Whitney's provincial government issued Regulation 17, curtailing the education rights of Ontario's French-speaking minority. For Fallon, Regulation 17 was sweet revenge for his 1888 dismissal by French-speaking clerics at the University of Ottawa. Franco-Ontarians were victims of raw prejudice and opportunism. In Ontario's 1914 election, Liberals vied with Tories in backing Regulation 17: the Tories won a landslide.

For Canada as a whole, Regulation 17 was another brutal, needless confrontation between French and English at a moment when Canadian unity would be tested as never before.

C anada went to war suddenly. The crisis that bubbled out of the Balkans in the summer of 1914 looked no worse than half a dozen predecessors had. Inexorably, alliance systems and mobilization plans clicked into place. Serbia, Russia, and France ranged against the Austro-Hungarian and German empires. At midnight on August 4, the British ultimatum to Berlin expired and another empire joined the war. From Quebec City to Vancouver, Canadians rejoiced. J.W. Dafoe of the *Winnipeg Free Press* declared Canada's own war on Prussian militarism. When MPs gathered in an emergency session, Sir Wilfrid Laurier was unequivocal: in Britain's hour of danger, Canada's only answer was "Ready, Aye Ready." Crowds of men in Montreal, Toronto, and Vancouver lined up to enlist.

Canadians were a little better prepared than they knew. Defence spending had grown sixfold since 1897. In 1913, sixty thousand militiamen had drilled in camps. Since 1909, most provinces, including Quebec, had imposed cadet training in their schools. Pre-war plans safeguarded ports, canals, and bridges from surprise attack. A detailed scheme existed to despatch a twenty-five-thousand-man Canadian Expeditionary Force within a month. Other preparations were less helpful. In 1902, influenced by Colonel Sam Hughes, Laurier's government had adopted the Ross rifle. It was highly accurate and it could be made in Canada, but it was long, heavy, and jammed easily.

The war crisis excited Canadians. In Parliament, a Liberal insisted that Borden's emergency legislation "omit no power that the Government may need." The War Measures Act met that test. Experts universally agreed that the war would be short. If massed armies did not settle the issue, economic collapse certainly would. As Minister of Militia, Sam Hughes scorned professionals, scrapped the mobilization plan they designed, and summoned volunteers to Valcartier, a brand new camp near Quebec. He appeared in full uniform to sort out the confusion he had caused. On October 2, a vast convoy left for England with 31,200 poorly trained soldiers.

Canadians marvelled. They also poured out their patriotism in voluntary effort. A Canadian Patriotic Fund collected donations for soldiers' families. A Military Hospitals Commission created facilities for the sick and wounded veterans. The pre-war militia regiments and patriotic civilians recruited close to half a million volunteers by early 1916 with scarcely a penny of public money. Churches, charities, the Red Cross, and women's organizations found interesting and sometimes useful ways to "do their bit," from buying machine guns to distributing white feathers as symbols of cowardice to healthy young civilian men. Patriots also forced dismissal of Germans and Austrians from public employment, banned the teaching of German in schools and universities, and pressured the city of Berlin to rename itself Kitchener. Miners in British Columbia went on strike to prevent employment of "enemy aliens," and, by May 1915, public clamour had forced the government to intern more than seven thousand mostly harmless people.

From the outset, the frugal practices of peacetime public finance were forgotten. At the best of times Sam Hughes was a spender, and the war gave him and his growing entourage of cronies all the excuse they needed. By 1915, the militia department was swallowing more than the entire government had spent in 1913. Less obvious but almost as serious was the financial appetite of the transcontinental railways. Cut off by the war from traditional money markets, with facilities badly needed to ship men and supplies, the Grand Trunk and the Canadian Northern gave Borden's government no choice but to support them.

As minister of finance, Sir Thomas White was no innovator. Only a horror of raising taxes and faith in a short war forced him into the first heavy Canadian borrowing in New York. Financiers insisted that Canadians would never lend money to their government. They were wrong. In 1915, desperation drove White to seek $50 million in a domestic war loan; Canadians gave him $100 million. Further loans in 1916 and 1917 were also oversubscribed. Victory Loans, directed at humbler citizens and backed by floods of advertising, delivered $400 million in 1917 and $600 million in 1918. While government revenue rose from $126 million to $233.7 million between 1913 and 1918, mostly due to higher tariffs, the national debt climbed from $434 million to $2463 million. White and his colleagues insisted that the cost of a war to end all wars might fairly be shared with later generations.

The burden would have been far greater without massive exports of wheat, timber, and Canadian-made munitions. Initially, the war only aggravated the prevailing depression. Hunger as well as patriotism drove thousands of young men into the Canadian Expeditionary Force. Industrialists, eager for business, got Hughes's backing to form a committee to bid for British artillery shell contracts. By the summer of 1915, the Shell Committee had orders worth $170 million, but greed, confusion, and inexperience allowed them to deliver only $5.5 million's worth. Beset by comparable problems of their own, the British demanded reorganization. The solution was an Imperial Munitions Board (IMB), officially a British agency, headed by a talented, hard-headed Canadian manager, Joseph Flavelle. By 1917, Flavelle's skills and experience as a bacon exporter had made the IMB the biggest business in Canada, with a quarter of a million workers and a turnover of $2 million a day. When the British, lacking foreign currency, curtailed their Canadian contracts, Flavelle neatly switched his market to a new ally, the United States. By the war's end, the IMB's own factories and its contractors produced ships, aircraft, chemicals, and explosives as well as shells.

The war also ended the depression in agriculture. With huge conscript armies trapped in the trenches, and Russia's wheat exports stopped by the war, the Allies needed all Canada could produce. Nature obliged with an unprecedented 15 million bushels of wheat in 1915. Prices soared. The pre-war conditions that should have returned the prairie dry belt to grazing were forgotten. In the later war years, yields dropped but farm profits climbed. Consumers accepted higher prices and shortages as the cost of war. Since farmers spent their new wealth on furniture and newfangled automobiles as well as on land and machinery, manufacturers also benefited. Employers and farmers soon regretted that so many men had been encouraged to go to war.

Manpower soon became the crucial resource of the war effort. By the end of 1914, the government had authorized fifty thousand men for the Canadian Expeditionary Force. By the summer of 1915, the target was a hundred and fifty thousand. A visit to England shocked Borden with both the magnitude of the struggle and the ineffectiveness of British wartime leadership. As if to set them an example, he raised Canada's manpower commitment to two hundred and fifty thousand, and in January 1916 he doubled it to half a million.

At the outset, Henri Bourassa had backed the war, but he added a prescient warning. The government, he suggested, should "ensure our own internal security before starting or pursuing an effort that it will perhaps not be in a state to sustain until the end." The government's own chief military adviser, Major General Willoughby Gwatkin, cautioned in 1915 that Canada might have trouble finding men for even two divisions in the trenches. Instead, by 1916, Hughes had committed the Dominion to four divisions with the promise of many more. In fact, men were found. When the old militia had exhausted its influence, politicians, businessmen, and local patriots accepted colonelcies from Hughes and raised still more battalions. Appeals to civic pride, sporting links, and a delight in wearing Highland regalia drew recruits. Clergy preached on Christian duty and women wore badges proclaiming "Knit or Fight." Patriotic doctors approved the young, the old, and the physically or mentally handicapped. Barriers of racial prejudice were lowered to recruit Aboriginals and Japanese Canadians, though black Canadian volunteers were referred to a construction unit.

Even when backed by social pressure, voluntary recruiting was highly selective. Seventy per cent of the men of the first contingent were British-born recent immigrants to Canada, with close ties to their homeland and harsh experience of a country where signs read: "No English need apply." In Winnipeg, Toronto, and English-speaking Montreal, recruiting pressure was more powerful than in rural districts or in regions like the Maritimes where roots went very deep.

In French Canada, the pressures were feeble indeed. No one distributed white feathers in Quebec City. The agencies that recruited in other provinces – the militia, local leaders, imperial patriots – in Quebec were weak or otherwise engaged. Historians often repeat a myth that a Methodist was put in charge of Quebec recruiting. In fact, no one was in charge of recruiting in Quebec or anywhere else until 1917. Lies, even widespread and innocently believed, remain lies. Still, it is easy to blame Sam Hughes and the government for recruiting failures in Quebec. No man was less fitted to understand French Canada than the tempestuous minister of militia. Though most of Borden's *nationaliste* colleagues loyally backed the war, they had won election by passionately opposing imperial adventures. Quebec Liberals enjoyed their discomfiture and Bourassa, rapidly losing interest in the European conflict, dismissed his former colleagues as "temporary nationalists" and even traitors. Ontario's Regulation 17 was a convenient distraction. The real enemies of French Canada were not Germans, insisted Bourassa, but "English-Canadian anglicisers, the Ontario intriguers, or Irish priests." As if to confirm the point, wartime nativism led the western provinces to annul French and minority education rights conceded years before.

French Canadians did not need Bourassa's editorials to keep them out of uniform. When Quebec's famous 22nd Battalion, the "Vandoos," was authorized in October 1914, it had difficulty filling its ranks. So did most of its successors. Few Quebeckers were moved by loyalty to Britain or France; unemployment or an urge for adventure and escape were the usual goads for enlisting. For the vast majority, the ordered familiarity of the farm or home town, well-paid work in the new munitions factories and textile mills, and a comfortable sense of isolation from a dangerous world were reason enough to stay home.

Canadians who did enlist became part of the British army. Not even the nationalistic Hughes claimed to control "his boys" in action, though he lustily condemned British tactics. Hughes's zest for chaos and cronyism complicated Canadian administration. In England by early 1916, three rival Canadian generals each claimed Hughes's full backing. Hundreds of CEF battalions arrived in Britain only to be broken up for reinforcements. Embittered soldiers blamed military bureaucrats. More knowledgeably, the staff blamed Hughes.

No more than in 1812 or 1885 were Canadians natural-born soldiers. They learned their business in the daily misery of trench warfare and in bloody battles made more dangerous by inexperienced officers and bad equipment. At the German gas attack at Ypres in April 1915, the 1st Division lost 6035 dead, wounded, and captured. Canadians stole British rifles to replace the useless Ross. At the St. Eloi craters in 1916, the 2nd Division suffered a painful setback because its generals could not locate their men. The test of battle eliminated inept officers and taught the survivors that precise staff work, careful preparation, and sensible but uncompromising discipline won battles and saved lives. The proof came at Easter 1917. After weeks of stockpiling, tunnelling, rehearsals, and bombardment, and sensible new infantry tactics, Sir Julian Byng sent all four divisions of the Canadian Corps to capture Vimy Ridge. After five days of fighting, the Allies could boast of the first unequivocal victory on the Western Front. Vimy was one of those great deeds, done together, which create nations. French and English could take equal pride in the victory.

Byng was British but his winning ways were inherited weeks later by his Canadian successor. Sir Arthur Currie was a pear-shaped soldier with a slightly shady pre-war record as a Victoria real estate speculator. The war revealed him as a cool, methodical soldier, fond of unconventional tactics and open to innovation. Instead of squandering men in an attack on Lens that summer, as his British superiors wanted, he captured nearby Hill 70. When, as he had predicted, the Germans tried to retake the position, Currie deployed his artillery to destroy them.

Currie's authority was stronger than Byng's because, in September 1916, Sir Robert Borden created an Overseas Ministry in London to manage Canadian forces in England and France. In November, after a tempest of rage and threats, Sam Hughes resigned. The chaos and conflict that affected every branch of Canadian administration, from chaplains to veterinarians, slowly vanished. By 1918, the British retained little more than tactical control of the Canadian units in France. Brilliant soldiers like Brigadier General A.G.L. McNaughton, a chemical engineering professor at McGill before the war, pioneered innovations in gunnery and military engineering. In military terms, if not yet in constitutional law, the war transformed Canada from a colony into a junior but sovereign ally. Administrative efficiency and hard-earned military success achieved the change.

Though the first powered flight in Canada occurred only in 1909 at Baddeck, Nova Scotia, Canadians won a reputation in the air. By war's end, almost a quarter of the pilots in the Royal Air Force were Canadians, some of them trained at British flying schools in Canada. Two Canadians, Major W.A. Bishop and Major Raymond Collishaw, ranked third and fifth among wartime air aces. Superior training methods helped. So did accents: it was hard for the British to know whether or not a Canadian was a gentleman. Having deplored a distinct Canadian navy, Borden's government approved a distinct Canadian air force only in the last months of the war. It never saw action. A few Canadians served with the Royal Navy, but Canada's own tiny navy was allowed only to hire trawlers to patrol for German U-boats outside Halifax harbour.

Experts have debated alternatives to the Allies' blood-soaked strategy of seeking victory on the Western Front. Skill, experience, and careful preparation could only reduce casualties. Taking Vimy Ridge cost 10,604 dead and wounded. Ordered to finish the grim British offensive at Passchendaele in October 1917, Currie protested that he would lose sixteen thousand men. The toll was 15,654. Keeping each of the four Canadian divisions in action required twenty thousand new soldiers a year. By 1917, they were no longer coming.

A year earlier, the patriotic leagues warned that their recruiting efforts were failing. To soften Quebec's hostility to the war effort, prominent Torontonians launched a "Bonne Entente" movement. Banquets and speeches failed to sweeten French-English relations. Many of the same men soon demanded conscription. The arguments became familiar: volunteering took the bravest and best young men of English Canada. When skilled workers joined up, industry suffered. Aware of a 1914 pledge of voluntary enlistment, the government did all it could. Borden finally put Arthur Mignault, a patriotic patent medicine maker, in charge of Quebec recruiting. A cabinet minister from Quebec tried (vainly) to raise a battalion. Borden also launched a voluntary national registration to identify potential recruits. Though suspicious that the scheme was a mere prelude to conscription, both the Quebec Catholic hierarchy and the Trades and Labor Congress urged compliance. A fifth of the registration cards were never returned. Among registrants who seemed eligible, almost none volunteered.

Save for his short, discouraging visit to London in 1915, Borden knew no more about British policy and strategy than he read in the papers. Once, in January 1916, frustration and ill health provoked him to write that Canadians would not put five hundred thousand men in the field "and willingly accept the position of having no more voice and receiving no more consideration than if we were toy automata." He tore up the letter and spent the year reforming Canada's creaking war administration and, in spare moments, urging sympathetic Americans to forsake their neutrality. December 1916 brought dramatic shifts in British politics, partly engineered by a Canadian expatriate, Max Aitken. David Lloyd George, a former Welsh radical and the only man in Britain's wartime government Borden now respected, headed a new coalition. Faced with hostile officials and a war effort sadly awry, Lloyd George summoned the Dominion premiers. "We want more men from them," he bluntly explained. "We can hardly ask them to make another great recruiting effort unless it is accompanied by an invitation to come over and discuss the situation with us."

On March 2, 1917, Borden and his fellow prime ministers learned the dreadful news. Russia was collapsing. The French army had mutinied. Germany's submarines threatened Britain with starvation. To Borden's delight, the Americans had entered the war, but years could pass before American military strength was mobilized. Lloyd George's purpose was served: Borden insisted on a new consultative Imperial War Cabinet, but the need for manpower had sunk in. Visits to Canadian camps confirmed the message. Lacking reinforcements, wounded men had to return to the fighting until they were dead or too terribly mangled to be useful. Though Borden halted Hughes's plans to enlarge the Corps, Canada's honour depended on keeping its four divisions at full strength. Victory at Vimy Ridge only hardened his resolve.

Later, Liberals claimed that Borden dreamed up conscription to save his party. Certainly the Tories were in trouble. The 1914 political truce had ended long ago. Since then, Tories had lost every provincial election. A wartime record of fumbling and ill-concealed scandals pointed to Laurier's comeback at the next election. But Borden was earnest and principled. Noisy patriots did not fool him: conscription would be unpopular across Canada. In Australia, voters had already rejected it and would do so again. But the prime minister saw no choice. With all the earnestness that drove him, Borden would keep faith with

Britain and with Canada's own young soldiers. On May 18, 1917, he announced that men would be selectively conscripted for service overseas.

Inevitably, conscription became a French-English debate. Opponents in English Canada – farmers, trade unionists, and pacifists – found few outlets for their views; French Canada was virtually unanimous in opposition. Henri Bourassa provided ready-made arguments. Borden, he declared, was a mere imperialist, pouring out Canadian lives and money at Britain's command. Canada's front line was in Canada, not France. Canadians should use the war to get rich by supplying the food and shells the belligerents needed. Such arguments enraged English-Canadian patriots. To Borden, they were servile and unworthy. Aware of their image as cold, materialistic people, Borden wanted to lead Canadians to a higher destiny. His reputation would perish in the attempt.

On the means Borden was very flexible. He would form a coalition with the Liberals and delay conscription until a general election. Laurier refused. With victory over the Tories imminent, surely Liberals would stay loyal. Liberal meetings in Toronto and Winnipeg trounced advocates of conscription. And if Laurier joined Borden, he would lose Quebec to Bourassa. Despite the evidence, Laurier was wrong. In Ontario and the West, the war had become the crusade that Dafoe had proclaimed in 1914. Out of the terrible fiery furnace of sacrifice, Canada must emerge purged of corruption and selfishness. It was a conviction that Liberals could share more easily than Tories. It lay behind the sudden triumph of women's suffrage and prohibition across the West in 1915 and 1916. By 1917, women in provinces from Ontario to British Columbia could vote, while both sexes had also lost the right to drink. Both causes remained frankly repugnant to Laurier, Quebec Liberals, and, for that matter, Henri Bourassa and the *nationalistes*. Hate the Tories as they might, reform Liberals like Newton Rowell, the party's Ontario leader, and Manitoba's J.W. Dafoe could see that Borden was in earnest about the war, and Laurier patently was not.

The prime minister was also a shrewder, abler politician than Laurier would ever admit. Reaching out to second-rank Liberals, Borden found them sympathetic but hesitant. Helped by his hard-faced solicitor general, Arthur Meighen, Borden armed himself with more weapons. A Military Voters' Act enfranchised soldiers; a Wartime Elections Act gave votes to soldiers' wives, sisters, and mothers and took it away from Canadians of enemy origin naturalized since 1902. Women, Meighen explained, would speak for men who had lost their lives; disenfranchised aliens would also be spared from conscription. It went without saying that they normally voted Liberal. The debate ended with closure. Almost at once, sensing that Laurier would lose, Liberal defections began. On October 6, Parliament dissolved, and the long-postponed election could follow. Five days later, Borden announced a coalition Union government, pledged to conscription, wartime prohibition, and the elimination of political patronage. It was a pledge Borden could never have won from his own party. The man who had grown to despise partyism could finally lead a government based on talent and patriotism – as he saw it.

With endorsements from eight out of nine provincial premiers (Quebec's Sir Lomer Gouin was the obvious exception) and almost every English-language newspaper, the Union government expected an easy victory. Outside Quebec the Liberal leadership was shattered. Unexpectedly, in the Maritimes and parts of the West, rank-and-file Liberals began to revive their party. Struggles to compress Tory and Liberal ambitions into a single Unionist candidacy provoked exasperating squabbles. On a western tour, Laurier drew large crowds. At Kitchener, with its German-speaking population, an anti-conscriptionist crowd howled down Borden. In late November, nervous ministers persuaded Borden to announce exemption from conscription for farmers' sons and soldiers' brothers. Finally the Union campaign got going. While Quebec extremists exulted at British defeats, respectable Ontario newspapers insisted that a vote for Laurier would allow Bourassa to rule all Canada and make the German Kaiser rejoice. English Canadians could believe that conscription would fall exclusively on "slackers" and French Canadians.

The result split Canada as no election ever had before: Borden took 153 seats, only 3 in Quebec; Laurier won 82, only 20 of them outside Quebec. As usual, seat totals were deceptive: without the military vote, Borden had only a hundred thousand more supporters than Laurier. Soldiers gave the government two hundred thousand votes and 14 more seats.

Designed by Meighen, the Military Service Act selected men on the basis of age and marital status and gave them three stages of appeal. During the months of campaigning, the act was in abeyance. Of 404,395 single men aged twenty to twenty-four, called as the first class, 380,510 appealed. Only twenty thousand appeared for training. "Freely denounced as an engine of oppression," one commentator observed, the act "contained so many safeguards against oppression that it had been made in no small degree inoperative." Quebec conscription tribunals, composed of a Conservative and a Liberal, granted blanket exemptions to *Canadiens* but, according to the central appeal judge, "applied conscription against the English-speaking minority in Quebec with a rigour unparalleled."

Unionists were soon busy with their program. Early in 1918, regulations prohibited the import, sale, and distribution of liquor for the duration of the war and one year after. On May 24, the federal franchise was at last open to women as well as men. The coalition made it a little easier to settle one part of the long, agonizing railway problem – Mackenzie and Mann's bankrupt Canadian Northern. Borden's new colleagues allowed him the solution he had advocated as long ago as 1904: public ownership. In return for money to rescue the Canadian Northern's heaviest creditor, the Bank of Commerce, the railway vanished into a new Canadian Government Railways system. The Grand Trunk would have to wait.

So would much else. In March of 1918, disaster struck the Allied cause. German armies, redeployed after the collapse of Russia, smashed through the British lines. The British Fifth Army dissolved. On the Easter weekend, anti-conscription riots broke out in Quebec City. They ended after soldiers, rushed from Toronto, fired on a furious crowd, killing four civilians. Future protesters would be conscripted on the spot, warned Ottawa. Since heavy losses seemed likely in France, the government cancelled exemptions under the Military Service Act. Just as seeding time began, farmers watched sons depart to the military depots and cursed the lying Unionist politicians.

More than farmers and French Canadians were bitter. Families mourned soldier sons and husbands. Inflation, moderate until 1916, soared out of control in 1917. Wages could not keep pace and more workers than ever turned to unions and to strikes. On December 6, 1917, the violence of war came home to a peaceful country. The blast from an exploding munitions ship devastated the working-class end of Halifax, killing 1630 people. Dazed survivors faced the worst blizzards in years. By early 1918, German U-boats began patrolling near Halifax, surfacing to sink and capture merchant ships. The navy's trawlers were helpless.

Amateurism and voluntarism had run their course. Behind the façade of business-dominated committees like the Patriotic Fund, government now controlled, regulated, and provided the money. Food and fuel controllers preached conservation, sought ingenious ways to increase production, and hunted for hoarders. Urged to conscript wealth as well as men, the finance minister, Sir Thomas White, cautiously imposed a Business Profits Tax and a War Income Tax. In 1918, only 31,130 Canadians were paying taxes through their new T-1 forms, for a total of $8 million. An "anti-loafing" regulation threatened jail for any man, sixteen to sixty, who was not gainfully employed. For the first time, the government authorized federal police forces to hunt for sedition. Radical unions and foreign-dominated socialist parties were suppressed and, after years of patriotic pressure, publications in "enemy" languages were outlawed. A wartime labour code affected unions more than employers. Collective bargaining and equal pay for men and women were recommended, but the right to strike was banned for the duration.

Overseas, the mood of exhaustion and despair was far heavier, but the Canadian Corps was exempt. By luck, it escaped all the major German offensives, and Currie grimly insisted on holding it together. Held in reserve in England since 1916, the 5th Division was broken up for reinforcements. The extra men made the Corps the strongest organization of its size on the British front. Borden returned to England that spring, angry at the waste of Passchendaele, furious when Currie reported on the sloth, incompetence, and lack of foresight of British generals. "Let the past bury its dead," he stormed at Lloyd George and his fellow prime ministers, "but for God's sake let us get down to earnest endeavour." During the summer Borden finally got a share in the British planning for a war which, it seemed, might well last until 1920. The British army must be husbanded and rebuilt. Perhaps a Russian front could be revived with Canadian help. In mid-August, Borden returned to Ottawa, trapped by a practical dilemma of imperial federalism – Canada could not manage without a prime minister, but no one else could represent it effectively in London. If anything, the war taught Borden the limits of Empire and the relative ease of dealing with wartime Washington. When diplomats could be sidestepped, Americans talked business and made decisions as the British never could. It was a disturbing thought in what might be only the middle of an interminable war.

Then, almost suddenly, the war rushed to a conclusion. On August 8, 1918, a Canadian and Australian attack near Amiens broke the German lines. Tanks, aircraft, and infantry worked with new efficiency. As the assault bogged down, Currie insisted on switching fronts. Again and again, Canadians attacked, suffering huge casualties but driving deeper than ever before imaginable. The conscripts were needed only at the end when, in early October, the Corps marched through still-green fields and undamaged towns. Retreating Germans fought to the final day at Mons, where the war had begun for the British in 1914. On November 11, at 11 a.m., the war ended for everybody.

The war cost Canada 60,661 dead; as many more returned mutilated in mind or body. During the fall of 1918, almost as many Canadians died from a strange, virulent influenza epidemic. The young and the talented shared in both tolls. For the survivors, nothing would ever be quite the same again.

DEAD ENDS | 4

Two contradictory hopes sustained most Canadians during the war years: on the one hand, they would find a new and finer world; on the other, they would return to the old one. Reformers could take heart in women's suffrage and prohibition. Reform-minded books ranged from a turgid tract on labour relations by Mackenzie King, *Industry and Humanity*, to Stephen Leacock's essay, "The Unsolved Riddle of Social Justice," with its surprising conclusion that the government "ought to supply work and pay for the unemployed, maintenance for the infirm and aged, and education and opportunity for the children." The conservative view was less literary: its proponents were too busy running businesses and the country to write much.

Reformers were also audible. Backed by a resolution adopted in Calgary in February 1919, a quarter of a million veterans demanded a $2000 re-establishment bonus. It seemed a fair return for years of earning only $1.10 a day while civilians prospered safely at home. Profiteers like Sir Joseph Flavelle, who had gained $1.7 million from his wartime bacon business, could pay the bill. The Union government offered a flinty resistance. Ministers insisted that Canada had done more than the Americans for war widows, orphans, and the disabled. Money for the able-bodied would only reinforce the paternalism of army life. Warned that "full re-establishment" would cost $1 billion, politicians, businessmen, and even some veterans' leaders turned against the bonus. When the pressure collapsed, the government seized the moment to "tighten up" on pensions and retraining for the disabled.

Organized labour seemed tougher and better organized. Union ranks had grown from 143,200 in 1915 to 378,000 by 1919. The expansion concealed sharp splits. In 1918, conservatives recaptured the leadership of the Trades and Labor Congress from the radicals who had wielded power since 1912. An angry minority, mostly from the West, swore to meet in Calgary in March 1919 to plot their strategy. When they met, an even more militant caucus from western cities took over the meeting. The excited majority cheered the Bolshevik revolution in Russia, called for a similar proletarian uprising in Canada, and so frightened Sir Thomas White in Ottawa that he proposed summoning a British cruiser to Vancouver harbour. Delegates dispersed to plan a "One Big Union," an organization of workers regardless of skill, to challenge the craft-based conservatism of the Trades and Labor Congress.

Except for the hot rhetoric, little of this had much to do with the Winnipeg General Strike in May–June 1919. Bob Russell, prime architect of the One Big Union, worked in vain to prevent the outbreak among his fellow machinists. The trouble was that a general strike in 1918 had won collective bargaining rights for Winnipeg's civic workers. Why not try again to help employees of Winnipeg's obdurate engineering industry? After an overwhelming vote of support from its twelve thousand members, Winnipeg's Labour Council proclaimed a general strike on

May 15. An astonishing thirty thousand Winnipeggers, from waiters to telephone operators, walked out. Other general strikes exploded from Vancouver to Amherst, Nova Scotia.

Strike organizers were slow to realize that their angry speeches, not their cautious deeds, alarmed Winnipeg's middle class. After a month without strike pay, most Winnipeg workers had had enough. Strikes elsewhere collapsed. But words on both sides got hotter. Winnipeg civic leaders, convinced that labour was plotting a Bolshevik revolution, got automatic support from Arthur Meighen, Manitoba's cabinet representative in Ottawa. Assured that "enemy aliens" were behind the strike, Parliament swiftly amended the law to allow easy deportation. Dawn arrests of strike leaders followed. On Saturday, June 21, crowds of veterans and their families filled the street in front of Winnipeg's city hall to protest the arrests. Mounted police charged the throng; special constables attacked with clubs. "Bloody Saturday" and the ensuing trials of the strike leaders (British or Canadian to a man) gave Winnipeg's workers a bitter memory of their ordeal. Driven back to the city's north end, they gave their neighbourhoods a durable allegiance to labour and socialist politics.

The strike's collapse and the sedition trials that followed doomed the attempt to create an organization of industrial workers known as One Big Union. Employer resistance, counterattacks by the craft unions, and bitter disputes among the OBU's own leaders left only fragments of its bold vision. The split was a foretaste of divisions to come. Within a few years, the TLC expelled its biggest Canadian affiliate, the Canadian Brotherhood of Railway Employees, because it rivalled an international union. A tiny Communist party, organized in a barn near Guelph in 1921, obeyed Moscow's orders to "bore from within" the labour movement, with divisive consequences. By 1927, the Communists switched to building their own labour organization, the Workers' Unity League. In Quebec, years of sermons and editorials combined with the resentments of the war years led in 1921 to the Canadian and Catholic Confederation of Labour. The dream of a strong, united, and radical Canadian labour movement dissolved for thirty years.

In contrast, bankers and businessmen won most of their post-war wishes. Days after the armistice, Sir Joseph Flavelle closed his munitions factories and put their assets up for sale. That was necessary and even wise, but bankers also felt free to apply their favourite inflation-fighter, high interest rates. Capital that was needed to adjust industry to peacetime purposes vanished. So did jobs. So did inflation, but not before farmers and smaller businesses had suffered financial disaster. Bankers and their admirers found deflation excellent. Fiscal righteousness was also profitable.

In 1917 the government had closed the Winnipeg Grain Exchange and created a single Wheat Board to market grain. Farmers grumbled and then rejoiced as prices soared to a record $3.15 a bushel. After the 1919 crop, the Wheat Board dissolved and free enterprise returned. Earlier rural grumbles salved the politicians' consciences; faith in the market did the rest. Despite serious crop failure after years of declining prairie productivity, wheat prices plummeted 45 per cent in two years. Farmers who had invested in land, machinery, and comforts in the confidence of high prices now had strong reasons for lamentation.

Unlike veterans and labour, farmers still had the power to be influential. In the war years, farmers had confirmed the political independence of the Canadian Council of Agriculture by endorsing a Farmers' Platform in 1916. Furious at Borden's conscription policies, farmers had marched on Ottawa and then backed stronger policies. Deliberately titled a "New National Policy," it included old demands for reciprocity, lower freight rates, and bank reform, as well as newer proposals for railway nationalization and a graduated income tax. In T.A. Crerar, Minister of Agriculture for the Unionists, farmers found a leader who wrote even ministerial letters on United Grain Growers' paper. After White's 1919 budget fell short of farmers' wishes, Crerar quit.

Sir Robert Borden seemed far removed from the domestic turbulence of 1919. He had left for Europe even before the armistice to achieve the war aims he had set for Canada. Sir Robert believed that Canada had now won her War for Independence. Inside or outside the Empire – Borden was no longer as sure as he had once been – Canada must become a sovereign power with a signature on the peace treaty and a seat in the new League of Nations. Borden's powerful patron, David Lloyd George, had no real objections. Once it was clear that the great powers would dominate both arrangements, Canada's concern could be met. It was the Americans who resisted, furious that the wily British leader would use mere colonies to give his country extra votes. On May 6, 1919, President Woodrow Wilson glumly withdrew his objections, but most Americans did not. Canada's membership in the League of Nations became an added argument for American isolationists, who protested British dominance in the organization. The United States stayed out, Canada stayed in, but the League was crippled. Borden's international dreams had reached a dead end.

Even in Canada, Borden's hard-won overseas triumphs were seen as symbolic, costly, and possibly dangerous. The prime minister's insistence that Parliament vote on the German peace treaty was dismissed by a leading Liberal, William Fielding, as "a colossal humbug"; Article x of the League Covenant, pledging members to mutual defence, was described by a French-Canadian MP as putting Canada "at the beck and call of a Council not responsible to the nation." Borden's Unionist colleagues resented his absence in the midst of so many domestic crises, at a time when the fate of his Union coalition was obviously in doubt. For all his earnestness and sense of duty, Borden had finally lost interest in politics. In July, he sailed down the St. Lawrence with Sir Lomer Gouin in a bold bid to win over Quebec's premier. Gouin was tempted; he had been running the province for Ottawa since the 1918 riots but political common sense finally triumphed: Gouin stayed and Borden went home. By fall, the prime minister was too ailing and exhausted to delay a long-awaited rest cure in the United States.

Buffeted from all sides, Borden's colleagues welcomed the rest cure because they could not agree on Borden's successor. They were not idle. A Royal Commission on Labour Relations gathered a long list of useful reforms, most of which would appear again in a generation. Civil service reform removed forty thousand government employees from patronage, robbing Unionists of much political influence. Titles of nobility, discredited by wartime profiteering and scandals, would no longer be granted (with a brief revival in the 1930s). As cynics expected, the income tax survived the war and grew dramatically in size and bite. One legacy of the influenza epidemic (and fears of wartime venereal disease) was a small Department of Health. An Air Board planned post-war aviation policy. Despite "tightening up," the government treated eight thousand sick and wounded veterans and maintained eighty thousand pensioners.

No problem had bigger impact than the railways. In 1919, the Grand Trunk followed the Canadian Northern, via receivership, into nationalization. With no Bank of Commerce to guard its interests, $180 million in watered shares simply evaporated, largely at the expense of English investors. Lord Shaughnessy of the Canadian Pacific offered to lease the entire national railway system, run it under the CPR, and charge any losses to the taxpayer. In this fashion, free enterprise would prevail and the CPR (with its eager partner, the Bank of Montreal) would profit immensely. Arthur Meighen bluntly rejected the scheme. Lord Shaughnessy was duly enraged, and Montreal's powerful financial and business community reflected his fury. Both Meighen and the Tories paid a price for responsible stewardship. While most Canadians saw Meighen as an austere exponent of free enterprise, in Montreal he was either the ultimate conscriptionist or a rabid socialist. His party lost its richest financial sources. For decades, the party of Canada's rich would verge on penury.

The government's railway policy had other consequences. In November 1918, the old, patronage-battered Intercolonial was forced into the public system, christened the Canadian National Railways in 1919. The ICR headquarters left Moncton for Toronto and then Montreal. To meet the entire system's debt charges, rates rose immediately to Central Canadian levels and, in September 1920, suffered a system-wide 47 per cent increase. Maritime protests were dismissed as the familiar whining of a too-favoured region. In fact, Maritimers were right. The ICR was *their* railway. Its regionally based rates not only supported local manufacturing, they also produced a regular profit. By 1925, the Maritimes' national market was gone. The British Empire Steel Company, owner of Cape Breton's steel and coal industry, reeled towards ruin amidst long, violent strikes over wage cuts. In half a decade, a hundred and fifty thousand Maritimers left the region. Lack of hydroelectricity, a lower coal tariff, and greedy profit-taking were all factors in the first great era of Maritime decline, but the loss of the ICR was decisive.

John Dafoe predicted in 1918 that no one in power in the post-war years could make friends. In October 1919, Ontario voters handed their provincial legislature to the United Farmers and a clutch of Labour members. With a premier, Ernest Drury, who had not even run in the election, a Farmer-Labour government took power. In February 1920, Crerar became leader of a national Progressive party. By 1921, farmers held power in Manitoba and Alberta. In Saskatchewan, a foxy Premier C.A. Dunning survived by making his Liberals look so Progressive that no one bothered to explain the difference. More than veterans or labour, farmers were English-speaking Canada's postwar juggernaut, sweeping up Tories and rather more Liberals.

On February 17, 1919, the venerable Sir Wilfrid died, sure as ever that he was about to regain power. To his French-Canadian followers, Laurier's ghost would be their guide to a successor. Lady Laurier sensibly thought that William Fielding might be the man to reunite a shattered party, but he had deserted in 1917. Young William Lyon Mackenzie King, too brash and ambitious to win the living Laurier's approval, was the beneficiary of the ghost. Had he not run as a Toronto-area Laurier candidate in 1917 and lost? Liberals gathered in a sweaty Ottawa exhibition hall in August 1919 for Canada's first party leadership convention. They agreed that the ex-labour minister was a bearable alternative. His youth and his expertise in modern notions like unions and management efficiency might help. King won on the third ballot.

King's antagonist would not be Robert Borden. The old prime minister returned to Ottawa in the spring of 1920 still sick and indecisive. Colleagues urged him to stay on. Meighen, bluntly, advised him to go. Weary, but trying to preserve Unionism, Borden preferred Thomas White or Sir Lomer Gouin as his successor. Both men refused. The Tory backbenchers wanted Meighen and, on July 10, 1920, they got him. "The only unpardonable sin in politics," claimed the new prime minister, "is lack of courage." Meighen had plenty. He was tough, hardworking, brilliant in speech and grasp. He was also as inflexible in his political principles as the plump and prolix King was flexible. When Progressives continued to win by-elections, Meighen ended the suspense and launched the longest federal election campaign in Canadian history – from September 1 to December 6, 1921.

Meighen needed time because he had a message. The tariff, he believed, could be as successful an issue in 1921 as it had been in 1911. King treated Progressives as "Liberals in a hurry"; Meighen flayed them with all his verbal brilliance. Crerar campaigned in Ontario and the West, but experience suggested that farmers would organize themselves. As for King's campaign, Meighen's description was not misleading: "Protection on apples in British Columbia, Free Trade in the Prairie Provinces and rural parts of Ontario, Protection in industrial centres of Ontario, Conscription in Quebec, and Humbug in the Maritimes." In a sense, it worked. Humbug and conscription gave King almost all his 116 seats. Outside Ontario and British Columbia, where he collected 50 seats, Meighen was routed. Farmers in Ontario and the West gave Crerar 65 seats. Winnipeg and Calgary each elected a Labour member. One of these, J.S. Woodsworth, a former Winnipeg clergyman and editor of a strike newspaper, insisted that Labour would sit for the first time as a separate party.

Canadians in 1921 voted in distinct regional patterns and elected their first minority Parliament. King now showed a single-minded skill in compromise. His task was daunting. On tariffs, railways, and much else, his conservative Quebec caucus had more in common with the Tories than with the Protestant, free-trade Progressives. Liberal ranks included both Laurierites and conscriptionists. As a labour negotiator, resolving opposite viewpoints with no visible opinions of his own, King had acquired experience he now needed. He discovered the little that united farmers and Quebeckers and swiftly exploited it. Both *Canadiens* and farmers despised imperialism and hated militarism. Service departments joined a single Department of National Defence. All he wanted, said its new minister, was something "simple and snappy." With J.W. Dafoe and a new undersecretary of state for external affairs, O.D. Skelton, King had ideal escorts to London. Schemes for imperial collaboration or even consultation met King's firm veto. Nationalists and *nationalistes* might not cheer, but they took quiet comfort. Lloyd George's appeal for aid in a possible war with the Turks at Chanak in 1922 inspired Meighen to utter an instinctive, "Ready, Aye Ready." From King, it drew resentful silence. The League of Nations was reminded by Senator Raoul Dandurand, president of its Assembly in 1925, that "Canada is a fire-proof house, far from the source of any conflagration." When more public gestures were needed, King sent another *Canadien*, Ernest Lapointe, to Washington in 1923 to sign the Halibut Treaty, ignoring proffered assistance from Great Britain.

If this seemed little, at home there was less. Not until 1924 was the tariff even modestly reduced – on items that exclusively troubled Tory Ontario. The Hudson Bay Railway, a prairie dream for thirty years, would come – but only when King got a majority. The Crowsnest Pass freight rate, suspended during the war, was restored – for wheat only – in 1923. The Maritimes, solid for King in 1921, got very little: surely the region was as Liberal as it needed to be. It was the West that needed pleasing and patience.

In 1923 Ontario's Farmer government was utterly defeated. Its mothers' allowances, county forests, and rural roads counted for little in the face of internal divisions. Voters now sneered at rural earnestness. King could exploit such weaknesses. Pragmatic farmer-politicians like Ernest Drury and Thomas Crerar were driven half-mad by rural ideologues, determined that farmers form a movement, not a party. Alberta's Henry Wise Wood preached that government must be based on groups of farmers, businessmen, and workers, not on political parties. Wood's "social corporatism" fitted awkwardly with voters who expected favours. Nor did farmers like what their representatives were doing for them. On the dubious argument that they were not really "politicians," Progressive MPs forbade Crerar from becoming leader of the opposition in 1922. Lacking a role of alternative government, the movement fell apart. Radicals debated freight rates, monetary theories, and Social Credit; pragmatists plotted how they could beneficially make peace with King.

In 1925 some were ready for a switch. So was Meighen. In opposition, he had worked ingeniously and hard. The Eastern provinces had united in a Maritimes Rights movement that just happened to be managed by Tories. By 1925, all three Maritime provincial governments were run by Conservatives. Elsewhere, Meighen could count on hard times since the war and what seemed to him the transparent futility of King's government. About Quebec, Meighen could do nothing, nor would he even try to buy votes in the West. If anyone really wanted the Hudson Bay Railway, he offered $3 million and no more. The outcome of the election, on October 29, 1925, was as good a victory as Meighen could have hoped to get: 116 seats and 47 per cent of the votes, to King's 99 seats and 40 per cent. The Progressives were cut to 9 per cent and 24 seats.

Yet King did not resign. Liberals raged privately at his "vanity and pomposity," his "predilection for strange and unworthy favourites," but when Meighen and King each presented the Progressives with his program, seven switched to King and his majority held. Defeated in his own seat, King went west to win Prince Albert, and he brought Saskatchewan's C.A. Dunning back with him to the cabinet. As finance minister, he gave Canadians a "prosperity budget" of tax cuts and giveaways, an experience few of them had known since 1906. Meighen's near-victory in 1925 demonstrated that Progressivism was dying and that the next contest would be a Liberal-Tory runoff. J.W. Dafoe was typical. In three elections he had avoided voting Liberal; now he saw no alternative.

First, there would be some unpleasantness. Prohibition, dead in most of Canada by 1924, persisted bravely south of the border, straining the morality of Canadian customs officers and the natural avarice of their superiors. A vigorous Tory MP, Harry Stevens, had evidence of the results: a malodorous scandal of kickbacks, cover-ups, and bribes reaching all the way to the minister of customs, Jacques Bureau. King swiftly hoisted the guilty minister to the safety of the Senate, but showed no signs of repentance. Tories raged and pure-minded Progressives squirmed. The upshot, after much uproar, was a vote of censure on King's government, which it was sure to lose. But first, King won a weekend adjournment. Then he headed to Rideau Hall to ask the governor general for a dissolution. Sir Julian Byng, shocked by the impropriety, refused. An equally shocked King urged him to check with London. The governor general refused so colonial a gesture. King indignantly resigned. Against good advice but full of loyalty to the governor general, Arthur Meighen accepted office. The Liberals then won a vote of censure against Meighen, and Byng gave him the election he had denied King.

Meighen never could understand the 1926 election. His opponent, the man who perennially insisted that "Parliament would decide," had been caught trying to run away from Parliament's decision. The man of insistent legalism had defied constitutional convention. King, too, may have been nonplussed by events, but luck was with him. In English-speaking Canada, the election issue had been settled by the prosperity budget and Meighen. The customs scandals aroused loyal Tories, but in good times muck smells like fertilizer. In Quebec, Liberals portrayed Byng as a British colonial governor, bullying the great rebel's grandson. And how many of the Tories' customs house crooks had been *Canadiens*? Meighen added Nova Scotia to his majorities in Ontario and British Columbia, but his 99 seats could still not match King's 128, nor the remnant of 20 Progressives and 3 Labourites. Meighen also endured the ultimate humiliation: defeat in his own riding.

In memory, the 1920s would shine as a golden era suspended between the Great War and the Great Depression. Only the last half decade actually qualified as golden, but economic growth was steady and remarkable. American prosperity poured over the border in the form of investment in branch plants, able to serve a British Empire sheltered behind an empire-wide tariff. Automobile, rubber, chemical, and clothing factories grew up around the lower Great Lakes in industrial cities like Hamilton, Oshawa, Windsor, St. Catharines, and also in Montreal. To supply both Canadian and American markets there was a prodigious prodding and digging away at the minerals of the Canadian Shield, from the Noranda copper properties in Quebec to the gold of Kirkland Lake and the nickel of Sudbury. When King finally launched the promised Hudson Bay Railway in 1927, it fulfilled an old tradition by opening up Flin Flon and the area beyond for the exploitation of its mineral wealth.

In 1920 the CNR earned $234 million, spent $231 million, and had the balance to retire its $1311-million debt. Instead of collapsing under the impossible debt load, the CNR staggered into the new decade. An American-born, British-seasoned railroader, Sir Henry Thornton, cheerfully accepted King's invitation to run the system. Thornton was traditional in insisting that expansion meant salvation, but he expanded with flair. The CNR added five thousand miles of track and built new locomotives, cars, and the grandest hotels the country had seen, from the Nova Scotian in Halifax to Jasper Park Lodge in the Rockies. The CNR bought ships to serve the West Indies, experimented with air service, and created a transcontinental network to send programs to "radio cars" on its luxurious passenger trains. It was the golden age of Canadian rail, but of all the potential dead ends in the decade this was the most certain.

Highways, the new transportation network, met American tourists at the border and led them to cities, scenery, and wherever they wanted. Roads became the largest new public investment of the decade, and telephone networks came close behind. Air was a third dimension of communication. Even before its official birth in 1923, the Royal Canadian Air Force showed that aircraft could be used to spot forest fires, deliver treaty money, and even catch smugglers. By surmounting mountain ranges and distances to deliver prospectors and supplies, bush pilots opened a hitherto neglected and little-known North. To the south, cars and trucks were having an even greater economic impact. Just as Canada's costly railway system had begun to rationalize and reform itself, road traffic became its most effective competitor. Canadians with $3250 to spend on a McLaughlin roadster or $850 for a Model T hardly worried. Provincial treasurers certainly did.

Almost every development of the 1920s contradicted national unity. American investment and American markets make Canada a north-south nation once again. British economic influence had slipped with wartime liquidation of investments; now it fell rapidly. Ottawa had managed railways; roads had been trivial enough to leave in provincial control. Now highways mattered. So did expansion of secondary education, new allowances for widows, the blind, and the disabled, and hospitals, and treatment for deadly diseases like syphilis or tuberculosis. Sir John A. Macdonald had planned an east-west country; branch-plant factories, mineral exploration, floods of American films, magazines, and radio programs usually linked Canadians to the United States. Was that why Meighen's 1911-style nationalism drew fainter echoes?

During the war, Ottawa had exercised any power it wanted. Now provinces grew more powerful, aided by an old ally. Guided by Lord Haldane's understanding of classic federalism, the Judicial Committee of the Privy Council lent a hand. In Haldane's eyes, the British North America Act's Section 91, with its "peace, order and good government" clause, was easily trumped by the provinces' power over "property and civil rights." Despite arguments from Ottawa and Quebec City, the Judicial Committee reinterpreted the BNA Act's 1867 wording to insist that women, as well as men, were "persons" and eligible for Senate appointments. The act, insisted British judges, was a "living tree" and subject to evolution. King accepted defeat but the first woman senator was a dependable Liberal, not one of the four western feminists who had fought the case. King also did what he could to find revenue for the added responsibilities assumed by provinces and, in good time for the 1930 election, ended a prairie provinces grievance by giving them full control of their land and natural resources.

Without duress, the federal government took few initiatives. In 1925, J.S. Woodsworth of the tiny Labour party extorted a promise of old-age pensions in exchange for support for a desperate King. The promise was kept in 1927 – Ottawa would meet half the cost of a meagre, means-tested pension for those over seventy. Compelled to pay the other half, most provinces hesitated. Nova Scotia found a novel way to raise its share: it legalized liquor sold in government-run stores, and used the profits to help its elderly. Other provinces followed suit. By ending prohibition, Ontario Tories, elected in 1923, bounced from deficit to surplus budgets.

The 1920s felt good for most people. Politics receded in favour of sports, movies, and American radio shows. Canada's diamond jubilee in 1927 featured the first nation-wide radio programming. An imperial conference agreed that Canada and her other white-ruled dominions should have formal sovereignty. First, Canada needed an amending formula for the BNA Act. Not even jubilee euphoria could convince Ottawa and the provinces to agree. While the British waited impatiently to adopt the Statute of Westminster, premiers Howard Ferguson of Ontario and Alexandre Taschereau of Quebec imposed their conditions: until they got their way, Canada's constitution would stay in London. Canadians might be independent, but they could not trust themselves to alter their own system of government fairly.

The diamond jubilee year generated tinselly nationalism, but nothing could hide the racial intolerance that flourished during and after the war years. A Manitoba author tried to create a more positive image of Canada's racial diversity by describing the provinces as a mosaic of cultures, but the diversity of languages and cultures seemed to give no pleasure. Bishop G.E. Lloyd of Saskatchewan, a colourful prairie pioneer, publicly denounced the "mongrelization" of Canada. Lloyd provoked an aging Sir Clifford Sifton to deliver his tolerant, if condescending, comments about "peasants in sheepskin coats." Later in the decade, the white hoods and flaming crosses of the Ku Klux Klan invaded Western Canada, threatening Catholics and "foreigners." Within a year, the Klan promoter had absconded with a hundred thousand dollars in membership funds, but the ugly message remained. In 1929 Saskatchewan voters elected a Tory government headed by J.T.M. Anderson, a respected educator whose book, *The Education of New Canadians*, demanded firm assimilation with "a true Canadian spirit and attachment to British institutions."

Nationalism and anxiety about alien forces made the West a natural birthplace for an interdenominational movement that ended in 1925 with the formation of the United Church of Canada. Methodists, Congregationalists, and all but a sturdy core of Presbyterians joined the new organization. Enthusiasts welcomed the new church as specifically Canadian and a challenge to a secular age. Others, with less idealism, saw it as a sensible business merger and an answer to the numerical challenge of the Catholics. The first moderator, George Pidgeon, firmly suppressed vestiges of the old Methodist radicalism; wealthy contributors must be encouraged. Church union exposed mainline Protestants to the challenge of fundamentalists on one side and rationalism and secularism on the other. And nothing could spare most churches from the costs of two great but divisive crusades: prohibition and the Great War.

Quebec had resisted both crusades and would fight until 1940 against a third: votes for women. In the post-war world, Quebec's traditional leaders felt their people to be more isolated and endangered than ever. The conscription crisis had not been as remote as Riel or the Ontario government's attack on the use of French in its schools. The Canadian majority had imposed its will, and taken Quebec's sons into an English-speaking army. Henri Bourassa, back in Parliament after 1921 as an independent, pleaded still for a bilingual, bicultural Canada, but he also abandoned forever the few radical ideas that earlier had inspired him. Bourassa followed a new intellectual style.

The new leader of Quebec nationalism was Abbé Lionel Groulx, a tireless elf of a man who taught the history of Quebec to generations of students at the new University of Montreal. Only within Quebec, argued Groulx and his disciples in *L'Action Française*, could a French and Catholic nationality be preserved. Survival demanded rejection, even in the cities, of external influence in the form of films, books, and magazines. On Sunday, January 9, 1927, Montreal's Laurier Palace cinema burned, killing seventy-eight children. Groulx's campaign to ban youngsters from movie theatres (and thereby the influence of American and British movies) triumphed within days.

Yet the triviality of the reform underlined the limits of the *Action Française* program. Montreal was a harsh, unhealthy city for too many of its people and, by 1931, two-thirds of the 818,377 Montrealers were *Canadiens*. But, for them as for most Canadians, cities seemed bright, lively, and crowded with the material rewards of the age. In good times Groulx's austere, moralistic nationalism commanded disciples, not a mass following. In the thriving 1920s, Groulx himself recognized that his cause had stalled.

The 1920s was the first decade of mass-produced culture. Films, magazines, gramophones with "hit" records, and professional sports all promised a lifestyle ordinary people could enjoy. Self-conscious elites could read *The Canadian Forum*, debate the merits of the Toronto-based artists in the Group of Seven or the Montreal School. Some even heard of Emily Carr's lonely work on the West Coast. Canadians boasted of the sailing feats of the *Bluenose* or hummed the songs of the Dumbells, the soldier-entertainers who sustained what little remained of wartime nostalgia, but real fame came from New York. Canada developed respected actors, musicians, and singers, but their renown was earned in New York, Paris, or London. The country's own frail culture shrivelled before the excitement and prosperity of the United States.

No cultural force broke down the international barriers more swiftly than radio. By the mid-1920s, powerful American stations carried signals into most populated parts of Canada, and the technology of a crystal set receiver was easy for a bright youngster. A royal commission on broadcasting, headed by Sir John Aird of the Bank of Commerce, recommended a BBC-style solution for Canada's chaotic airwaves. The choice, claimed one of Aird's supporters, was "the State or the States." Canada, with its frugal comforts, its low wages, its backwater vision of itself, was culturally challenged. Would the competition do some good?

THE DEPRESSION | 5

G reat events have complex causes. Few now date the Great Depression of the 1930s from the Wall Street Crash of October 1929. Although the slump was a symptom of a much wider sickness, there are not many who still believe the contemporary preachers who blamed it on rising skirts, falling morals, lack of prayer, and a self-indulgent insistence on living beyond one's means.

In 1929 it cost over $10,000 a year to live the resplendent life depicted in the rotogravure supplements; only 13,477 Canadian families acknowledged such an income. The federal Department of Labour insisted that a family needed $1200 to $1500 a year to maintain a "minimum standard of decency." Sixty per cent of working men and 82 per cent of working women earned less than $1000 a year. By any definition, most people were as poor as Canadians had been for generations. Depressions did not occur because ordinary people lived beyond their means. In fact, a British economist, John Maynard Keynes, would soon argue that the economy shut down because too many people had no means to buy what it could produce. Most Canadians fitted this category.

In Canada, the immediate cause of the Depression was not the Wall Street Crash but an enormous 1928 wheat crop. A decade of immigration had filled the last, most infertile prairie land. As times improved, prairie farmers had forgotten politics. Instead, they listened to a persuasive American lawyer named Aaron Sapiro. Rather than going to the Wheat Board or the Grain Exchange, Sapiro said, why not pool the wheat harvest and sell it with the bargaining power of any good cartel? Thousands of farmers joined the Wheat Pool, prospered, and added to their acreage. The idea worked brilliantly – as long as there was no glut and no serious competition. By 1928, there were both: 567 million bushels at a Pool-guaranteed price of $1.28 a bushel, to be sold in a world that could now buy much more cheaply from the United States, Argentina, Australia, and even the Soviet Union.

Of course, no one worried too much in 1929. Prosperity now seemed permanent, though, as some brokers warned their clients, the market needed just a tiny "correction." Inventories were too large. Capital investment was a trifle optimistic. On the prairies, salesmen confessed that orders were down. Business prophets cautiously reminded their customers that economies, like people, needed an occasional rest. Slowly, and then irreversibly, an economic system based on credit, confidence, and massive resource exports began running down the cycle. Far away, buyers cut or cancelled orders for timber, fish, and base metals. Construction slowed. Industrialists checked their shrinking order books, and ordered wage cuts, half-time work, even a temporary shutdown. No one could be astonished; a prosperous decade had already experienced two depressions, in 1920 and 1923.

Politicians in the 1920s were seldom faced with economic indicators or unemployment statistics. The few available figures were collected by the Department of Labour through a haphazard system of local reports and published monthly in its *Labour Gazette*. In 1929, the *Gazette* found about 3 per cent of its sample looking for jobs; a year later, the total had reached 11 per cent, or 530,000 men and women. That was alarming but not unprecedented. Provincial governments, pestering Ottawa for relief measures, were undoubtedly playing politics. They were also dodging their constitutional responsibility for social welfare. Proud of his soberly balanced budget, Mackenzie King was outraged that Tory premiers should mine votes from an unpleasant but short-lived downturn. He would not give one cent, he told the House of Commons on April 3, 1930, "for these alleged unemployment purposes." He would confer with the more needy prairie premiers, but as for provincial governments that diametrically opposed him, "I would not give them a five-cent piece."

Such blunt comments were out of character, but the prime minister felt quite removed from the economic calamity that was beginning to preoccupy Canadians. He had determined on a 1930 election long before his current spiritualist added her blessing, and his current finance minister, C.A. Dunning, duly cut the federal sales tax to one per cent. Veterans must be grateful for new allowances, the prairies would reward the Liberals for giving them control over their natural resources, nationalists would applaud the promised Statute of Westminster, and Quebec would again be reminded of conscription and the Tories.

Then there was the Opposition. In 1927 the Tories had followed the Liberal example with an American-style leadership convention in Winnipeg. The winner was Richard Bedford Bennett, a New Brunswick–born Calgary corporation lawyer who had managed national registration but opposed conscription in 1917. His friendship with the heiress to the fortune of Ottawa's E.B. Eddy lumber company brought him a vast inheritance. As a youth Bennett had pledged total abstinence, and he fought temptation with candy and sugar. He was a big, plump man with a booming voice, a domineering manner, and a capacity for generosity that he kept utterly secret. A lonely bachelor, Bennett carried an aura of the business competence that the era already worshipped. King considered his opponent far inferior to Meighen. About Bennett's intellect, King was right. In electoral terms, King was wrong.

The Depression was Bennett's chance. The "five-cent piece" speech was soon burnished in memory as proof of King's callousness. "Mackenzie King promises you conferences," trumpeted Bennett, "I promise you action." Quebec farmers were told to blame their misery on imports of New Zealand butter. Bennett would save them. The Liberals had allowed a one-sided imperial preference; Bennett would demand full reciprocity. In the crisis, the United States had hoisted tariffs. Bennett would do so too, but, in his hands, protection would "blast a way into the markets of the world." Even doubters stayed to marvel. After the years of anaemic compromise and shuffling evasion, here was self-confidence and dynamism. As a businessman rich enough to finance his party's entire campaign, Bennett would solve the Depression. On July 28, Bennett won the kind of triumph Tories had not seen since the days of Sir John A. Macdonald: 137 seats to 91 for King and a rump of only 12 for the Progressives. To prove that this was the age of miracles, Bennett won 16 rural Quebec seats.

If vigour could have demolished the Depression, it would have faded within a year of the election. Bennett summoned the new Parliament for September 1930, forced through the biggest tariff increases since 1879, and ordered $20 million in emergency relief. He insisted added protection would guarantee twenty-five thousand industrial jobs. In London for the Imperial Conference of 1930 – signing the Statute of Westminster in place of King – Bennett joined his old friend, Lord Beaverbrook, in a vain crusade for an Empire-based exclusive trading system. Two years later, after Britain's own efforts for free trade had utterly failed, an Imperial Economic Conference in Ottawa gave Bennett a belated victory. Desperate for any agreement, the British lowered their tariff barriers to Canada in return for no more than Bennett's pledge not to raise his 50 per cent protection any higher. British politicians complained that Bennett had bullied them mercilessly. Canadian financiers and industrialists had good reason to rejoice.

While Canadians found themselves in a trade war with a steadily more protectionist United States, Bennett made a determined bid to launch the long-contemplated St. Lawrence Deep Waterway project. A treaty with President Herbert Hoover's Republican administration passed all the way to the American Senate, where Atlantic state senators killed it for the sake of their harbours. Thousands of potential construction jobs vanished, but Bennett poured still more money into provincial relief projects, adding close to $1 billion to the national debt. The Wheat Pool, utterly ruined when its advance payments to farmers far exceeded the price for their wheat, survived only because Bennett provided secret subsidies. Canada's chartered banks preened themselves on surviving without a bankruptcy, but Bennett compelled them to accept a central Bank of Canada – though the government held only a minority of the shares.

Bennett's most unexpected creation was the Canadian Radio Broadcasting Commission (CRBC). Prodded by young enthusiasts in the Canadian Radio League, Bennett took up the Aird Commission report with unexpected interest. A Judicial Committee decision, surprising only because of its past preferences, confirmed that broadcasting was a federal responsibility. Born in 1932, at the depth of the Depression, the CRBC was a sadly underfinanced compromise. It was also a Canadian stake in public broadcasting in a decade when radio became the only mass medium almost everyone could afford. As the Depression deepened, many found their radio sets were the only escape from besetting hopelessness. This was no ordinary depression, in which savings vanished and city families slipped home to the security of the farm. As J.S. Woodsworth told Parliament, "If they went out today, they would meet another army of unemployed coming back from the country to the city." People in Ottawa, he reported, took refuge in garbage dumps. Bennett's own files bulged with reports of misery. Even the aged daughter of a former prime minister was reported to be on the verge of starvation.

Unemployment insurance had been a Liberal policy in 1919. Only unions now pleaded for it: editors and experts insisted that it would subsidize idleness. Instead, they claimed, wages must fall until everyone would find work. It took time. By 1933, the government's crude statistics reported 23 per cent out of work. A third of Canada's manufacturing jobs had vanished. Net farm income fell from $417 million in 1929 to $109 million in 1933. Those with work found some compensations. Until 1932–33, prices fell faster than wages. A 15 per cent wage cut imposed on civil servants by Ottawa and imitated by most provinces and other major employers left living standards undamaged. The prosperous few could enjoy themselves with an obliviousness to wider suffering that wealth seems to confer. Newspapers and radio helped. Media in the 1930s accepted a solemn duty to trivialize or ignore the misery of millions. Lush Hollywood musicals and adventure films filled neighbourhood movie theatres. Air races, professional sports, and the exotic junketing of reporters such as the *Toronto Star*'s Gordon Sinclair allowed the public to escape. The birth of the Dionne quintuplets on May 28, 1934, at Callander, Ontario, provided reporters, politicians, business promoters, and members of the medical profession with another chance for fame and fortune. The "quints" were exposed like zoo animals.

The unemployed would eagerly have shared in the escape, but relief procedures, designed to force the idle to work, crushed self-respect. Relief officials insisted that cars, telephones, pets, ornaments, comfortable furniture, and all but a single bare light fixture be sacrificed. Recipients collected food vouchers, sought medical care from an overworked contract doctor, and visited a municipal depot to collect used clothing. Men shovelled snow, chopped wood, or pulled weeds for their relief benefits. Since women did not work, provision was seldom made for their clothing or personal needs. The young profession of social work sold its expertise in detecting fraud and waste.

Misery on relief was deliberate public policy. Even at the depths of the Depression, editors and business leaders insisted that jobs were available if men would only hunt for them. One result was that single unemployed men were sent packing by relief officials. Thousands rode boxcars to British Columbia. On the way, some froze to death or were murdered. Provincial governments established work camps for single men. Bennett's government followed suit in 1933, using the Department of National Defence to run camps behind a discreet façade of civilian administration. Men hacking at bush or restoring historic fortifications cost a dollar a day. After their expenses were deducted, twenty cents remained as their pay.

The employed knew that thousands were waiting for a chance to replace them. Some employers fired women because men needed work; others replaced men with women because they accepted lower pay. There were few strikes. The Communist-led Workers Unity League organized vigorously, but its efforts often ended in failure and even bloodshed. Bred in the doctrine of self-help, individual Canadians seemed tragically willing to accept responsibility for their plight. Some literally died rather than accept relief. Slowly guilt turn to despair and then, as the depth and duration of the Depression exceeded every memory, to deep but unfocused resentment. Some urban politicians like Montreal's Camillien Houde or Vancouver's Gerry McGeer sought to help the unemployed. Since tax revenues had collapsed, Houde's parks, playgrounds, and public urinals – known locally as "camilliens" – led Montreal to bankruptcy.

Nowhere was destitution greater than across the prairie West. Eastern Canadian farmers suffered falling prices and occasional foreclosures, but there was food to eat, and the rural population actually increased. In the West, proclaimed "the greatest farmland in the world," the 1930s yielded literal starvation. The collapse of world grain markets would have been catastrophe enough, but people would have eaten. In 1929, drought devastated much of the harvest, and for nine more years crop conditions denied the prairies a satisfactory harvest. In 1931, the wind began lifting the dry topsoil in great black clouds. In 1932, the first great plague of grasshoppers devoured every green thing, plus clothing and tool handles. In 1933, drought, hail, rust, and frost joined the grasshoppers, as though all nature's forces had united to give prairie settlers notice to quit. Thousands obeyed, fleeing the region, or hauling their families and remaining livestock north to the parkland belt. Some ventured to the Peace River country. A battered remnant stayed and, in a collaboration of farmers and scientists, learned to fight the encroaching desert with trash cover, contour ploughing, and new strains of wheat. Huge acreages, sold for cultivation because of the greed of railways and governments, returned to the grazing role for which they were appropriate.

Settling the prairie West had been Canada's proudest achievement. In 1928, only British Columbia boasted a higher per capita income than Alberta's $548. At $478, Saskatchewan stood fourth.

By 1933, at a mere $135 a person, Saskatchewan was the poorest province in Canada. Her government was bankrupt and her people gratefully welcomed trainloads of food and used clothing sent as charity from other regions. Even Depression-battered Newfoundland sent salt cod; the poor Westerners, not knowing what to do with it, soaked it, boiled it, and, if they could not stand the taste of wet socks, used it to plug holes in their roofs.

Bennett's bold speeches and dynamic policies provided no adequate answer to the spreading misery. Within the available orthodoxies, no government could. By espousing protection, Canada merely echoed beggar-my-neighbour policies that deepened the worldwide depression. In opposition, the Liberals offered no alternatives. Their defeat in 1930, they soon discovered, had been a stroke of luck. The Tories were in trouble, and Mackenzie King had no intention of helping them out with his own ideas. King's fourteen-point program of 1933 set high standards for vagueness and contradiction. The Liberals, King pledged, would "liberalize internal trade" and create "a more equitable distribution of wealth." Such phrases were deliberately meaningless. At heart, King was satisfied that the economy was working as badly as could be expected when Liberals were out of power.

Bennett was unlikely to take anyone's advice, least of all King's. A lonely, domineering man, inhabiting an extensive suite in the Château Laurier, Bennett was portrayed by Arch Dale, the *Winnipeg Free Press* cartoonist, as conducting cabinet meetings with himself in every chair. His wealth and corpulence now inspired loathing, not reassurance. Goaded by his own sense of failure, Bennett's reaction was to strike out. Bennett pledged to crush communism "with the iron heel of ruthlessness."

The labour crises in 1919 had added Section 98 to the Criminal Code: a sweeping description of sedition accompanied

by prison terms and possible deportation. In 1931, the government seized leaders of the small Communist party. Chief
Justice Sir William Mulock (a former Laurier minister and
King's first patron) condemned the men with every appearance
of relish. Book censorship became a duty of customs officials.
The Royal Canadian Mounted Police, expanded in 1920 from
the old Royal North West Mounted Police, served Bennett as a
secret service and riot police. Though Communists *were* involved
in much of the unrest that accompanied the Depression, many
Canadians saw strikers, hunger marchers, and even rioters as
fellow humans, fighting for jobs, wages, and a little dignity.

There had to be alternatives, but few were emerging. Among
the country's leading intellectuals, the University of Toronto
economic historian Harold Innis lectured his junior and more
radical colleagues against venturing to mingle their ideas with
contemporary politics. The United Church of Canada, heir to a
reforming Methodist tradition, worried about its finances and
prudently proclaimed moral depravity a greater evil than economic misery. J.W. Dafoe, editor of the influential *Winnipeg
Free Press*, urged Liberals to find new ideas and then damned
anything that strayed from his laissez-faire individualism.

The ferment came, as had almost every radical idea of the
1920s, from Calgary. One doctrine was already familiar: William
Irvine, Woodsworth's partner in the 1921 Parliament, had promoted Social Credit. Brainchild of an English engineer, it
argued that the gap between the return to a producer and the
final price of the product created "poverty in the midst of
plenty." In the 1920s it was a theory; by 1932, it was harsh reality.
William Aberhart, a Calgary high school principal and fundamentalist radio preacher, took up the Social Credit message.
Rarely have medium and message been better combined. A
gospel-reared audience, frightened by debt, insecurity, and
sudden poverty, responded to simple economics taught with

images of thieves, moneylenders, and social dividends. The radicalism of overthrowing the entire financial system seemed less when the temples of Canadian banking would crash in the distant East. Besides, wasn't Mr. Aberhart of the Prophetic Bible Institute a man of God, not a politician like the corrupt opportunists in Ottawa, Toronto, and Edmonton?

Social Credit mingled radical and conservative messages in brilliant counterpoint. Another idea was less ambiguous, if more complex. Canadian socialism had shattered with the Bolshevik revolution of 1917. Communists became the disciples of Lenin and Stalin and servants of Soviet policy. The divided remnants shared little more than a commitment to democracy. Craft unionists of the Trades and Labor Congress had fled politics in the 1920s, and nothing in the 1930s would entice the TLC's aging, frightened leaders back. The wreck of the federal Progressives left a radical remnant, the "Ginger Group," more correctly called the "co-operating independents." Among them, only the slight, bearded ex-clergyman and pacifist, J.S. Woodsworth, had both a strategy and patience. Someday, Canada must have a version of Britain's Labour Party, complete with intellectuals, riding associations, trade union affiliates, and MPs. The Depression gave Woodsworth an opportunity to build such a party.

In 1932, a few academics ignored Innis's advice and formed the League for Social Reconstruction. Woodsworth became honorary president. In Calgary that summer, delegates to the regular meeting of western labour parties found that the economic crisis had attracted members of farmer and socialist parties and even A.R. Mosher from the All-Canadian Congress of Labour, a TLC rival. With Woodsworth's shepherding, the meeting launched a "Co-operative Commonwealth Federation (Farmer Labour Socialist)," or CCF. A year later in Regina, the first national convention of the CCF survived bitter debates and adopted a manifesto. The document's chief author was

Professor Frank Underhill of the University of Toronto, but delegates added a dramatic conclusion: "No CCF government will rest content until it has eradicated capitalism and put into operation the full programme of socialized planning which will lead to the establishment in Canada of the co-operative commonwealth." More cautiously, Woodsworth reminded listeners that socialism came from "the good old Latin word for 'friend,'" and promised an authentic Canadian version of the idea.

Unlike Social Credit, whose study groups and mass radio audiences swept it almost silently toward power, the CCF was exposed and embattled from birth. By 1934, it could boast hundreds of clubs and an organization in most provinces. It had also been denounced by business leaders and editors, repudiated by the TLC, and condemned as a danger to Catholicism by the coadjutor bishop of Montreal. For good measure, the disciplined militants of the Communist party were as keen to wreck the rival CCF as to undermine R.B. Bennett, and with rather better chance of success. Social Credit, in contrast, remained within Alberta and Saskatchewan, under the sweep of Aberhart's powerful radio message.

Third parties usually look more frightening before elections than afterwards. The CCF started strong. In 1933, building on an old labour-socialist tradition in British Columbia, the CCF won second place. A Liberal, T. Duff Pattullo, triumphed on a slogan of "Work and Wages." In 1934 an engaging young onion farmer from Elgin County named Mitchell F. Hepburn pledged to go left where few would follow, and turned Ontario Liberal for the first time since 1902. The CCF won a single labour seat. A Liberal victory in Saskatchewan under former premier Jimmy Gardiner was predictable. Not a single Tory supporter survived, and the opposition was CCF.

Not even the Depression could make many Canadians embrace socialism. Small businessmen and supporters of a modified status quo found a hero in Harry Stevens, a British Columbia Tory who had been hero of the customs scandal. As minister of trade and commerce, Stevens turned into a crusader. A small merchant himself, Stevens understood how big companies controlled markets. In the Depression, big merchandisers had protected their rich profit margins by squeezing smaller suppliers and independent retailers. The proof was in the price spread between the primary producer and the ultimate consumer. Stevens demanded an investigation, and a parliamentary committee found ample evidence of price-gouging, starvation wages, sweated labour, and predatory practices. The report named powerful retailers like Eaton's and Simpson's. Harry Stevens and his main backer, Toronto clothier Warren K. Cook, were delighted. Bennett was not. When the prime minister tried to suppress Stevens's views and drove him from the cabinet, millions of Canadians accepted the ex-minister as a crusading hero.

Canadian heroes were scarce. Until 1932, people saw no alternative leaders. Americans were faring no better under Herbert Hoover. Then, as Canadians heard on their radios, Franklin Delano Roosevelt swept into the White House and began the long drama of the New Deal. A generation of Canadians became instinctive Democrats. Roosevelt's radio image may have been artificial, but it transcended borders. For the first time, Canadians coveted their neighbours' political leadership. Not even Bennett was immune to Roosevelt's spell. Privately he had writhed at the sneers about shantytown "Bennettburghs" and horse-drawn automobiles called "Bennett buggies." All his life, Bennett had seen himself as a dynamic, successful figure. Frustration now drove him to imitate Roosevelt. In 1927, Canada had opened a legation in Washington. Bennett chose his brother-in-law, W.D. Herridge, for the post. A man of ideas, Herridge urged Bennett to adopt the style and perhaps even some of the content of the New Deal. Bennett was game. Herridge drafted speeches and Bennett demanded radio time. On January 3, 1935, he began.

Canadians listened dutifully and then with astonishment, none more so than Bennett's Tory associates. The substance was not new; Bennett's flamboyant, uncompromising language was. If the CCF's Woodsworth had seized the microphone, the words might have been similar. "There can be no permanent recovery without reform," Bennett declared. "And, to my mind, reform means Government intervention. It means Government control and regulation. It means the end of *laisser faire*." It meant unemployment insurance, minimum wages, maximum hours of work, marketing legislation for farmers, and measures against price-fixing. Stevens had proposed a federal trade commission. Bennett would create one.

In one speech, Bennett regained the initiative. Then he fell ill. When he recovered, he hurried to England for the Silver Jubilee of King George V. When he returned, Mackenzie King had found a line: if Bennett's New Deal was good, it was Liberal policy; if it was not, it was typical Tory dictatorship. In either case, King declared, most of Bennett's program was beyond Ottawa's constitutional powers. Meanwhile, old Tories and business interests had orchestrated opposition. By the time Bennett tabled the Dominion Trade and Industry Commission Act, Harry Stevens had left his party and on July 7, 1935, he announced a new one. Within five days Stevens had a program and a title: the Reconstruction party. Its target would be those thousands of Canadians who still hoped for reformed capitalism.

By summer, Canadians wondered whether Bennett even remembered his January cry for reform. In May, Communist organizers pulled men out of the shabby, demoralizing relief camps in British Columbia. The men came eagerly. Surely there had to be more to life than labouring under army discipline for twenty cents a day. More than a thousand piled on boxcars for an "On-to-Ottawa" trek. Bennett ordered the march halted at Regina. In Ottawa he met the leaders, exchanging a tornado of insults with Arthur "Slim" Evans, the trek leader. On Dominion Day, RCMP and city police in Regina broke up a trekkers' public meeting. A policeman was beaten to death. Even so, most sympathy lay with the trekkers.

On August 22, Aberhart's Social Crediters annihilated Alberta's Farmer government. The simple certainties of two-party politics dissolved. CCFers, Reconstructionists, Communists, and Social Crediters vied with Liberals and Conservatives for votes. Pounding out the old verities of tariff and Empire, Bennett poured his own money into the Tory campaign and ignored all that had happened in some of the worst years most in his audiences had experienced. Mackenzie King caught the frightened mood with a slogan, "King or Chaos." The hysteria was reflected by Quebec's premier, Alexandre Taschereau. In 1930, he had admitted that Bennett might be "a safe man"; now, raged Taschereau, the Tory leader had "launched into a Socialistic venture bordering on Communism."

King was confident enough not to make promises. He was right. No Parliament had ever been so lopsided: 173 Liberals faced only 40 Tories, and 17 Social Crediters. Woodsworth led only 6 CCFers with double the Social Credit vote. Stevens won as many votes as Woodsworth and one seat, his own. In Canada, third parties could help the winner gain more seats and power. Had Canadians shown excessive caution in choosing King? The Liberal majority is deceiving: King gained a smaller percentage of votes in 1935 than in 1930. Canadians had so many choices they could not make up their minds.

King's luck worked twice, with defeat in 1930 and victory in 1935. It worked again. In the months before the election, Bennett and the Americans had finally negotiated the Reciprocity Treaty both countries had toyed with since 1866. Within weeks of the Liberal victory, King went to Washington to collect the prize. Its Tory origins were conveniently forgotten.

King's new government was more positive than its program. In 1937, the Bank of Canada became a purely public institution without private shareholders. The feeble CRBC, which had angered King by programming Tory election propaganda, was replaced by a stronger Canadian Broadcasting Corporation. King's transport minister, an American-born engineer and contractor, C.D. Howe, launched the government-owned Trans-Canada Airlines (TCA).

Across North America, the Depression reached bottom in 1932. Then the economy climbed painfully out of the trough. Perhaps Bennett's policies helped. They certainly rewarded the business and financial backers of his party. Their sectors of the economy suffered less pain; humbler Canadians suffered much more. Between 1933 and 1937, business recovery climbed to a peak, while incomes and employment lagged behind. In the United States, more by intuition than by guidance from John Maynard Keynes, Roosevelt had discovered that purchasing power was a key to recovery. If the British North America Act had not been used to checkmate his monetary ideas, Alberta's new premier might have fallen on the same solution. Social Credit's $25 "prosperity certificates" were, after all, an unusual form of purchasing power. Hidden among the better-educated young mandarins in Ottawa, similarly heterodox notions were circulating, though clad in conventional economic jargon. A combination of sympathetic and unknowing Liberal ministers and the relapse of the economy in 1938 gave Canada its first Keynesian budget in 1939. Younger officials cautiously spoke of a "stimulative deficit," though the experiment was obscured by a far greater stimulus: war.

King's opposition came from provincial premiers, not Parliament. Pattullo, Hepburn, and Aberhart had broken the tradition of grey, invisible provincial leadership. In 1936, they were joined by another premier, Maurice Duplessis. Not since 1897 had the Liberal hold on Quebec been broken. As leader of the tiny provincial Conservative party, Duplessis could never have managed it, but, like Honoré Mercier, he united the extremes. The pretext this time was not Riel but the Depression, and Premier Taschereau's corrupt links with the English-dominated "trusts." For Quebec, the Depression was a national as well as an economic issue. Nationalistic young Liberals abandoned their party; Duplessis scooped them up in a Union Nationale, pledged to social reform and nationalization of the worst oppressors, including the electricity trust. Once Duplessis won, young Liberal reformers were set aside. Duplessis governed in his own style, courted the Church and persecuted Communists, unionists, and Jehovah's Witnesses with an ingenious application of "property and civil rights." A "Padlock Law" allowed police to lock up premises used for undefined "Communist" purposes. Duplessis welcomed business, and Montreal's English-speaking leaders knew how to respond.

Duplessis's style was a variant of a new pattern. The Depression had shown the constitutional and fiscal weaknesses of Canada and its provinces. If Canada hoped to be a modern industrial society, drastic changes were needed. None of the new premiers agreed. They had captured the hopes of voters by arguing that style, not fresh ideas, would cure the Depression. Ontario's Mitch Hepburn summoned the press to watch him fire senior career officials. He auctioned off government limousines at a football stadium to show he was a man of the people – then bought new ones. At the same time, in his suite at Toronto's Royal York Hotel, Hepburn discovered sensual pleasures known to few other Elgin County onion farmers. He became the guest and confidant of financiers, speculators, and the handsome mining promoter, George McCullagh, new owner of an amalgamated *Globe and Mail*.

In 1937, General Motors employees at Oshawa contrasted soaring company profits with their latest pay cut and decided to organize. Organizers summoned from the bold new Congress of Industrial Organizations (CIO) in the United States made Ontario less comfortable for American investors. When workers struck at General Motors, Hepburn did his best to defeat them. Ultimately, the company buckled. Industrial unionism held its small bridgehead at Oshawa, but Hepburn had arguments and cash to win a smashing re-election that same year. Other premiers took note. So did the Tories, some of whom had backed the Oshawa strikers.

The Depression forced thoughtful Canadians to realize how a feeble central government and penniless provinces crippled any collective response to economic crisis. Most of Bennett's five New Deal laws failed at the Judicial Committee. Provincial premiers like Hepburn, Pattullo, Duplessis, Aberhart, and Nova Scotia's charismatic Angus L. Macdonald had no reason to want more power in Ottawa, but why would Ottawa hand over taxing powers to political rivals? To find answers, King turned to a Royal Commission on Dominion-Provincial Relations, headed by Newton Rowell and Joseph Sirois. Aberhart refused to meet it; only premiers of poor provinces took much interest. Politics and the British North America Act locked Canadians into their Depression misery.

In time, Canada might have recovered. Instead, a worldwide tragedy became Canada's salvation.

PART IV

MIDDLE AGE, MIDDLE POWER

I | MR. KING'S WAR

After passage of the Statute of Westminster in 1931, Canada could exercise an independent voice in the world. The experiment of a shared imperial foreign policy had failed. The end of the Anglo-Japanese alliance, demanded by Canada to placate American opinion, was its major achievement. Having lost a valuable Asian ally, the British lost any appetite for sharing vital decisions; the dominions had even less taste for imperial burdens. In 1926, Lord Balfour's proposal of a "British Commonwealth of Nations," linked by no more than sentiment, tradition, and a common monarch, seemed to be the only acceptable survivor of the imperial dream. Three centuries of colonial rule ended without rancour.

Post-war Canada was no keener on League of Nations commitments. Even more than Americans, Canadians rejoiced that the Atlantic separated them from the sordid diplomacy and quarrelsome politics of the Old World. They could enjoy the luxury of near-disarmament. At Geneva, King and his undersecretary, O.D. Skelton, did little more than preach to the delegates assembled regularly for what Skelton termed "The

League of European Victors." Few Canadians needed to be persuaded that the Versailles settlement had been short-sighted;
even fewer would die to uphold its terms. Long before he
rewrote economics, John Maynard Keynes convinced a generation that the harsh, punitive treaty would lead to a new war.
He was, of course, right. Even before Mackenzie King, Sir
Robert Borden had bemoaned Article x, the League's mutual
security provision.

In the 1920s and 1930s, Canadians were isolationists,
indifferent to the Old World. Even Canadians with strong
British loyalties halted their allegiance at the English Channel.
The conservative, Catholic leaders of French Canada found
everything to abhor in German and French socialism and
Soviet communism but much to admire in Mussolini's fascism
or Franco's Spanish Falange, though not the overt paganism of
Hitler's Third Reich. Canadians of neither French nor British
origin followed European issues more closely. The tiny
Communist party recruited cadres from Finns, Ukrainians,
and Jews with memories of tsarist Russia. Nazi and fascist
organizations recruited among German and Italian Canadians.

In the 1920s, King found that his eternal "no" in external relations and defence provided useful common ground for his
coalition of prairie and Quebec support. He needed no refresher
training when he returned to power in the more dangerous
world of 1935. Japan had invaded Manchuria in 1931; in 1933,
Hitler's Germany defied the arms limitations imposed at
Versailles. Soon the direction, if not the ultimate extent, of Nazi
policies became apparent. As King took office, League diplomats at Geneva were devising sanctions to deter Mussolini from
invading a helpless Ethiopia. Left on his own during the change
of government, Canada's permanent official at the League, W.A.
Riddell, proposed adding oil to the embargo; no other commodity would more surely slow the Italian war machine.

Riddell's initiative became the "Canadian Resolution." In Ottawa, Mackenzie King was horrified: had Riddell committed Canada to defying Italy? If so, he had offended French Canadians who saw no harm in Mussolini's imperial adventure. The "Canadian Resolution" discreetly disappeared. Instead, the League received a homily from King on the virtues of conciliation and a reminder of the Dominion's interests: "Canada's first duty to the League and to the British Empire," King explained in 1936, "is, if possible, to keep this country united."

Canada's attitude did not cause the Second World War. Like New Zealand, which valiantly upheld the cause of collective security, Canada's influence was tiny. It was also clear. The twelve hundred Canadians who went to Spain to fight Franco faced a two-year jail sentence under a bill rushed through Parliament. (A third of them did not survive service in the International Brigade.) Jewish refugees, fleeing Hitler's concentration camps, were unwelcome to King's Quebec lieutenant, Ernest Lapointe, or to influential anti-Semites across Canada. "None is too many" wrote Frederick Blair, the civil servant who managed immigration. In the autumn of 1938, King rejoiced like most Canadians after the British prime minister, Neville Chamberlain, returned from Munich with the promise of "peace in our time." J.W. Dafoe of the *Winnipeg Free Press* sounded curmudgeonly when he headed his editorial, "What's the Cheering For?"

If Britain had gone to war over Czechoslovakia that autumn, King knew that even his divided country would have had to follow. Reluctantly, he began preparing Canada for the ordeal. Fifteen years of major change in the weapons of war had left Canada's forces virtually unarmed. Forethought about rearmament might avoid the heavy casualties that had led to conscription in 1917. Building up the young Royal Canadian Air Force and the Royal Canadian Navy would strengthen coastal defences and avert charges of imperial subservience. The army, Canada's pride and heaviest burden in the earlier war, would have lowest priority.

Rearmament included a new dimension in Canadian policy: defence links with the United States. A flood of American tourists, investment, and mass culture had accelerated Americanization, but until Roosevelt, nothing altered Washington's traditional indifference to Canada. As much as the dynamism of the New Deal, Roosevelt's "Good Neighbor Policy" transformed Canadian-American relations. Economic links strengthened after the 1935 trade agreement, but more followed. By 1935, it was no longer science fiction to expect enemy bombers, refuelled at a hidden Arctic base, to sweep down on American cities. U.S. security was threatened by Canada's vast, undefended territory. Subtly, Canada found itself positioned behind the 120-year-old Monroe Doctrine that Washington would defend against any European assault on the North American continent.

At Kingston in 1938 to receive an honorary degree from Queen's University, Roosevelt assured his audience that "the people of the United States will not stand idly by if domination of Canadian soil is threatened by any other empire." A delighted Mackenzie King promptly promised that Canada, too, understood her obligations: invaders must not be allowed to use her soil to attack the United States. It was a firmer guarantee than King had ever given Britain.

By early 1939, war was inevitable. Appeasement had failed. French-Canadian Liberals were sternly brought into line by Ernest Lapointe. King's pledge about conscription helped: "So long as this government may be in power, no such measure shall be enacted." The pledge was promptly echoed by Bennett's successor, Robert Manion. In a further brilliant stroke, King stage-managed Canada's first royal visit. The monarchy had been shaken by the abdication of Edward VIII in 1937. In June 1939, Edward's successor, a shy, stammering George VI, and his radiant queen crossed the Dominion. A whiff of glamour excited Depression-weary Canadians. The glow lasted into September, when German tanks rumbled across the Polish frontier.

On September 3, 1939, Britain went to war. Unofficially, so did Canada. Before politicians could assemble in Ottawa, the War Measures Act was proclaimed and meagre forces moved to war stations. King had promised that "Parliament would decide" on war, but only two Quebec nationalists and J.S. Woodsworth, the CCF leader, dissented. Canada officially entered the war on September 10 more united than anyone could have imagined a year earlier. When André Laurendeau, a young nationalist, sought supporters to denounce the war, he found too few to matter. Across Canada the unemployed flocked to militia armouries to enlist: two Montreal regiments filled their ranks first.

It was not clear what should happen next. Precedent took over. As in 1914, a 1st Canadian Infantry Division was approved and sailed in December. Its commander, Major-General Andrew McNaughton, was selected as a known foe of conscription. Then King remembered his pre-war worries, and army war plans suffered drastic cuts. While French and British troops settled down to a "phoney war" on the frontier, Canada's government discussed how war orders might pull the economy out of a depression that still claimed half a million unemployed. The British offered a solution. Flyers in the earlier war had trained in Canada's secure skies; would Canada consider a far larger program? After much ill-tempered haggling, in December 1939 King and British negotiators announced a British Commonwealth Air Training Plan (BCATP), designed to train twenty thousand pilots a year. Canada would pay $350 million of the $600 million cost and provide most of the trainees. At King's insistence, the British reluctantly described the BCATP as Canada's major contribution to the Allied effort.

The government rejoiced: its money would be spent in Canada. Britain would pay for airmen once they reached England, and it was inconceivable that aircrew casualties could ever lead to conscription. Let other countries provide the cannon fodder.

Polling, in its infancy, showed that most Canadians were also satisfied. In October, Duplessis sought a new mandate from Quebec voters, offering himself as national saviour against Ottawa and conscription. Lapointe sent other federal ministers criss-crossing the province, repeating pledges against conscription and warning they would resign and leave Quebec voiceless if Duplessis won. Liberals, under Adélard Godbout, swept the province. In Ontario, Mitch Hepburn pursued his old vendetta with King by denouncing the national war effort as half-hearted. Mackenzie King used Hepburn's attack to justify a snap election. He summoned MPs to Ottawa, forced them to listen to a throne speech, and dissolved Parliament before they could reply. Outmanoeuvred and floundering, Bennett's successor, Robert Manion, re-christened his Tories as the National Government party. No one cheered. The CCF, divided by the war and their leader's pacifism, did little. Voters gave Liberals their most one-sided margin in history: 51.5 per cent of the popular vote and 181 seats to only 40 for the Tories, 10 for Social Credit, and 8 for the CCF. King had a mandate for his kind of war. Personally defeated, Manion resigned.

Canada waged war with one guiding light: avoid the errors of 1914–18. From October 1939, a Wartime Prices and Trade Board stood guard against profiteering and inflation. Through the cautious Trades and Labor Congress, labour was consulted. Each policy decision was scrutinized for any possible threat of conscription. Above all, King avoided Borden's fatal mistake: sacrificing himself and his party to the cause of Allied victory. The higher cause of national unity and Liberalism prevented talk of the last man or the last dollar.

Suddenly, such a philosophy seemed inappropriate. On April 9, 1940, Hitler struck at Norway. By June 4, the British had lifted its army from Dunkirk. Eight days later, France sought an armistice with Germany. Britain and her dominions stood alone against Hitler and Mussolini. In Britain, Canadian troops stood in the front lines against a German invasion. Behind them, a shattered British army struggled to re-arm.

Every feature of Canada's war effort was transformed. Instead of a single division, Canada's overseas army must grow to five divisions, maybe more. Since German submarines could block the Atlantic to allied convoys, Canada must build and man scores of warships. Meanwhile Canada must also provide aircraft for the air training plan. All must be done in desperate haste and without experience or training.

In the summer of 1940, Parliament passed a National Resources Mobilization Act (NRMA) – conscription for home defence. When Montreal's tempestuous mayor, Camillien Houde, denounced national registration, few opposed his prompt internment. Canada was in danger. Even Americans could help. On August 18, 1940, Roosevelt summoned Mackenzie King to Ogdensburg, New York. A scribbled memorandum recorded their agreement: a Permanent Joint Board of Defence would "consider in the broad sense the defense of the north half of the western hemisphere." A delighted King rejoiced that he had brought the two great English-speaking powers together. Winston Churchill, the new British prime minister, responded that "there were two views about that." He saw that Ogdensburg represented Canada's transfer from one empire to another.

Few Canadians had the detachment or historical grasp for such reflections. The crisis of 1940 created a mood of total war, at least on the home front. Its symbol was not King but his new minister of munitions and supply, C.D. Howe. Howe quickly grasped that almost anything Canada produced would be useful somewhere. An entrepreneur in government, Howe gradually won the confidence and then the devotion of industrial leaders and businessmen. Some came to work in Ottawa for a symbolic dollar a year, managing crown corporations, controlling scarce commodities, scouring the United States for machine tools and aircraft engines. Tax concessions, credit, and $1.5 billion in direct investment unleashed the huge industrial potential that had lain idle in the 1930s, and then added to it at a rate few countries have experienced in peace or war. By 1943, 1.2 million Canadians worked in war industries, often in factories that had not existed in 1939.

Howe and his officials worried little about costs or consequences. J.L. Ilsley, a dour Nova Scotian and King's finance minister after 1940, found the money. His frugality accidentally coincided with the Keynesian principles of his younger officials. Recalling how the public borrowing of the earlier war had fuelled inflation, Ilsley insisted that this time Canada would pay most of its way by direct taxes and selling bonds to individuals. The Rowell-Sirois Report, published in 1940, recommended sweeping redistribution of federal-provincial finances. Premiers from the richer provinces bluntly rejected the proposals, but the war gave Ottawa all the power it needed to take over direct taxes. Provincial governments could choose between grants equal to pre-war revenue or having Ottawa absorb their debt burden.

Within five years, federal revenue from income, corporate, and inheritance taxes rose sixfold. Over six years, Ottawa had borrowed $12 billion, half of it from individuals. During the first two years of the war, prices climbed 15 per cent. In 1941 Ottawa imposed sweeping wage and price controls, enforced by the Wartime Prices and Trade Board: for the rest of the war, inflation was held to a mere 3 per cent. Donald Gordon, the hard-drinking Scot who ran the Wartime Prices and Trade Board, got much of the credit, but Ilsley's tough fiscal policies made the real difference.

Howe's massive production program helped defray the costs of war. Two-thirds of Canadian war production went to the Allies. As in the earlier war, there was a catch. By the end of 1940, Britain's reserves of gold and American dollars were used up. Not only could Britain not afford to buy from Canada, it could not provide the currency Canadians needed to buy vital components from the United States. The British accepted Roosevelt's solution: "lend-lease," with repayment at the end of the war. For Canada, lend-lease would have meant post-war economic paralysis. Officials found an answer in the 1917 experience. On April 20, 1941, King met Roosevelt at Hyde Park, his Hudson River estate, and signed an agreement integrating the Canadian and American economies. Orders for Britain would be charged to the British lend-lease account. With E.P. Taylor, a youthful beer magnate, as principal agent, Howe soon exceeded the $250 million ceiling the Hyde Park agreement imposed on Canadian munitions sales to the United States. There were no protests from Washington.

As for Britain's debt to Canada, not even the takeover of almost a billion dollars of British direct investment could meet it. By war's end, the Canadian government had approved $4 billion in direct aid and forgiven huge loans to Britain and her allies. Since almost all the money was spent in Canada, charity stayed beneficially at home.

Wartime prosperity was tangible. Wages were frozen but they were certain. More and more women joined the workforce, and this time the social barriers against wives and mothers collapsed. Governments even experimented nervously with day nurseries. Full employment gave Canadians money to spend, but war needs absorbed scarce raw materials, foreign exchange, and factory space. Regulations under the War Measures Act imposed exchange controls, banned non-essential imports, and ended production of civilian cars, toys, jewellery, silk stockings, and a host of hotly desired items. In January 1942, Canadians used their first ration coupons for basic food items. By European standards, hardships and sacrifices were slight, and many Canadians found the war years a bright contrast with the grim Depression. Discomfort and disruption contributed to a mood of common purpose and a sense that Canada had rediscovered its youth and vigour. Boring jobs or military routine had at least lifted people from pre-war ruts.

On December 7, 1941, the Japanese attack on Pearl Harbor suddenly brought the war closer. Canada declared war on Japan. Two battalions of infantry, sent on a hopeless mission to defend Hong Kong, were the first significant Canadian losses of the war. Frightened British Columbians clamoured for protection. Ottawa sent thirty-four thousand soldiers, most of them conscripted by the National Resources Mobilization Act. Under the shabby pretext that Japanese Canadians needed protection from their angry neighbours, the government also evacuated nineteen thousand men, women, and children to the B.C. interior, auctioning their property for derisory prices. It was an inexcusable act, born out of half a century of racial prejudice. Generals, admirals, and the RCMP protested that there was no military need for the internment. Politics sufficed.

The war with Japan demonstrated the realities of Canada's role in continental defence. To defend Alaska, the United States poured men and equipment into the task of reaching the remote territory by road and of piping oil from Norman Wells to a refinery at Whitehorse to support a likely theatre of war. Together, the Alaska Highway and the Canol project cost $270 million. At the height of construction, thirty-three thousand Americans were at work in Canada, unmoved by the minor details of Canadian sovereignty. Warned by the British high commissioner, Ottawa despatched a "Special Commissioner" with his own aircraft. Ottawa also repaid the Americans, even for airfields and bases that were never needed. Only in the 1950s did Washington concede Canada's claims to its vast Arctic domain.

By bringing the United States into the war against all of the Axis powers, Japan helped ensure an eventual Allied victory. So had Hitler when he invaded the Soviet Union in the summer of 1941. The strength of the two superpowers was not yet apparent in 1942, while Britain experienced the most stunning disasters of her war, the fall of Singapore and the loss of Tobruk.

Amidst defeats and inexplicable catastrophes, many Canadians felt that they had done too little in the war. By transferring most of the British Commonwealth Air Training Plan's graduates to the RAF, King's government had deliberately sacrificed a powerful, autonomous Canadian air force. Until that decision was reversed, most Canadian flyers served with the British, but their contribution was buried in RAF news releases. The navy's dreary and dangerous role of escorting Atlantic convoys attracted little publicity. King himself refused to allow Canadian troops to be sent to the most active British theatre, the North African desert. Guilt about that decision prodded the government into the tragic Hong Kong commitment. Compared with their First World War experience, Canadians felt they were on the sidelines.

In 1940, Canadians had endorsed a lacklustre war effort. By 1942, supporters of total war gained fresh support. By appealing for greater sacrifice, the government encouraged a widespread belief that everything possible must be done for victory. Newspaper headlines, broadcasts, and warnings of the horrors of a Nazi or Japanese triumph fuelled demands for action. One word symbolized a Canada utterly committed to victory: *conscription*. Tories and anti–Mackenzie King Liberals like Hepburn seized the issue. Arthur Meighen, summoned from retirement to lead his party, announced that he would make conscription his cause.

King acted with deft opportunism. Conscription would be put to the people in a plebiscite. Only they could release the government from its earlier pledge. Robbed of his issue, Meighen went down to defeat at the hands of the CCF. It was a warning that old-fashioned patriotism might be the strongest political current in wartime Canada, but not the only one. In the April plebiscite, 64 per cent of Canadians voted to free the government: 80 per cent of Manitobans, 82 per cent of Ontarians – and 28 per cent of Quebeckers, the people to whom the pledge had really been made. This was the betrayal Duplessis and the nationalists had warned against. A host of nationalists, young and old, had rallied opposition. Lawyers and journalists like André Laurendeau and Jean Drapeau (a future mayor of Montreal), and even a twenty-three-year-old Pierre Elliott Trudeau, joined the campaign and shared the defeat. In Quebec, the 1942 plebiscite became another bitter memory.

King had not finished, of course. The National Resources Mobilization Act was amended, but Parliament would have to vote again before conscripts went overseas. It was, he explained, "not necessarily conscription, but conscription if necessary." Lapointe was dead by now, but for Pierre Cardin, the ranking Quebec cabinet minister in Ottawa, it was enough conscription to bring his resignation. For J.L. Ralston, the dogged, honest minister of national defence, King's compromise was needless and he, too, resigned. Then he relented, but the resignation stayed in King's desk.

The conscription issue of 1942 was one of those savagely divisive symbolic distractions from reality that Canadian politics so often generates. Manpower was already an issue, as a population so uselessly surplus in the 1930s proved inadequate for military and industrial needs in wartime. Innovation helped a little. By the summer of 1941, all three armed services had cautiously established women's branches. National Selective Service

(NSS), established in October 1941, extended its authority. By September, no employer could hire or fire without giving notice to NSS. Men and young women were compelled to register; those considered "underemployed" could be compelled to take a specified job.

Industrial or military conscription could allocate manpower in Canada; it could not solve recruiting problems for the armed forces. The Royal Canadian Air Force (RCAF) was an obvious favourite for young men eager for adventure. The needs of the Royal Canadian Navy (RCN) were easily met, though there was a crippling shortage of qualified technicians. The army was the Cinderella service. Talk of a new, mechanized army fooled no one. Experience proved that front-line infantry needed high mental and physical standards to survive. To the prime minister, high rejection rates showed that the generals were sabotaging voluntary recruiting. The generals used every stratagem the army could devise to persuade NRMA men to "go active." Many agreed. Others refused, and a tough core of NRMA men, proof against any threat or promise, gloried in the abusive term of "zombie." Fully trained and fit, they remained in uniform because coastal communities demanded their presence and because Ralston knew they were his only reserve of infantry reinforcements.

A mixture of policy and luck had so far saved Canadians from heavy war casualties. While other Allies, including Australia and New Zealand, bore the brunt of fighting, Canada's overseas army remained on guard in England. As King had hoped, air and naval losses so far were small, in part because it took a lot of training before aircrew could join operations. Canadians took enormous pride in the dramatic expansion of their fleet of corvettes, frigates, and other small warships. They did not know that the ships were often too ill-equipped and the crews too ill-trained to defend convoys effectively. Since German U-boats concentrated on merchant ships, not on their escorts, it was civilian seamen who paid the price while the RCN learned its job. Most of them were foreigners. Though long-range aircraft proved to be decisive weapons against submarines, the RCAF gave low priority to coastal patrols. Canadian admirals resented British criticism. Canadian officials insisted on installing inferior Canadian-made radar and rejected other costly electronic gear as unproven.

At the crisis of the Battle of the Atlantic in the winter of 1943, failure in convoy battles forced the withdrawal of Canadian escort groups for training and re-equipment. Canadian naval authorities never acknowledged the humiliation, but all three Allied partners learned from it. In March 1943, Canada was assigned its own sector of the Atlantic under Rear Admiral L.W. Murray. The RCAF finally acquired long-range aircraft, and Canadian ships returned to battle ready to match a courageous and wily underwater enemy. By war's end, Canadians claimed the third largest navy in the world – 373 warships and ninety thousand men and women.

Winning the Battle of the Atlantic meant only that a massive Allied build-up in England was possible. Allied military and political leaders differed sharply over the next step. Canadians played no role in such decisions, and neither Churchill nor Roosevelt sought King's advice. Unlike Sir Robert Borden, King was content to be photographed with Allied leaders on the terrace of the Château Frontenac in Quebec City and to leave the fate of Canadian soldiers and airmen to their wisdom. With the exception of the stubbornly independent General McNaughton, few Canadian senior officers had their own thoughts to offer. Trained between the wars in British military schools, veterans of the tiny permanent force accepted British leadership, even if they often resented a British air of superiority.

Senior RCAF officers, for example, fully shared the Royal Air Force's faith in the bomber offensive against Germany. Belated

"Canadianization" eventually produced forty-five RCAF squadrons overseas, flying everything from Spitfires to transport planes, but the largest RCAF formation was 6 Bomber Group. Its eleven squadrons included only some of the thousands of Canadians who flew and died in the most controversial major operation of the war, the four-year bomber offensive against Germany. Even Canadianization was controversial as 6 Group struggled with problems of morale, inexperience, and outdated aircraft. Like the navy's, the RCAF's eventual achievements were won at a high price. Part of the cost was 9980 young men who died in the bomber offensive (more Canadians than fell in the long advance from Normandy to Germany). So much for King's expectation that air war could never lead to heavy casualties. In all, the RCAF lost 17,101 men. It also became the fourth largest air force in the world.

Many young men avoided the army because their fathers remembered the First World War. Nonetheless, it became the largest of the services, with 730,000 men and women. General McNaughton eventually won his battle for a highly mechanized force. Mackenzie King had recognized the old general's passionate opposition to conscription and his conviction, inherited from the earlier war, that science and technology could save lives. With five infantry and armoured divisions in England, the army trained for years, but it lacked the vital stage of battle experience. While land operations raised the risk of conscription, the army's inactivity seemed to prove that Canada was not playing her part.

Years of waiting made it almost impossible for Canadian generals to reject or even to criticize plans to raid Dieppe. The landing on August 19, 1942, was the most conspicuous Canadian disaster of the war. Of 4963 troops who set out for Dieppe, 907 died; 1946 remained as prisoners. Canadians have never stopped seeking scapegoats, from McNaughton to the debonair Lord

Louis Mountbatten. A less innocent nation might have recognized that amphibious operations are a risky form of war and that inexperience doubles the risk. Common sense should have argued for the kind of equipment and fire support that could have brought success. The bloody experience at Dieppe helped convince generals and politicians that costly new resources would be needed for a real invasion of Europe.

Pressure soon resumed for further operations. To gain battle experience, the 1st Division shared in the Sicily landing in July 1943. A month of fighting turned green soldiers into an effective fighting force. It also brought such public acclaim that Mackenzie King insisted on sending an additional formation – the 5th Armoured Division – and a corps headquarters to join the Italian campaign. Angrily opposed to the destruction of his army, mistrusted by Ralston and his British superiors, General McNaughton was removed. The symbolism of a Canadian army in the field survived with the promise to include other Allied formations. Meanwhile, British, American, and Canadian troops crossed to the Italian mainland, ran into relentless German resistance, and discovered that mud, trenches, and bloody offensives had not vanished in 1918.

On June 6, 1944, Canadian sailors, airmen, and soldiers shared in the D-Day landings. The 3rd Infantry Division was one of five Allied assault formations. Canadians lost 1074 casualties, fewer than expected. It was only a down payment. Weeks of bitter fighting followed to defend the beachhead, capture Caen, and press against tough, well-led German armies. Savage battles in Normandy's hills, fields, and hedgerows, aggravated by inferior weapons and unskilled generals, cost the 2nd and 3rd Canadian Divisions the heaviest losses of any of the formations under British command. The 4th Armoured Division, the spearhead in closing the Falaise Gap, was almost as hard hit. While a hundred thousand Canadians fought in Normandy, their comrades in Italy launched two major offensives, breaking the Hitler Line in June and the Gothic Line in the autumn. In the separate theatres, Canadians lost twenty-three thousand men, most of them trained infantry. They would have to be replaced.

This was the crisis King had feared throughout the war. Everyone could be blamed, from staff officers who allowed too many men to remain in support units, to generals who demanded victories to enhance their careers. By splitting the Canadians and sending unneeded troops to Italy, the prime minister himself had aggravated the problem with a double system of administration and reinforcements. The fact remained, as J.L. Ralston saw for himself, that infantry reinforcement pools were empty. Canadians soon knew it too. Major Conn Smythe, a popular Toronto sportsman wounded in Normandy, made it his business to report how untrained replacements stumbled into German fire. To Ralston, there was only one answer: conscription was now necessary. The NRMA men must be sent.

For King, conscription was still unthinkable. The war had virtually been won. Surely so huge an army could find a few thousand volunteers. There must be a plot by the generals, or even his more conservative ministers, to destroy him. Resourceful as ever, he checked on Ralston's earlier resignation and contacted Ralston's enemy, General McNaughton. On November 14, the cabinet learned that McNaughton was the new defence minister. Ralston rose, shook hands with his colleagues, and silently left.

The rest was uneasy anticlimax. King's opponents were dumbfounded. McNaughton's charisma had no impact on hardened "zombies." In British Columbia, Major-General George Pearkes, who commanded most of them, sent in his resignation. In Ottawa, McNaughton's senior staff officers reported that volunteers could not be found. To the ingenious King, this represented an opportune "general's mutiny," enough to frighten wavering ministers and Quebec backbenchers. A shaken, discredited McNaughton confessed failure. King himself told Parliament that fifteen thousand NRMA conscripts would be sent to Europe. He was upheld 143 to 70, with 34 Quebec Liberals dissenting.

The crisis was not over. There were riots in Montreal. At Terrace, British Columbia, a brigade of NRMA men mutinied for almost a week before senior officers persuaded them to submit. On February 5, McNaughton lost a by-election in Ontario. In the end, the conscripts were hardly needed. After the costly battle for the Scheldt estuary in October, Canadians went into winter quarters in Holland and Belgium. At Canadian insistence, the two divisions in Italy travelled to the Netherlands, a long, needless journey that kept them from harm. The final offensive that drove into Germany and the flooded Netherlands cost Canada six thousand casualties, but very few of them were conscripts. On May 6, Germany surrendered. Japan followed suit on August 14. Pure accident had again made the bitter conscription crisis unnecessary.

2 | PROSPERITY

The costs of war were high for Canada: forty-three thousand men and women had died; the national debt had quadrupled. Yet casualties were far lower than they had been in the First World War, and they came from a larger population. Most of the money, including virtually all of the mutual aid, had been spent in Canada, doubling the gross national product and creating industries that would enrich the post-war economy. Ordinary Canadians lived hard, frugal, wartime lives, but most of them always had. Wartime incomes and savings had created reserves of spending power that a previous generation could hardly have imagined. Despite wartime shortages, Canadian consumer spending rose 40 per cent between 1938 and 1944. The plain fact is that Canada did well out of the war.

Indeed most Canadians had both yearned for and feared the war's end. The growth in support for the CCF was the clearest symptom of suspicions that peace would restore the unemployment and hopelessness of the Depression. The wartime feat of ending unemployment, stopping inflation, and redistributing spending power had made the Depression seem all the more unnecessary, but only the CCF promised to carry wartime planning, controls, and massive public spending into the post-war world. In 1943, Ontario voters narrowly favoured George Drew's Conservatives to replace the Liberals, but the CCF had come from nowhere to close second place. A few months later, a Gallup poll reported that the CCF edged out both traditional parties in public support. In June 1944, the CCF under Tommy Douglas swept Saskatchewan and formed the first socialist government anywhere in North America.

Liberals and Conservatives felt the wartime mood. It was evident as much in innumerable evening forums and debates, in journalism and radio commentaries, as in political movements or opinion polls. In their latest bid for electoral support, Tories turned for leadership to the respected Progressive premier of Manitoba, John Bracken. Part of his price was adding "Progressive" to the party title. Being "Progressive Conservative" might also reflect the public demand for change. Communists, too, gained from the war. In 1939, the party was banned for supporting Moscow's alliance with Hitler. Soon after the Nazis invaded Russia, Canada's Communists surfaced as "Labour Progressive" and basked in the glory of the powerful Red Army. They used their considerable labour cadres to ban wartime strikes and attack the hated CCF. The CCF fought back, winning frustrated union militants.

The real initiative lay, as ever, with the government. Even in 1940, the belated adoption of unemployment insurance had promised at least one difference in post-war Canada. By late 1942, Allied victory seemed certain. Citizens and their government could begin to think about post-war reconstruction, but the right direction was by no means clear. A committee of distinguished academics urged the adoption of a comprehensive system of social insurance for health, income, and old age, and a massive program of public works. This initiative was embodied in a 1943 report by Leonard Marsh, a McGill University professor and former CCFer.

A brilliant team of civil servants gathered by Clifford Clark, deputy minister of finance, deftly gutted Marsh's report. Clark's approach was fiscally cautious but conceptually radical. While Marsh had ignored constitutional obstacles, Clark urged restructuring of federalism to give Ottawa fiscal powers to manage the national economy in proper Keynesian fashion. Provinces would be financed so that the richest and the poorest could each provide a comparable level of services, avoiding the terrible inequities made apparent by the Depression. The influence of the abandoned Rowell-Sirois Report was no coincidence. W.A. Mackintosh, a major Rowell-Sirois contributor, was Clark's alter ego. Louis St. Laurent, an eminent Quebec City lawyer and the commission's counsel, entered King's cabinet in 1941 as successor to Ernest Lapointe. Another contributor, Brooke Claxton, became the minister of a new Department of Health and Welfare in 1944.

The "mandarins," as Clark and his team of civil servants were soon called, gained immense influence and prestige, yet their power depended entirely on the prime minister. When labour problems, seething for years, finally burst in 1943, costing the economy a million days in strikes, King himself engineered the government response. The problem, as Mr. Justice Charles McTague of the National War Labour Board had no trouble proving, lay with Canada's lack of procedures for union recognition and orderly bargaining. Reluctantly persuaded by the argument and even more by defection of labour votes to the CCF, King approved PC 1003, the Wartime Labour Relations Order, in early 1944. Canadian unionists gained rights to organize enjoyed by American labour since 1935. When the war ended, PC 1003 became the basis for federal and most provincial labour legislation. Its immediate effect was a dramatic drop in strikes for the rest of the war.

Family allowances were also urged by Ian Mackenzie, the minister of pensions, by Marsh, and by McTague's board. For decades, reformers had recommended them as the most effective way to solve the most obvious cause of family poverty: low incomes among parents. King had been horrified by the cost and the threat to individualism. He was converted by the growth of CCF support, flattery about his image as a reformer, and by the example of his secretary, J.W. Pickersgill: growing up as a war widow's son on a government pension had not sapped his initiative. Typically, King's resolve was strengthened by discovering that the same ministers and backbenchers who demanded conscription were often fervent opponents of family allowances. Charlotte Whitton, social worker and leading Conservative, tactlessly underlined a discreet Liberal argument for family allowances, complaining that the allowance would be a special subsidy for French Canada's large families. (The big winner turned out to be Saskatchewan.)

By 1945 King's government had acquired all the enemies ten years of power and six years of bitterly controversial decisions could earn. If opposition parties needed encouragement, they found it in Britain, where voters decisively rejected their powerful wartime leader, Winston Churchill, for the untried Labour party of Clement Attlee. John Bracken and the CCF's M.J. Coldwell each took comfort from the example. In Quebec, conscription and loyalty to Ottawa destroyed Godbout's Liberals; Maurice Duplessis and the Union Nationale had been back in power since 1944.

Yet King's infinite caution and flexibility had their rewards. Even Quebec anti-conscriptionists who ran as independents preferred him to any other leader, especially after Bracken promised to send conscripts to fight the Japanese. King's "New

Social Order," adorned by family allowances (organized in mid-campaign) and the promise of a health insurance plan, offered security without CCF socialism. Leaders of the Trades and Labor Congress endorsed the Liberals. More secretly and effectively, so did the Communists, splitting votes in labour constituencies that the CCF smugly took for granted. A crude but effective scare-mongering campaign, financed by business, gave the CCF its *coup de grâce*. On June 4, George Drew swept to a one-sided Tory victory in Ontario; a week later, King gave the Liberals a much narrower federal success with 125 seats against 67 for Bracken, 28 for Coldwell's CCF (almost all from the West), and 13 for Social Credit. Twelve independents, mostly from Quebec, gave King a margin of safety. Soldier-voters defeated the prime minister in Prince Albert. It was only a minor humiliation.

The Liberals faced a divided opposition and the post-war challenges. It was not an easy prospect. Whatever their promised plans and programs, cabinet members could easily recall the painful aftermath of the earlier war.

On May 6, 1945, jubilant sailors wrecked downtown Halifax. At home and overseas, soldiers and airmen demanded prompt demobilization. Britain, a major trading partner, was bankrupt. American generosity had shrivelled as the war's end approached. Roosevelt was dead; isolationist Republicans were rampant in Congress. In 1944, Canadian war production had eased off and some industries had switched back to civilian purposes, but the task was daunting and costly. Canadians, in their comfortable oasis, were impatient and demanding, but the rest of the world was shattered – perhaps beyond recovery – and Canada had to trade to live.

Canada played as modest a role as she could in the Pacific War. Ottawa's demand that Canadian servicemen volunteer to fight Japan led to embarrassment when the only major Canadian unit in the Far East, a cruiser, voted itself out of action and sailed for home. On the other hand, as long as the war continued, so did the government's limitless emergency powers. When King summoned provincial premiers to Ottawa on August 6, 1945, federal authority loomed over the meeting. Neither Drew nor Duplessis was impressed. Already nervous at the extent of Clifford Clark's fiscal proposals, King promised cooperation, not coercion. The premiers found their weapon: delay. Almost a year passed before finance department mandarins conceded that economic centralism was dead, but the basic federal-provincial antagonism survived.

For a time, so did Ottawa's power, prestige, and its grip on tax revenues. Clark's scheme faded but his goal of relative equalization evolved into complicated formulas and agreements by which all the provinces but Quebec and, for a time, Ontario "rented" their direct tax fields to Ottawa in return for compensation. The wartime invention of payroll deductions eased the unpopularity of being tax collector to all Canada.

One minister at least had been utterly sanguine about Canada's post-war prospects. C.D. Howe despised the moanings of what he called "the Security Brigade." King offered him the chance to head an ill-defined Department of Reconstruction. Howe accepted, but only if he retained the sweeping powers of his wartime role. Canada needed "reconversion," Howe insisted, not reconstruction. His weapons were generous credits for investment and exports, a minimum of regulations, and "accelerated depreciation," an ingenious tax device that protected investors from loss if the economy turned sour and allowed them to turn a quick buck if it thrived. Howe unashamedly developed the crown corporations he had launched before and during the war. An aircraft industry would back up his earliest public venture in 1937, Trans-Canada Airlines. Polymer Corporation at Sarnia and Eldorado Nuclear at Port Hope would prove that Canadians could expand the frontiers of science and technology. Meanwhile, as "Howe's Boys" left their dollar-a-year jobs to return to the seats of private power, they remained a loyal network and a source of support that Howe alone could tap.

Howe was prudent. A government white paper by W.A. Mackintosh in 1945 promised full employment; Howe substituted "high and stable level of employment." Either commitment seemed bold. It was soon apparent, though, that the post-war depression would not happen. Instead, Canada was booming. Military forces melted away, their transition to civilian life eased by the gratuities, grants, and educational opportunities their fathers had sought in vain after the First World War. By the summer of 1947, Canada's armed forces had dwindled from a million to only forty thousand members. Only fifteen thousand veterans collected out-of-work benefits. A limping housing industry was infected by Howe's dynamism, insatiable post-war demand, and a National Housing Act that made mortgages available to families that had never dared apply for them before. By 1947, builders were producing houses faster than couples were marrying, making up for years when families had doubled up. Three-quarters of the new buildings were individual homes, monotonous boxes scattered across cheerless suburban developments to fulfil the pioneer expectation that each Canadian was entitled to land and individuality.

One by-product of prosperity brought no joy to Howe or his friends, but it was as vital to continued growth as their tax concessions. In 1945 strikers at the Ford Motor Company in Windsor won the Rand Formula, a uniquely Canadian form of union security. Employees need not join a union, but they had to "pay the freight" for its benefits. In 1946 the brash new industrial unions tested their wartime gains with a co-ordinated nationwide bid for higher wages. Strikes in the British Columbia forests and in Eastern Canada's basic steel, electrical, and rubber industries cost more working days than in any year since 1919, but now there was little violence, and most unions won modest concessions. Instead of eliminating unions, employers learned to live with them. Most workers gained enough purchasing power to sustain the post-war economic boom.

More than dollars were needed. Canadians could not escape their battered world or even the disorders of their own economy. Business pressed the government into "orderly de-control," but meat and butter rationing returned late in 1945. Gas and tire rationing ended, but liquor stayed diluted (as it still is) and controlled. Farmers, harvesting bumper crops since the summer of 1939, had prospered beyond their dreams in the war years. Could a hungry Europe afford the dollars to buy Canadian products? James Gardiner, the minister of agriculture, preened himself on selling a huge wheat deal to the British. Other British orders were possible only after a $1.5 billion Canadian loan, fully a third as much as Washington provided. Even this was no answer to Canada's most urgent problem: lack of American currency. In 1947, King's government took drastic measures to save its dollar reserves: exchange controls, a ban on luxury imports, licensing of major purchases, and a limit on the cash tourists could take south.

Economic arguments made little impact on Washington. Congress had gone solidly Republican in 1946. Business was business again. It took a far more frightening crisis to capture American concern.

Even before the Allied armies met at the Elbe in May 1945, the wartime alliance was falling apart. Canada knew little of the details, only that, even more than the First World War, this one had been a war between the world's great powers. Canadian voters in 1945 were assured that Mackenzie King had enormous influence in the world. If so, he did not use it. Canadian diplomats, as able a team of officials as would ever serve the country, organized on the "functional principle" – Canada would demand a voice only when it had a major role to play. When Canadians were asked to feed refugees or provide raw material, they must be consulted. At Bretton Woods in 1944, when bankers launched the International Monetary Fund and the World Bank to prevent renewal of the currency crises of the 1930s, a Canadian delegation under Louis Rasminsky made useful, "constructive" proposals. At Dumbarton Oaks and San Francisco, where the United Nations was shaped and launched, unlike the bumptious Australians, Mackenzie King's delegation made no trouble for the major powers, kept its disquiet to itself, and met its modest goals.

Only two world powers now mattered: the United States and the Soviet Union. To her acute discomfort, Canada lay between them. Her allegiance was clear. Stalin's Russia was a tyranny as atrocious as Hitler's, tolerable only to the self-deceived or the would-be totalitarian. Russia was also a deeply wounded and profoundly frightened power. No nation had lost more in the war, and its huge armies offered no safeguard against the kind of bombs that had annihilated Hiroshima and Nagasaki and driven Japan from the war. Canadian officials learned early of the desperate Russian bid to equal the nuclear balance. In September 1945, a Soviet embassy cipher clerk, Igor Gouzenko, shared secrets of a Communist spy ring that reached into King's own office. Official Ottawa's shock was almost matched by its revulsion at having to deal with the problem. Eventually Gouzenko's evidence sent officials, professors, and the lone Communist MP to prison. King and most of his advisers doubted that Stalin was really bent on world conquest. The brutal seizure of eastern European countries, they believed, merely established a vast buffer zone for a nervous but inward-looking Soviet empire.

Others differed. Americans had been as eager as Canadians

to demobilize. Now Washington insisted that Russia posed a threat to North America. The 1940 arrangements at Ogdensburg, Roosevelt had insisted, were permanent. Canadians realized that defending themselves to American satisfaction was the price of sovereignty. If Americans did the job, independence would fade. "If we do enough to assure the United States," confessed Major-General Maurice Pope, "we shall have done a good deal more than a cold assessment of the risk would indicate to be necessary." On February 13, 1947, a bilateral defence agreement asserted that Canadian forces would henceforth use American arms, equipment, and tactics, share facilities, and co-operate with the United States. Continentalism now had a military dimension. Another British link had withered.

In 1946 the continental threat was remote – a bogey to promote American rearmament. Western Europe was another matter. Only Britain maintained respectable military strength; her continental neighbours were now virtually defenceless against invasion or subversion. Canada's foreign exchange crisis, with its threat to peacetime reconversion, was a tenth as serious as those of western European countries. Without American credit, European recovery was hopeless. In Washington, business was business, but not if Europe fell to the Communists. Action was needed. The European Recovery Program, or Marshall Plan, launched in 1948, was a vast outpouring of American material and financial aid. To Canadian delight, American congressmen allowed Europe's Marshall Plan credits to be applied in other "American" countries. Canada's 1947 exchange crisis was over.

Europe's security crisis continued. In February 1948, Czech Communists, backed by the Soviet garrison, seized power. Days later, Jan Masaryk, symbol of Czech resistance to Hitler, fell from a window. It was "suicide," claimed the new regime in Prague. The West recalled the price paid by Czechs for pre-war appeasement. Next, Soviet troops blockaded the British,

American, and French zones of Berlin. The United States and Britain mobilized an airlift to feed Berlin. Canada did not join, but even Mackenzie King had now been shaken from his habitual caution. Not even Duplessis's Quebec would condemn resistance to communism. First, though, Canada waited for the Americans. In June 1948, Congress endorsed a new western alliance. Ten months later, in April 1949, the North Atlantic Treaty Organization was proclaimed. At Canada's insistence, the twelve members pledged to be more than a defence league; in fact, they wanted rearmament on the cheap. Committed to buy American-style weapons, Canada, for example, could generously spare the British equipment it had stockpiled in 1945.

Canadian post-war diplomacy was moralizing and self-important, but it had finally escaped from Britain and King's fussy oversight. In 1946 the old prime minister had handed external affairs to Louis St. Laurent. A conservative corporation lawyer, St. Laurent was Quebecker enough to be unimpressed by the symbols and sentiment of the British connection, but he was no provincialist. In the controversy over federal fiscal proposals, he bluntly backed the centralizers. Quebec would always complain, he explained, but Quebeckers also admired government that did things for them. St. Laurent was fascinated by Canada's potential role in the world. He backed officials such as his new undersecretary, Lester Pearson, who insisted that Canada was now a "middle power," with influence in the United Nations, NATO, and the emerging multiracial Commonwealth. St. Laurent helped persuade India to remain in the Commonwealth after 1947, when its instincts were to break all imperial ties. Other emerging colonies would follow that lead.

Of all Canada's connections, Washington now mattered most. Wartime experience had shown Canadian officials how insensitive a great democracy could be when its own interests were concerned. Moreover, rebuffs and criticism could easily drive Americans back to their old isolationism. Not only would Europe be vulnerable; Canadians would find themselves alone with their huge and often heedless neighbour.

In June 1950, North Korean tanks rolled deep into South Korea. Few Canadians could find the small peninsula on a map, and fewer knew its history as a Japanese colony or its post-war partition. South Korea was a test of collective security in a Cold War turned hot. A dying session of Parliament approved the dispatch of three destroyers; when the war went badly for troops under UN colours, the government agreed to recruit a special infantry brigade from veterans. Three years of fighting cost Canada 1642 casualties, 309 of them fatal. The United States and South Korea bore the heavy brunt of costs and losses.

Meanwhile, the Korean War raised a terrifying thought: was the invasion a Soviet-ordered diversion, leaving western Europe defenceless? The fear spurred NATO rearmament. No longer could it be cheap and leisurely. Early in 1951, Ottawa announced substantial new military commitments: twelve fighter squadrons and an infantry brigade for Europe; two more brigades available as immediate support; a fleet of Canadian-built destroyer escorts to withstand any new Battle of the Atlantic. Canada's forces would grow to a hundred and twenty thousand men; new weapons and equipment would cost $5 billion. As Canada undertook its first serious peacetime mobilization, C.D. Howe received fresh economic powers.

It was no longer Mackenzie King's Canada. Having served as prime minister longer than anyone in British history, King agreed to go. A Liberal convention in August 1948 chose his only possible successor: Louis St. Laurent. The architect of modern Canadian Liberalism, with its seemingly permanent hold on power, King retired, as he had served, with little love from Canadians and less respect than he deserved. St. Laurent was instantly more popular: a courtly, dignified man, a permissive autocrat who left ministers to manage their departments. He was conservative, too, and the many unfulfilled promises of King's 1945 program remained as good as new. But St. Laurent began with a bonus.

Wartime Canada had again staked a claim to Newfoundland, sending thousands of troops to the island to match the American garrison. Between them, the wartime visitors had brought a brief, unfamiliar prosperity to the island, but it was the islanders themselves who would choose their fate. The British commission of government, established in 1934, was about to end. The logical choice, to almost everyone but a small, bespectacled former broadcaster named Joey Smallwood, was a return to responsible government. By reaching past the island's merchant elite by way of the broadcast proceedings of the constitutional convention, Smallwood persuaded Newfoundlanders to make Confederation an option. After a second 1948 referendum, Smallwood emerged with a narrow majority for union with Canada. On March 31, 1949, Newfoundland entered Confederation. Her 350,000 people had been won by social benefits, fiscal guarantees, and, above all, by the hope that prosperous, expanding Canada would haul Newfoundland from its historic poverty. The merchants and lawyers of St. John's were unpersuaded.

Proud of the overdue completion of Canada, Liberals sought a new mandate. The Conservatives offered their fifth new leader in a decade. George Drew was handsome, articulate, and had won Ontario twice. Though his government had been more progressive than Hepburn's, Drew was an unabashed Tory and pro-conscription imperialist. When Drew sought an electoral alliance with Duplessis in the name of their anti-Ottawa axis, Liberals in Quebec and Ontario were ecstatic. The image of a Drew-Duplessis alliance, with Camillien Houde in the background, exploited ugly memories. For his part, Drew played indelicately with the neurotic anti-communism that won votes for Senator Joe McCarthy in the United States. Communism, Liberalism, and the CCF were lumped in a socialist stew.

Over the grubby politics of 1949 floated the avuncular image of Louis St. Laurent, addressing his audiences through their children, offering benign platitudes fit for a summer campaign in a country fully aware of its good fortune. The result was a landslide – 193 Liberals to a mere 41 Tories, 13 CCFers, and 10 Social Credit. In Newfoundland, only a resentful St. John's bucked the Liberal trend.

Canadians had voted for prosperity. The Cold War rearmament and Korea had restored an economy that had begun to flag in 1949. American investment fell off in the early post-war years, leaving Canadians to finance their own boom, but in the 1950s capital poured into Canada. Corporations built or expanded branch plants to supply Canadians with the cars, radios, refrigerators, and, after 1952, television sets they could now afford. Even more foreign investment was directed at unlocking Canadian resources. Oil and gas discoveries in the Turner Valley had given Alberta a modest pre-war petroleum industry, but nothing prepared the province for the huge oil finds at Leduc, outside Edmonton, in 1947. By 1956 Alberta supplied three-quarters of Canadian needs, and as much as possible was exported to the United States, though Arab oil was much cheaper. At Chalk River, Ontario, in 1952, Canadian scientists began preliminary work on an even newer energy source: the CANDU, or Canadian Deuterium Uranium, reactor. Rearmament and the American development of nuclear weapons created a demand for uranium and a long list of nonferrous metals.

Transportation was still a major Canadian industry. New railways reached north to Lynn Lake, Manitoba, for nickel; to Pine Point in the Northwest Territories for nickel and zinc, and to Labrador's Knob Lake to develop one of the world's richest iron ore deposits. The Mesabi Range reserves that sustained American heavy industry were close to depletion, and Labrador became the best alternative. The long debate over the St. Lawrence Seaway ended just as Canada decided to proceed on its own with a hydroelectric development. After five years of building, the billion-dollar project was finished in 1959. In 1948 Ottawa promised $150 million to the provinces to develop a Trans-Canada Highway for an increasingly road-bound population. It was finished in 1965 at a cost of almost $1 billion. Meanwhile pipelines carried Alberta crude oil east to the lakehead at Superior, Wisconsin, and west over the mountains to British Columbia. Engineers prepared to tackle two of Canada's great hydroelectric projects, Churchill Falls in Labrador and the Columbia River in British Columbia.

Critics complained that the developments did more for the United States than for a purely Canadian economy. New railways and pipelines reached into the North, but their termini were often in the United States. Trade, like investment, was increasingly bilateral; efforts to increase Canadian exports to Britain were dismissed as imperial echoes. As in the 1920s, some academic voices complained that key sectors of Canada's economy had fallen under foreign control and that more would follow. Most Canadians were too delighted with their new prosperity to worry. Economic nationalism had no place in the minds of C.D. Howe or his associates.

Even in Quebec, where Duplessis's regime was entrenched in an old-fashioned alliance of Catholicism and conservative nationalism, foreign investors were discreet partners. Like Liberal premiers before him, Duplessis welcomed the revenue and the jobs and let wages look after themselves. When Catholic unionists at Asbestos struck their American employers in 1949, provincial police provided management with strong-armed support. The resulting violence shocked Catholic leaders and pulled unions across Canada into unprecedented solidarity with the Quebec-based syndicates. Later, the Asbestos strike would be interpreted by one observer, Pierre Elliott Trudeau, as the symbolic beginning of a new kind of Quebec nationalism. At the time, it was much more a reflection of a common Canadian demand to share in the new prosperity and a North American standard of living. No more than Cape Bretoners or Ontarians would Quebec workers still accept deprivation for themselves and their families as the price of *la survivance*. Nor, given the cornucopia of apparently limitless Canadian wealth, did they have to. Maurice Duplessis won votes by giving Quebec her own flag in 1948 – a blue and white emblem mythically linked to the 1758 victory over the English at Carillon – but in daily life, *Canadiens* became more North American.

The 1951 census found 14 million Canadians. It quietly revealed another fact: a third of Canadians were poor, most of them elderly, rural, or tied to the have-not regions; too many of them were native people and Métis. Yet earlier censuses, from 1921 to 1941, had found that two-thirds of Canadians were poor. Now the poor formed a minority. Like all the best social revolutions, this one passed unnoticed. How had it happened? Family allowances, unionization, and, above all, steady incomes and a little to spare helped most families. Federal housing policy helped people break out of slum housing, find a home in the suburbs, buy a second-hand car, live healthier lives, and push their children to stay a few years longer in school. Canadians routinely enjoyed the one- or two-week paid holidays that union contracts won for members and non-unionists alike. A consumer society created new sectors of service and white-collar employment. So did the growth of government. The embittered meanness of pre-war Canada faded.

Canadians celebrated their better life with a baby boom. During the Depression, immigration and birth rates had both tumbled. Only in the 1880s had Canada's population grown so slowly. That changed. By 1947, natural increase alone added 2 per cent a year. Women left the workforce through choice because a single salary could support most families. Prosperity encouraged children; it allowed them to be fed and educated to a standard no generation of Canadians had experienced. The 1950s saw a demand for new schools, teachers, and, in due course, expanded colleges and universities.

Natural growth was supplemented by the largest flood of immigration since Sir Clifford Sifton's day. Between 1945 and 1957, a million and a half people came to Canada, including war brides, concentration camp victims, perhaps some of their oppressors, and thirty-five thousand refugees from the 1956 Hungarian uprising. Many brought industrial skills; very few came to farm. They fitted into a Canada that was now over-whelmingly urban. By 1956, half the people of British Columbia lived in Vancouver or Victoria; a third of Quebeckers clustered in Montreal and its sprawling suburbs. While five hundred thousand of the newcomers came from the British Isles and a hundred thousand came from the United States, many post-war immigrants had no links with either founding culture or even with the eastern European roots of Sifton-era arrivals. Perhaps prosperity and economic growth made Canadians tolerant.

Tolerance did not come at once. After the Holocaust, once-widespread anti-Semitism became despicable, but in 1947 Mackenzie King reassured Canadians that their country would guard its European character. Could a Commonwealth leader retain racist policies? St. Laurent thought not. Family reunion made the case to resume limited Asian immigration. Middle-class demand for home helpers opened a narrow door for West Indian women. King's policy survived to the 1970s, but the exceptions undermined old rules.

Diversity brought surprisingly little friction or cultural antagonism. Indeed, newcomers made their own demands for a more sophisticated, culturally varied Canada. Puritan conformity cracked when immigrants and Canadian-born alike chafed at old drinking laws, "blue" Sundays, and restaurants that served bad food and no wine. Canadian family practices, in turn, strained Old World traditions of parental authority and female roles.

Change was controversial. The United Church, dominant among Protestants but threatened by the largely Catholic influx of immigrants, defended the Sabbath and condemned liquor. Roman Catholic votes kept birth control an offence under the Criminal Code and resisted divorce law reform. In the 1930s, divorces in Canada hovered between one hundred and two hundred a year; by the 1950s, six to seven thousand marriages a year ended in divorce. As usual, Canadians blamed the United States for exporting loose morals and permissiveness, with films, radio, and television as the vehicles. The Canadian Broadcasting Corporation developed three radio networks, only to be outflanked by television. In 1952 the CBC launched television stations in Toronto and Montreal. High costs of TV production forced the CBC to buy most of its English programs from American networks and to concentrate resources on a coast-to-coast microwave link-up that united viewers for special national occasions such as *Hockey Night in Canada*. A single French channel, experimental, even amateurish, created a single Quebec audience as English CBC never could.

In 1949, St. Laurent reluctantly approved a Royal Commission on the Arts and Letters in Canada. While St. Laurent had few qualms about meddling with provincial control of culture, he had robust reservations about "subsidising ballet dancers." The commission's report in 1951, firmly guided by its wealthy and cultured chairman, Vincent Massey, argued forcefully that the government must do precisely that if Canadians were to share in performing and creative arts and to develop universities worthy of the name. The report lay where it landed. The arts struggled on: Vancouver's symphony orchestra played in an arena and Canada's art treasures hid behind the dinosaurs in the dusty National Museum. When Paul-Émile Borduas and colleagues published *Refus Global*, a radical manifesto against Quebec's traditionalism, Borduas promptly lost his job in a government art school.

Prosperity and immigration soon built pressures politicians noticed. In 1953, Stratford's Shakespeare festival opened in a tent. The Théâtre du Nouveau Monde opened in Montreal. As a matter of civic pride, cities began erecting theatres. The nadir of the arts in Canada, the late 1940s, evolved into growth. At least some people in an affluent Canada, far from being horror-struck at the thought of subsidizing ballet dancers, began to wonder why they had not done so before. Artists and musicians became cultural icons and models. In 1957, the death of a trio of millionaires, Sir James Dunn, Isaak Killam, and Harold Crabtree, produced such a windfall of inheritance taxes that the federal government launched the Canada Council and endowed it with $100 million, half for capital grants to universities, the rest for scholarships, loans, and grants. Ottawa cautiously became a patron of the arts and awaited the critics.

Later, Canadians complained that the 1950s were boring, marked only by the successive fads of American popular culture. Politics, too, were predictable and routine, grey and repetitive. In a 1953 national election, the sober competence of St. Laurent and Howe, the regular government surpluses, and a discreet trickle of pre-election goodies made the Liberals proof against George Drew's bluster and evidence of scandal in the expanding defence department. The government lost twenty seats but the popular vote was hardly altered from 1949. Thoughtful observers assessed the results and wondered whether constitutional reforms might be desirable. Canada seemed bound for permanent one-party government.

3 | RECESSION

I n the 1950s, Canadians seemed to live in a permanently prosperous, internationally esteemed, and increasingly united country. Ottawa's mandarins, prestige undimmed from the war, applied orthodox doctrines of macroeconomic management. In 1952, as the royal succession passed to a young Queen Elizabeth II, the self-important Vincent Massey became the first Canadian-born governor general. Abroad, Canadian diplomats tried to be confidants of both the Third World and the West. Social and regional tensions faded. The CCF was in decline. Worried by stagnant membership and the costs of rivalry, Canada's two largest labour organizations merged in 1956 as the Canadian Labour Congress (CLC). Federal-provincial conferences were decorous. Few provincial premiers were now Liberals, but most followed Ontario's affable Leslie Frost in a spirit of "live and let live." Only Maurice Duplessis made war on Ottawa, though even he preferred compromise.

Problems persisted, although few of the 15 million affluent Canadians hunted for them. Keynesian macroeconomics amounted to little more than Joseph's advice to the Egyptian pharaoh: run a surplus in good times to cover a deficit in bad times. In 1949 and 1953, economic downturns coincided with pre-election budgets. Liberal politicians and mandarins congratulated each other when re-election coincided with recovery. Yet the pharaoh had not had to manage a federal democracy. By the mid-1950s, the provinces, not Ottawa, were the big spenders. A baby boom, urbanization, and prosperity demanded hospitals, water and sewer systems, and highways for the two-thirds of Canadians who now owned cars. Ontario and British Columbia clamoured for money as loudly as their poorer neighbours, for they were doing the most expensive growing.

Canada's post-war international role was another Liberal bonus. Tories (and Duplessis) deplored foreign aid, and the CCF condemned German rearmament. Neither approach won many votes. Most Canadians, even in Quebec, accepted commitments to NATO, Korea, and world hunger. Brooke Claxton, the defence minister and a Montreal MP, even believed that, with St. Laurent as prime minister, conscription could have been possible. Canadian intellectuals deplored Communist-hunting by American politicians, and Canadian diplomats worried about aggressive American foreign policies. NATO had been a way of curbing Washington's rashness, but Republicans, elected in 1952, began switching from costly, conscripted conventional forces to a "massive deterrent" of strategic bombers. American taxpayers might like "a bigger bang for the buck"; allies like Canada worried about how to restrain an American trigger finger. Anxiety grew because United States policy makers needed to convince allies and enemies alike that they would, indeed, risk a nuclear holocaust to defend the interests of the United States.

However, two older allies turned Canada's external policy into a Liberal problem. The Anglo-French invasion of Egypt in October 1956 split the Commonwealth. Canada lined up with newer, non-white members and, more gratefully, with the

United States to deplore the Anglo-French move. At the United Nations, Lester Pearson performed a diplomatic miracle by securing the UN's first peacekeeping force to cover an Anglo-French and, simultaneously, an Israeli withdrawal. His rewards were a Nobel Peace Prize and denunciations at home.

Opinion polls in 1956 showed modest majority support for Britain. Were these the same Canadians who grumbled as St. Laurent created a distinct Canadian citizenship, abolished appeals to the Privy Council in London, and removed crowns, Union Jacks, and other historic symbolism from the public scene? The Suez affair gave British sympathizers a focus for their discontent.

So did another event in an unusually active year. Bent on linking Alberta natural gas with Quebec and Ontario markets, C.D. Howe sought fast parliamentary approval to give a pipeline contract to a Canadian-American consortium. The project fitted national and nationalist goals, but Tory tacticians agreed that obstruction would drive Howe into one of his increasingly explosive rages. They succeeded. Howe insisted on his deadline; the Liberal majority imposed closure and jeered when the opposition protested. A hitherto respected Speaker retreated into partisan subservience. The ensuing struggle lasted long enough for most Canadians to take notice. The issue itself was unimportant: the pipeline was built without further controversy. What people noticed was political arrogance. Liberals had been too long in power.

George Drew's own chronic arrogance might have saved the Liberals, but in December 1956, ill health forced the Tories to find a successor. John Diefenbaker was quite unlike any previous Canadian party leader. First elected in 1940, Diefenbaker held his party's lone Saskatchewan seat by dint of preacher-style rhetoric and devotion to the underdog. He had as little in common with Tory financiers as he had with Ottawa civil servants, but his backers knew that Diefenbaker could find support where no one had ever voted Conservative before. They were right. The Liberals also knew Diefenbaker, and dismissed him.

June 1957 was early to hold an election, but St. Laurent was now seventy-six and he could be used only once more. This time, economic wisdom called for restraint on pre-election bonuses. Old-age pensioners would have to be satisfied by a six-dollar increase. Western farmers grumbled about huge unsold stocks of grain, but the blame lay with the American's giveaway export programs, not with Ottawa. Besides, the West never voted Tory. A Liberal victory was a foregone conclusion. Experts and pollsters agreed. The experts also noted that Diefenbaker was impressive, especially to voters who had missed out on post-war wealth and power. His populist rhetoric and sarcasm targeted both Liberals and bureaucrats with their taxes and "tight money." The pension increase was scorned as the work of the "six-buck" boys. Still, had voters ever shot Santa Claus?

Many Canadians went to bed on June 10 convinced, as some magazine headlines claimed, that St. Laurent would be returned by a reduced majority. Instead, voters elected 112 Conservatives and only 105 Liberals. A quarter of the voters had shifted from the Liberals to Diefenbaker, incidentally boosting the CCF to 25 seats and Social Credit to 19. In Port Arthur, a CCFer, Douglas Fisher, defeated C.D. Howe himself.

St. Laurent refused to cling to power. By June 21, John Diefenbaker led a new, inexperienced government. The change was refreshing. Civil servants remembered to be neutral and dutifully faced new masters. Suspicions were mutual and, for Diefenbaker and some of his associates, never alleviated. The Liberal strategy was plain. St. Laurent resigned the leadership, and his decimated caucus sat demurely silent, giving Diefenbaker time to hang himself. In January 1958 a Liberal convention chose Nobel Prize–winner Lester Pearson. A renowned diplomat with a lisp and a reputation as a friendly, uncomplicated baseball fan seemed a sure winner. Pearson seems to have thought so too. Fresh from his convention victory, he invited Diefenbaker to resign and hand power back to the Liberals. Even some Liberals blanched.

Too late. Pearson saw that he had blundered. So did Diefenbaker. Pointing to unrepentant Liberal arrogance, he immediately called an election. Pearson's election promises sounded phoney for a party that had held office for twenty-two years. When Liberals blamed the Tories for the harsh recession that gripped Canada in 1958, Diefenbaker proved that the previous government had foreseen the crisis. Diefenbaker's spectacular theatrical skills on radio, television, and at public meetings allowed him to dominate the campaign. Audiences sat hushed as he summoned them to "catch the vision of the kind of Canada this can be." Liberals and intellectuals could fume that it was all humbug, but it worked.

Indeed, Diebenbaker's speeches were hardly necessary. When the election began, Tory support stood at 50 per cent. Canadians were captivated by their new government. The Liberals disintegrated. Minor parties seemed irrelevant. Waverers could join a certain winner. Diefenbaker had ignored Quebec when he sought the leadership and during the 1957 campaign. In 1958, Tory strategy was simple: "*n'isolons pas Québec*," said party advertisements – Quebec would not be isolated. In 1957, Frost had ended his neutrality and delivered Ontario to the Tories. This time Duplessis deployed the Union Nationale machine. Quebec Liberal MPs, who had scarcely ever campaigned, barely knew what hit them. On March 31, 1958, Conservatives, many of them Duplessis nominees, took 50 of Quebec's 75 seats. Across Canada, Diefenbaker won 53.6 per cent of the popular vote. Only Borden in 1917 had ever done better. The Conservatives won 208 seats, the Liberals held 49 (not one of them in Western Canada), the CCF dwindled to 8, and Social Credit vanished.

The 1958 campaign was more a referendum than an election: Diefenbaker was the issue and most Canadians approved. Only Newfoundland stayed Liberal. In 1957, the western provinces elected more CCFers than Conservatives; nine months later they were solid for Diefenbaker, and Conservative votes doubled. It was the kind of majority that Diefenbaker's hero, Sir John A. Macdonald, once claimed "could corrupt a committee of archangels." It evoked automatic sympathy for a tiny opposition, and it persuaded journalists, self-important by nature, to assume the role of critic. It was not hard to find things to condemn. Ministers were inexperienced and sometimes inept; some civil servants were disloyal, and others resented that their loyalty was suspect. Above all, the prime minister himself seemed uneasy about his majority and eager to prove his record as a defender of Parliament, allowing endless debate. The mere volume of sound from Parliament, liberated from the cavalier condescension of St. Laurent's ministers, persuaded Canadians that there must be much to criticize.

So there was, but much was accomplished too. Diefenbaker's "vision" was conceived by an adviser as a development plan for Canada's North; it became a catch-all for miscellaneous but useful projects like the South Saskatchewan dam, a railway to lead-zinc deposits at Pine Point on Great Slave Lake, and the development of Frobisher Bay on Baffin Island. A procession of royal commissions, headed by impeccable Tories, produced awkwardly radical reports. Mr. Justice Emmett Hall provided unanswerable arguments for medicare, as well as over-optimistic forecasts on its costs. Kenneth Carter's Royal Commission on Taxation infuriated the wealthy a decade later by insisting that income from capital gains should be as taxable as a paycheque. Grattan O'Leary, a veteran Tory editor, embarrassed Ottawa and annoyed Washington with a report that would have banned U.S. magazines from competing for Canadian advertising.

For the first time in memory, the West was in power in Ottawa and the Quebeckers who arrived in 1958 were too late for major cabinet posts. It never occurred to Diefenbaker that his election prospects depended on making room for them. Donald Fleming, finance minister and voice of traditional eastern Toryism, carried little weight. He had run against Diefenbaker for the leadership in 1956. Western ministers like Alvin Hamilton, Howard Green, and George Pearkes had the prime minister's ear. So had prairie populists. Old-age pensions rose sharply. Amidst free-enterprise rhetoric, the government adopted costly price supports for twenty-four farm products and kept the Wheat Board. An Agricultural Rehabilitation and Development Act (ARDA) helped some farmers to prosper and others to leave the land. In 1960, Diefenbaker managed to sell the huge western wheat surplus to China. Washington grumbled at Canada giving aid to the Communists, but western farm incomes tripled. With advice from a royal commission and from a new National Energy Board, the government forced Ontario to be a market for Alberta's high-priced oil. Quebec and the Maritimes were free to benefit from cheap imports.

Diefenbaker's most cherished project, a Canadian Bill of Rights, grew out of his prairie experience and memories of the discrimination he himself had suffered, even in Tory circles, for his foreign-sounding name. Passed by Parliament in 1960, with copies immediately distributed to millions of Canadians by a sympathetic toothpaste manufacturer, the bill promised much, though it could not bind provinces or even subsequent Parliaments. It also ignored the rights French Canadians had sought for generations. To Diefenbaker, who preached "unhyphenated Canadianism," cultural and language rights were irrelevant or divisive. It was a widespread western view. Quebeckers, Diefenbaker felt, should be pleased that Ottawa now sent them bilingual cheques.

Even with a huge majority, power gave traditional Tories far less pleasure than they had hoped. Their biggest party bonus was the result of a Liberal-appointed royal commission. A 1957 report accepted an old demand by private broadcasters that the CBC be stripped of its regulatory powers. In 1958 the Conservatives established and staffed a new Board of Broadcast Governors. Among its early decisions was approval of a private network (CTV) to rival the CBC's national television coverage. John Bassett, an energetic Toronto Conservative and part-owner of the CTV network, was the chief beneficiary.

Opposition parties almost always champion provincial rights. In power, Diefenbaker had costly promises to fulfil. In 1957, when tax rental agreements ended, St. Laurent had bluntly told the provinces that, like Quebec, they would have 10 per cent of federal income and corporation taxes. Ottawa could collect more, but provincial taxpayers would feel it. More was needed because hospital insurance had become the latest and most costly of over a dozen shared programs. Diefenbaker allowed Ottawa's share of income taxes to fall from 90 to 84 per cent by 1962, but federal-provincial relations grew more acrimonious. A long-sought constitutional amending formula almost won approval until Quebec backed out: its demand to control unemployment insurance had been rejected. British Columbia's Premier W.A.C. Bennett repudiated a Canadian-American agreement to develop Columbia River power and then demanded control of offshore resources. Joey Smallwood cried betrayal when Ottawa insisted on the letter of Newfoundland's terms of Confederation in 1949 instead of Smallwood's more generous interpretation. His fury grew when Diefenbaker refused RCMP reinforcements to crush a 1959 loggers' strike.

Such battles were a reassertion of history. Ottawa's immense post-war power and the harmony of federal-provincial relations had been unusual. So, too, was Canada's post-war industrial strength. A clear economic strategy, with tough priorities, heavy investment, and conscious sacrifice of inefficient industrial sectors might have given Canada a durable, if specialized, industrial future. Instead, her defeated enemies chose that route to prosperity while Canadians enjoyed a flood of foreign investment. Simply being North American had seemed a sufficient guarantee of permanent affluence. It was not. Brief recessions in 1949 and 1953–54 gave warnings. Canada's return to the vulnerability of a resource exporter was concealed by pride in the new hydroelectric projects and pipelines and in the Seaway.

With the conservatism of success, the Liberals had reverted to traditional monetarist techniques of high interest rates to curb inflation. The latest governor of the Bank of Canada, James Coyne, was a fan of the policy. His strategy of "tight money" provided Tories with a campaign issue in 1957, but, as recession deepened and inflation faded, Coyne's policies persisted. Canadians, he insisted, must tighten their belts and pay their way. A professed nationalist, Coyne found arguments from the warnings in the report of the Liberal-appointed Royal Commission on Canada's Economic Prospects, headed by a wealthy Toronto accountant, Walter Gordon. Foreign investors now controlled key Canadian industries and resources, Gordon warned, threatening Canada's sovereignty. Yet the Bank's high interest rates attracted foreign money while they dampened Canadian business and industrial expansion. As a nationalist, Coyne did more harm than good.

Diefenbaker's government inherited far worse problems from the Liberals than he and most Canadians realized, while the huge majority left him no excuses. Europe's new Common Market threatened old Canadian markets. Giant supertankers, developed when the Suez Canal was blocked in 1956, cut the price of oil and threatened Alberta's main industry. Diefenbaker's solution, banning imported oil west of the Ottawa river, angered Ontario. Another problem was $6.4 billion in Victory Bonds, maturing fifteen years after the war. Reconversion of the bonds at higher interest cost money, but James Coyne claimed that bondholders should have enjoyed even higher rates. Believing the expert, Canadians blamed Diefenbaker. The prime minister blamed Coyne. Conservative politicians denounced Coyne for arranging a $25,000 pension for himself, not for policies that neither they nor most Canadians probably understood. In the end, Coyne went, but not without damaging the Tory regime with the voters.

Despite Coyne and a substantial ignorance of economic mysteries, Diefenbaker's policies did more to ease the recession than contemporaries recognized. His spending was the despair of Donald Fleming. While the finance minister promised surpluses, squeezed civil service salaries, froze hiring, and demanded restraint, annually he had to confess yet another deficit. Between 1957 and 1961, government spending rose 32 per cent. A winter works program taught the construction industry to work year-round. Grants to universities doubled, and a federal technical and vocational training program expanded schools and kept hundreds of thousands of students from an overcrowded labour market. Unemployment figures hid the fact that employment and output both grew. Yet Diefenbaker's own political style led Canadians to look at appearances, not facts, and the image was a damning contrast to the Liberals' apparent record of efficiency and success.

Economic chaos was matched in Canada's international relations. With rhetorical thunder, Diefenbaker pledged a 15 per cent shift of Canadian trade from the United States to Britain. The figure, taken from the air, was absurd. Though the British examined the proposal seriously, Ottawa instead raised tariffs. Diefenbaker toured the world, seeking to inherit Pearson's prestige, revelling in the links with Britain and the monarchy.

Initially embarrassed that leadership on the issue fell to him, Diefenbaker was soon delighted by his part in excluding South Africa from the Commonwealth in 1961. Among innumerable repugnant policies of Commonwealth members, apartheid alone was deemed intolerable. Having condemned Canada's Suez role in 1956, the Conservatives took a share of UN peace-keeping duties in the Congo in 1960. When UN soldiers were beaten and abused without the right of self-defence, and a corrupt and brutal dictator emerged from the chaos, no one could take pride in the outcome.

Whatever the attractions and risks in the world, economics and defence bound Canada steadily closer to the United States. China, and later the Soviet Union, might buy Canadian wheat, but the bilateral trend was steady. Each year, Canadian-American trade grew, while manufactured exports to other countries declined. Walter Gordon's 1957 report on Canada's economic prospects helped push Diefenbaker toward economic nationalism. A new law required corporations and labour unions to report their affairs so that the degree of foreign influence might at last be measured.

American dependence on the deterrent and Soviet develop-ment of both nuclear weapons and the means to deliver them to American cities made continental defence a priority. Late in the 1940s, the Liberals had authorized a Canadian-designed fighter plane, the CF-100, and a Canadian role in building three radar warning lines. Replacing the CF-100 with a supersonic fighter, the Avro-Arrow CF-105, was essential, exciting, and so costly that it would not have survived a Liberal victory in 1957. Even plans for a single North American Air Defence Command (NORAD) were too touchy to be settled before the 1957 election.

In power, with the aged General George Pearkes as defence minister, Diefenbaker acted decisively. Before officials could warn of its risks, Diefenbaker approved the NORAD agreement.

The Arrow was a tougher problem. Suspicious of Liberal contractors, warned that costs would rise and that no new buyers
could be found, the prime minister cancelled the project on
February 20, 1959. In one day, Avro fired fourteen thousand
engineers, scientists, and skilled workers. Within a week, all five
prototypes were demolished. Diefenbaker added confusion to
anger. The age of the missile had arrived, he claimed; both
bombers and fighters were obsolete. The Arrow's replacement
was indeed the Bomarc missile, but it was useful only against
manned bombers, and only if supplemented by F-101 fighters,
which the Americans had relegated to their reserves. National
pride was doubly hurt. So was Diefenbaker's credibility.

The Bomarcs were dubious weapons, useful only with nuclear
warheads. An antinuclear crusade, launched in Britain, spread
to Canada to be endorsed by women's groups and by both the
Liberals and the CCF. It also appealed to the rigid moralism and
anti-Americanism of Howard Green, Diefenbaker's latest secretary of state for external affairs. Canada, the government
announced, would not acquire nuclear weapons. Or perhaps it
would. Or did it even know? Every major weapons system
ordered for Canada's NATO and NORAD commitments, from
Bomarcs and F-101s to "Honest John" surface-to-surface missiles, depended on nuclear warheads. Diefenbaker denied it: the
weapons were non-nuclear. Only the ignorant or the resolutely
unmilitary believed him. In Canada, such people are numerous.

Cancelling the Arrow proved to be the last tough decision
Diefenbaker was willing to make. The ensuing confusion and
deception undermined his reputation with allies and Canadian
opinion-makers alike. Not even peace activists could trust him.
In Washington, Diefenbaker's contradictions and Green's
evident hostility might have been tolerated by an aging, compla-
cent Republican administration, but a dynamic new president,
John F. Kennedy, saw them differently. Diefenbaker instinctively

disliked Kennedy. The feeling was mutual. As with Roosevelt and Bennett in the 1930s, some Canadians contrasted their own leader with the handsome, articulate American and were embarrassed. The image of Camelot persuaded younger members of the Canadian elite that they were too sophisticated for the fire and brimstone or the crude evasions of their own national leader.

There were alternatives, though none was as charismatic as Kennedy. Under Pearson, the Liberals shed many veterans of the St. Laurent era. Assured by Conservative fumbling that Liberalism was still the way to power, ambitious younger politicians emerged to rebuild party organizations, notably in the major cities. New Canadians, angry at sharp Tory restrictions against immigration imposed in 1957, recalled which party had brought them to Canada. Business leaders recollected the competence of the St. Laurent–Howe era. Newer policies, some of them proposed but unnoticed during the 1958 debacle, brightened the Liberal image.

A competitor was a regenerated and renamed CCF. The post-merger Canadian Labour Congress settled its differences about endorsing the CCF by agreeing to form a new left-wing party. A battered CCF agreed. By 1960, a New Party movement was under way, with the CCF's guiding genius, David Lewis, in control. Two thousand delegates met in a steaming Ottawa in August 1961. Veteran CCF and labour organizers managed the business and delivered the leadership to the CCF premier of Saskatchewan, Tommy Douglas. A surprise delegation of left-wing Quebeckers committed the convention to a "two-nations" version of Canada. Rank-and-filers ignored pleas to avoid a title that could be abbreviated and voted for "New Democratic Party." It became at once the NDP.

Liberals and New Democrats seemed more powerful than they were. Liberal organizers neglected the rural ridings where

King had patiently hunted supporters. Some CCFers warned that the NDP's new labour image would be a hard sell among prairie farmers. Both parties were designed to split sophisticated urban voters, the most fragile and flighty element of the 1958 Tory coalition. Dangerous but unnoticed was Social Credit, less in the West than in rural Quebec, where a spellbinding used-car dealer named Réal Caouette quietly created a hinterland movement of people angry at governments, taxes, and change.

No one much cared: there was much more exciting news in Quebec City. In 1959 Duplessis died. His Union Nationale had been a personal regime, a tight, authoritarian machine with which *Le Chef* could guard his endangered people. Even the Church, for all its seeming influence, had depended utterly on Duplessis for funds to run its imposing empire of hospitals, schools, and orphanages. Beyond ruthless use of patronage and an electoral machine that did not shrink from violence and fraud, Duplessis had depended on his wars with Ottawa to harvest votes. Successive Liberal leaders were dismissed as "travelling salesmen" of federalism. Now *Le Chef* was gone. Soon, so was his able and reforming successor, Paul Sauvé. By backing Diefenbaker, the Union Nationale had gained patronage and lost independence. The initiative now lay with Jean Lesage, once Pearson's parliamentary assistant, a man whose aloof dignity contrasted with the vulgarity of the Duplessis era.

Il faut que ça change, proclaimed the Liberal slogans, to be echoed by younger, better-educated Quebec voters, shaped by the 1950s to demand more of life and of government than the Church or Duplessis had allowed them. When Lesage won the 1960 election, most Canadians welcomed the message and saw a superbly talented new government take shape: Paul Gérin-Lajoie, René Lévesque, and Georges Lapalme attracted comparable talent to the task of modernizing Quebec. Canadians were slower to overhear the other slogan of the 1960 victory: *maîtres chez nous*. The state would replace the Church and the land as the fundamental instrument of *Canadien* survival. Unless something dramatic happened in Ottawa, that state would be *Québécois*; its logical direction was independence.

On June 10, 1962, Diefenbaker faced the electorate. Guided by polls and a mid-campaign economic crisis in which the dollar was sharply devalued, the experts predicted a Liberal victory. Liberals issued a "Diefenbuck" as a reminder of Tory competence and dispatched a "truth squad" to report on Diefenbaker's lies. The tactics backfired. In was the Liberals' own campaign that sagged. Lester Pearson did not excite Canadians, and he had a huge margin to trim. Voters elected 112 Conservatives, 100 Liberals, 19 New Democrats, and an astonishing 30 Social Crediters, all but four from Réal Caouette's grassroots Quebec campaign. With their help, Diefenbaker could still govern. He did so, with even deeper suspicions of officials and colleagues. Only the West remained true and solid.

The defence issue should have gone away. After all, Canadian governments always let politics rule military decisions. Diefenbaker heeded Howard Green and believed his anti-nuclear mail. The Bomarcs, finally inserted in their silos at North Bay and La Macaza, were armed with sandbags. The F-101s were safer unarmed. Decisions could wait. In October 1962, Soviet missiles created a crisis and forced decisions. For a few tense days in October 1962, President Kennedy waged a war of nuclear bluff against Soviet strategic will. Canada did not play. NORAD in the United States moved to readiness; its Canadian element, covering New York and Pittsburgh as well as Toronto and Montreal, officially did not.

Whatever they might have felt later, at the time most Canadians were appalled. Polls reflected a dramatic switch in favour of acquiring nuclear warheads. Lester Pearson switched with the polls. In January 1963, he dropped his anti-nuclear stand in a single speech in Scarborough. Humiliated past endurance by his chief, the defence minister, now Douglas Harkness, resigned. A series of American statements, deliberate or accidental, refuted Diefenbaker's public speeches. A blunt State Department release summarized American opinion and the plain facts: Canada had proposed no arrangement "sufficiently practical to contribute effectively to North American defence." It was a bombshell.

Confident that the flood of letters he received reflected public opinion, Diefenbaker refused modest overtures to Caouette's Créditistes that might have kept their votes. Polls, he felt, were for dogs. On February 5 Caouette abandoned the sinking government. So did more Tory ministers. An election followed.

Within days, the nuclear weapons issue vanished. Diefenbaker promised a full statement on defence. It never appeared. Instead, he denounced the White House for engineering his downfall. Almost no newspapers backed Diefenbaker – no one, he boasted, but the people. In much of urban Canada, Tories sat out the campaign. Pearson's campaign, programmed to imitate the Kennedy victory of 1960, stumbled and backfired but this time it did not fail – quite. On April 8, Pearson won 129 seats to Diefenbaker's 95. The NDP won 17, Social Credit 24. Not since 1925 had Liberals faced a minority government. The Mackenzie King alliance of Quebec and the prairies against Tory Ontario was gone. Of 48 prairie seats, Diefenbaker's Tories held 41. The two central provinces gave Pearson all but 30 of his supporters. In Quebec, two elections cut Progressive Conservative voter support from 50 to 19 per cent.

In five years the national consensus of 1958 had dissolved. Old regional rivalries and frustrations found new shapes, but they had all their old virulence.

4 | CONFUSION

The elite, more than ordinary Canadians, abandoned Diefenbaker. They yearned for the effortless competence of post-war Ottawa and for smooth relations with Washington. Many humbler voters, frightened by the recession, recalled the ancestral wisdom that "Liberal times are good times"; but only in the West had Diefenbaker's times been good. And newer Canadians remembered the regime that had welcomed them.

Like other Canadians, Pearson took Liberal efficiency and good times for granted. Few guessed his own priority: French Canada. Outside Quebec, most Canadians rejoiced at the so-called "Quiet Revolution" and approved in 1962 when René Lévesque bullied Jean Lesage into making hydro nationalization a provincial election issue: publicly owned electricity would make Quebec more like other provinces. The outcome was a rout for the Union Nationale. Displacement of Church control of schools by a new department of education in 1964 looked Canadian too. Quebec would have a high-school system like other provinces. Surely Canada would be more united.

Diefenbaker brushed aside Quebec ministers when they tried to explain the significance of such developments. In 1961 the NDP encountered the radical new Quebec nationalism, absorbed the catchphrases, and continued on its own familiar, centralizing way. It never got another chance in French Canada. Pearson, unilingual and unpolitical, had a diplomat's ears. In a 1962 speech unnoticed outside Quebec, Pearson recognized that *Canadiens* would control their economic and cultural destiny; to remain loyal to Canada, they must also play an equal role in Ottawa. In 1963, he launched a powerful Royal Commission on Bilingualism and Biculturalism, as much to educate as to find answers. André Laurendeau, who was later to become the reflective editor of *Le Devoir*, and Davidson Dunton, former head of the CBC, were joint chairmen. As a start, French became a language heard in the Liberal cabinet and caucus.

Bereft of any powerful Quebec Liberals, Pearson chose his own Quebeckers: able, decent men, often with his own lack of gut political instinct. In vengeful opposition, Diefenbaker was back in his element. Quebec ministers were often humiliated by his attacks. An irresolute prime minister and a minority government seemed helpless in their defence.

However, Quebeckers were not alone in their humiliation. Walter Gordon, inspiration of economic nationalism in the 1950s, had been Pearson's ally and economic adviser in rebuilding the party. As finance minister, he was key to Pearson's pledge that Liberals would begin with "Sixty Days of Decision." Gordon's first act was a confused, poorly argued budget. Never in Canadian memory had parts of a budget been hauled back for revision. Opposition parties tasted Liberal blood, and soon a procession of scandals provided a national spectacle.

Pearson's insistence on a simple maple leaf flag as national emblem in place of the traditional Red Ensign provoked indignant protests from the Royal Canadian Legion convention where he unveiled it in 1964. Diefenbaker's caucus denounced the so-called "Pearson pennant," and for months Parliament was trapped in the uproar. Finally, a compromise emerged: red on white with a single stylized leaf. National unity was not an obvious by-product.

Liberals had not restored efficiency; few people watching the parliamentary cacophony gave the Liberals credit for reviving prosperity. Economic recovery was real enough, but it had begun in 1961 as Chinese and then Soviet wheat sales spread their impact. Thanks to wheat as a leading staple, Canada entered a new era of export surpluses. Liberals deserved credit for adopting an old and controversial solution to Canada's troubled branch-plant automotive industry. In January 1965, the Auto Pact erased the border for firms in Canada and the United States making cars and parts. The first outcome was an impressive boom in Ontario's manufacturing towns. In the mid-1960s Ottawa rarely got much credit for economic achievements. The Conservatives' success with the Agricultural Rehabilitation and Development Act (ARDA) inspired a procession of acronymic programs from the Liberals. Canadians absorbed a new American belief that costly agencies with well-paid officials could somehow lift neglected regions from poverty.

In the 1960s, most provinces aspired to grandeur. Quebec's huge Manicouagan hydro dam satisfied René Lévesque's claim to the obvious – that Québécois could be brilliant engineers. Toronto had acquired its first subway line in 1954 and a second by 1960; Montreal must follow suit in time for a grandiose world's fair in 1967. Nova Scotia boasted a Volvo assembly plant; Quebec matched it with Peugeot. In 1962, amidst doctors' strikes, Saskatchewan's aging CCF government introduced universal, pre-paid health insurance or "medicare." Doctors yielded after winning fee-for-service payment. Their incomes soared. To finish educating baby boomers, provinces expanded old universities and most added new ones. In a single announcement, Ontario created a collection of twenty-two community colleges exclusively for skills training. In British Columbia, Premier W.A.C. Bennett's government developed cheap Columbia River power and sold it to the Americans to finance Bennett's own hydroelectric scheme on the Peace River. To the despair of General A.G.L. McNaughton, ending his career as co-chairman of the International Joint Commission, the Pearson government limply acquiesced.

The pendulum of power swung back to the provinces as it had done before, but it would swing even farther if they could get more money. The need was clear enough. The baby boom grew more costly with age. Post-secondary education, experts now claimed, was the key to economic growth and social justice. Both seemed desirable. So was medicare. Liberals had promised health insurance since 1919 but left it to the provinces. Saskatchewan had acted. Some premiers, including Ontario's John Robarts, professed philosophical objections. Others merely shuddered at the cost. Ottawa had to find the money. Why else had Pearson promised a new era of "co-operative federalism"?

A major Liberal promise in 1963 was a national scheme of contributory portable old-age pensions. Who cared that the plan invaded provincial jurisdiction? Premiers did. They also saw that a contributory plan would create a huge capital fund years before big payouts began. Ontario's John Robarts, as a Tory, had no love for the scheme, but the Liberal premier of Quebec, Jean Lesage, was more awkward. His politics of grandeur cost money. Surpluses, squirrelled away by the frugal Duplessis, had vanished. Buying private electricity companies used up Quebec's credit, and the province still needed to build universities and secondary schools. Provincial voters grumbled about Lesage's heavy taxes. In fact, Lesage was running a staggering deficit. Rural Quebec threatened one flank; radical nationalists in Lesage's own government cited terrorist bomb blasts to press their case for more powers. A magazine poll in 1964 showed that 13 per cent of Quebeckers wanted independence.

Pearson and the premiers met in Quebec City in 1964 to discuss the pension plan, and a tradition of affable federal-provincial relations died. Behind police guards, amid bomb threats, Canadian politicians discovered that the normally cool, dignified Lesage was angry, defiant, and drunk. Even more significant, the pension plan his officials unveiled was better designed and better argued than the federal version. Ottawa's mystic expertise had vanished. Paradoxically, the humiliation helped save the federal plan. Sensing that Confederation might crumble if Ottawa's plan collapsed, Ontario's Robarts backed Ottawa – at a price. A new Canada Pension Plan must be funded, like the Quebec version. Quebec would still opt out, but the other provinces would get CPP funds to invest as they chose until the day when pensions must be paid. A crisis had passed but neither Pearson nor his officials would easily recover their prestige.

Surely Canada's external standing would be safe with the Liberals. Pearson had found an easy rapport with John F. Kennedy; he resembled the tweedy, liberal-minded academics with whom the young president surrounded himself. Canada immediately accepted nuclear warheads for its new weapons, with all the safeguards Washington had promised. A white paper by Paul Hellyer, Pearson's defence minister, reassured anti-war activists that the first priority for the Canadian armed forces would be peacekeeping. New equipment would be non-nuclear, and military strength would be trimmed to pay for it. Allies were content. Few readers noticed a small, explicit promise: the armed forces would also be unified.

Washington, however, was not serene. Gordon's ill-fated budget initially included a takeover tax on foreign purchases of Canadian businesses. The O'Leary Report, shelved by Diefenbaker, led to a law promoting Canadian magazines by discouraging Canadian advertising in foreign periodicals. Fear of Washington lobbyists led to exemptions for *Time* and *Reader's Digest*. More trouble grew out of Ottawa's reluctant decision to place the Seafarers' International Union (SIU) in trusteeship and to prosecute its American leader, Hal Banks. Banks jumped bail and fled to the United States; the SIU showed no repentance, and Canadian officials had to seek help in Washington. SIU blandishments meant more to the Kennedy administration than Canadian indignation.

On the whole, Canadian-American relations improved. Liberal policies imitated Kennedy's "New Frontier." A "Company of Young Canadians" was a strife-ridden imitation of the Peace Corps. Overdue concern for Canada's blacks and Indians was a guilty acknowledgement that Canada, too, had civil rights problems. Kennedy's assassination on November 22, 1963, was a blow a generation of Canadians would not forget.

Kennedy's successor, Lyndon Johnson, offered no such rapport. Few Canadians at the time recognized the sterility of Kennedy's record or the practical idealism of Lyndon Johnson's "War on Poverty." Privately, Pearson had questioned the wisdom of Kennedy's policies on Cuba and the Far East. By continuing his predecessor's Vietnam entanglement, Johnson took the United States into a real war by February 1965. Vietnam was not Korea. Full of moral righteousness, Canadians condemned the war, and Pearson expressed their disapproval in Philadelphia in April 1965. It was a speech few Canadians would have welcomed from an American leader, and President Johnson was not a tolerant man. He summoned Pearson and dressed him down: "Lester," he told the Canadian, "you peed on my carpet." His outrage forced an apology from the prime minister. Talk of special relationships ended.

Often, in 1965, leading Liberals reviewed opinion polls, a fractious Parliament, and their own achievements – chiefly the flag and the Canada Pension Plan – and pondered how pleasant life would be with a majority. It seemed easy. The Conservatives were preoccupied with plots against Diefenbaker. Social Credit split into English- and French-speaking factions. A July announcement of medicare by 1968 would silence the NDP. Canada was prosperous, and even the West would welcome the latest wheat sales to Russia. Pearson was reluctant, but his friend, Walter Gordon, was persuasive. On September 7, uncertainty faintly sounding in his voice, Pearson made his public case for an election.

While Liberal voters annihilated Diefenbaker, the prime minister decided to remain in Ottawa, bearing the burdens of state, safe from the electorate. The plan failed. Electioneering was Diefenbaker's joy. Reluctant Tories, dragooned into line by the party's brightest organizer, Edwin Goodman, found funds and candidates. Their leader gleefully threw Liberals on the defensive to the delight of rural and small-town audiences. The Liberal campaign floundered and even ran short of money. As usual, Pearson could not help it much. On November 8, voters returned a virtually identical House of Commons – 131 Liberals, 97 Conservatives, 21 New Democrats, 9 of Caouette's Créditistes, and a rump of 5 Social Crediters. Only Tommy Douglas took comfort from the campaign. His NDP profited from disillusion to reach a new plateau: 18 per cent of the vote. In Quebec, the dynamic Robert Cliche almost won the NDP seat.

Cliche might have done even better without the only Liberal coup of the campaign. More than ever, Pearson needed a powerful Quebec lieutenant. His choice was Jean Marchand, leader of Quebec's formerly Catholic *syndicats* and the man who had steered them away from the Canadian Labour Congress and the NDP. Marchand refused to come alone. One partner, Gérard

Pelletier, editor of *La Presse*, was welcome. The other, Pierre Elliott Trudeau, was not. Ostensibly a law professor, Trudeau had the reputation of being a wealthy intellectual dilettante who edited a radical magazine, *Cité libre*, and denounced Pearson for switching on nuclear weapons in 1963. Marchand insisted, and safe seats were found for the "three wise men."

Marchand was influential. Since the Conservatives froze civil service salaries in a struggle to balance their budgets, federal employees had demanded collective bargaining. All major federal parties had agreed. By 1965, many civil servants also demanded the right to strike. As an ex-civil servant, Pearson was appalled. As minister of manpower, Marchand was not. Quebec had allowed its provincial employees to strike without disaster, and Marchand's own union had profited; Ottawa must follow suit. The Public Service Staff Relations Act in 1967 gave federal employees a free choice and a chance to choose between compulsory arbitration and going on strike.

Marchand was too sanguine. A younger generation of workers, free of Depression memories, demanded even more than their leaders recommended. A violent wildcat strike at Hamilton in the summer of 1966 fuelled a year of labour turmoil. Canadians survived the first railway strike since 1950. An illegal postal strike drew unexpected sympathy for ill-paid sorters and letter carriers. Public opinion forced a generous settlement. Hospital workers and even teachers joined their first picket lines. Buying labour peace was costly. To avoid a crippling St. Lawrence Seaway strike, a government arbitrator imposed a 30 per cent wage increase. Without remotely considering the arguments, editorials called the settlement "the Pearson Formula" and raged at the government's folly.

The seaway was needed because Montreal was about to become an international showplace. Preparing for Canada's centennial was a sour joke. Some Canadians insisted that an

aloofness to windy boosterism and flag-waving was part of the
national identity. The opportunism of communities, groups,
and publishers jostling for a cornucopia of centennial grants
made easy satire. One town promised to burn its outhouses;
another would build a pad for flying saucers. No centennial
project matched the magnitude of Montreal's. Mayor Jean
Drapeau dreamed up the idea of a world-class exposition, sold
it to the international community, and virtually blackmailed
Ottawa and Quebec City into underwriting his efforts. Despite
Canada's vast empty spaces, the fair would be staged on islands
in the St. Lawrence, built with earth excavated for the city's new
subway line. Of all the absurdities of centennial year, Expo '67
easily took the prize. For a city with crowded slums and without
proper sewage treatment, it was a gross extravagance.

Even Quebeckers were tired of the politics of grandeur. In
1966, they rejected Lesage and elected Daniel Johnson's Union
Nationale. The party had shed some of its conservatism and
burnished its nationalism. Johnson's slogan was *Québec d'abord*
("Quebec first"), discreetly translated for English-speakers as "A
better Quebec for all Quebeckers." The French was more
precise. Johnson won because rural voters resented the cost of
Liberal reforms, but the new government changed little.
Instead, Johnson confronted Ottawa with new, uncompromising demands for fiscal transfers. He also asserted Quebec's role
in the world. In France's President Charles de Gaulle, Johnson
had an eager patron. Since the war, de Gaulle had sought
vengeance for humiliations he had suffered at the hands of his
Anglo-Saxon allies. It was irrelevant to him that most Quebec
opinion had favoured his wartime enemies in Vichy.

Financial demands were familiar; seeking an international
role was not. Pearson was furious. As usual, he also felt helpless.
Even the Lesage government had argued that Quebec had a
right to be involved in treaties that affected its constitutional

responsibilities in education or culture. For Daniel Johnson, external aggrandizement was a cheap and popular issue. The French cheerfully made life miserable for Canada's ambassador, and bluntly refused to welcome General Georges Vanier, Canada's governor general.

Meanwhile, Pearson discovered unsuspected virtues in the least wanted member of the "three wise men." As a parliamentary assistant, Pierre Elliott Trudeau offered Pearson unexpected and welcome advice about Quebec. Appointed minister of justice in April 1967, he showed a zeal for reform and a flair for refuting critics. It was not in the tradition of Ernest Lapointe for a Quebec Liberal to proclaim that the state had no business in the bedrooms of the nation, that homosexuality was not criminal, or that divorce reform was overdue.

Even more valuable was Trudeau's hard distinction between the national and the provincial rights of French Canadians. Like Pearson, Trudeau was committed to requiring equal opportunities for French and English in the federal government and in as much of Canada as could be persuaded. Unlike Pearson, he had a firm, perhaps unrealistic, belief that the functions of the federal government could be clearly defined. Years earlier, Trudeau had lectured on the dangers of centralization, but where the federal role was clear, he insisted, provinces had no business. Trudeau felt free of the ancestral tribalism of Quebec nationalism and scornful of those who remained in what he called "the wigwam." Talent, boldness, and inherited wealth had taken him to Harvard, the Sorbonne, and the London School of Economics, and he believed others could do so too. Trudeau had travelled the globe. If St. Laurent, Laurier, and Cartier had burst the limits of Quebec to see themselves as Canadians, Trudeau had no limits at all.

Suddenly and quite unexpectedly, Canadians also seemed liberated from parochialism. Once centennial year arrived, the sneers and the cynicism died away. To their own astonishment, a host of Canadians looked about themselves and felt proud. Celebrating turned out to be fun, and the organization of the celebration proved more efficient than most people had expected. To national astonishment and delight, Montreal's Expo '67 opened on schedule. In a suffusing glow of pride, Canadians realized that they had sponsored an artistic and innovative success.

In 1967, most Canadians felt smugly superior to their American neighbours, as the U.S. was torn with urban riots and sank deeper into the morass of Vietnam. Boosterism was in fashion. Mordecai Richler, an expatriate Montrealer who had deplored Canada's feeble cultural nationalism, now confessed that he no longer yearned for the day when the border would vanish. "Vietnam and Ronald Reagan," he wrote in 1967, "have tempered my enthusiasm. Looked at another way, yes, we are nicer. And suddenly that's important."

Not everyone agreed. Angry at Canadian criticism of his Vietnam policies, President Lyndon Johnson paid a cold, per-functory centennial visit. Quebec separatists fashioned licence-plate tags proclaiming *100 ans d'injustice*. The violent student riots that had greeted a 1964 royal visit to Quebec were not repeated when the Queen opened Expo, but massive police pre-cautions were unsettling reminders. The visit of Charles de Gaulle was a carefully orchestrated contrast. Daniel Johnson and Paris virtually excluded Ottawa from the arrangements. The French president landed at Quebec and rode in a triumphal motorcade up the valley of the St. Lawrence, revelling in the glittering welcome that Premier Johnson had promised. At Montreal on July 14, the old general strode to the city hall balcony to deliver his regal greeting. He concluded, arms out-stretched, *Vive Montréal! Vive le Québec! Vive le Québec libre!*"

Had vanity, mischief, or calculation led de Gaulle to shout

the slogan of Quebec independence? It hardly mattered. He had wreaked his vengeance on the Anglo-Saxons. The euphoria of 1967 dissolved. "Canadians do not need to be liberated," sputtered a furious Pearson. Unwelcome in Ottawa, de Gaulle promptly returned to France. English Canada echoed the prime minister. Quebec responded defensively and angrily. *Le Devoir*'s Claude Ryan scolded Pearson for causing hysteria and fear; 60 per cent of Quebeckers condemned the prime minister's counterblast. The Saint-Jean-Baptiste Society summoned its local worthies to an *Etats généraux* and solemnly demanded associate statehood for Quebec, on a basis of full equality with the rest of Canada. René Lévesque, whose years of television commentary had made him the best-known of Lesage's ministers, issued *Option Québec* in September, a clear demand for Quebec independence. When fellow Liberals hesitantly rejected Lévesque's program, he left the party. On November 18, 1967, Lévesque launched his Mouvement souveraineté-association.

In Canada's hundredth year, the forces of disintegration had found a compelling leader and a program. The logic and the example of a world of liberation movements had come to Quebec. The old, tiresome arguments about language and powers and money would end if Québécois were the majority and English Quebeckers could suffer the humiliations of a minority. It was the logic of Papineau, Mercier, and Duplessis, carried to its modern conclusion. Young, ambitious Québécois, frustrated by the persistent dominance of Montreal's English-speaking commercial elite, resentful of the burden of mastering a second language, found independence irresistibly seductive. For a decade, English Canadians had bored Quebeckers with the question "What does Quebec want?" René Lévesque had furnished a clear, disturbing answer.

The next question was what Canada would do about it. For a start, the country would change, testing whether centennial euphoria really meant a new willingness to live on as a transcontinental nation. After all, Québécois were not the only force for change. Post-war immigrants wanted a Canada without allegiance to old British ways, and their children embraced transatlantic freedoms and materialism. Even the armed forces, usually scorned or ignored in peacetime, became a controversial symbol of change. A stubborn, ambitious Paul Hellyer had been entirely in earnest about unification. A unified force in a single green uniform would win him renown for originality and efficiency. His chosen military commander, General Jean-Victor Allard, rejoiced that it would also "Canadianize" British-style uniforms and traditions. Protests by admirals, generals, and air marshals were dismissed as mutinous threats to civil supremacy. On Canada's hundredth birthday, the three armed forces reluctantly became one.

Other changes came even harder. Late in 1967, the Royal Commission on Bilingualism and Biculturalism delivered its first report. The recommendations were predictable, sweeping, and now inescapable: the federal government must not only provide services in both official languages, it must provide a working environment where French as well as English Canadians could work in equal comfort.

More than language, uniforms, and symbols needed changing. A revolution in the status of women began hesitantly in the wake of Enovid, the first apparently safe oral contraceptive. It steadily gathered momentum. Pearson's sole woman minister, Judy LaMarsh, demanded a Royal Commission on the Status of Women. Across the country, women's organizations mobilized, consulted members, and discovered, to their delight or horror, that the old maternal feminism was largely discredited. With their lives increasingly defined by education and work, women would settle for no status less than equality, from pension rights to pay scales.

Other problems, smaller or more urgent, were handed to mere task forces. Embarrassment at the "Pearson Formula" led, in 1966, to a study of labour relations. To ease his political demotion, Walter Gordon sponsored a task force on foreign ownership, headed by a sympathetic but hitherto anti-nationalist economist, Melville H. Watkins.

If Canadians gave any message in 1965, it was that most of them wanted new political leadership. By 1967, New Democrats ranked with their rivals in the polls, but John Diefenbaker ignored the hint. The result was a harsh, year-long battle between his loyalists and the party's youth, financiers, and urban supporters. Having engineered Diefenbaker's overthrow, Dalton Camp, a Toronto advertising executive, sponsored Robert Stanfield, the premier of Nova Scotia. A man of wit, integrity, and painfully cautious speech, Stanfield faced Diefenbaker at his most malevolent. Having been persuaded to quit, the former prime minister made a final leadership bid, he claimed, to fight a convention resolution endorsing a Canada of two nations. Stanfield won a bitterly divided party, with a caucus dedicated to his rival.

Lester Pearson, on the other hand, went quietly, content with his achievements and painfully aware that even the untried Stanfield had soared in the opinion polls as Canadians welcomed a new face. The Liberal succession drew half a dozen cabinet ministers, from the nakedly ambitious Paul Hellyer to aging veterans of the St. Laurent era such as Robert Winters and Paul Martin. All the aspirants defied two Liberal traditions: the alternation of leaders from Ontario and Quebec, and a preference for inexperience. Laurier, King, and even St. Laurent had served briefer apprenticeships than had the more obvious claimants.

In November 1967, Ontario's Premier John Robarts summoned premiers to Toronto for a "Confederation of Tomorrow" conference, keeping an election promise, and acting on his own deep desire to save the country. Canadians watched Daniel Johnson dominate the proceedings with a vision of a divisive future few of them welcomed. In February 1968, the premiers met again in Ottawa. This time, television watchers saw the new minister of justice answer Johnson with a brutality few could remember hearing from a federal official. Pierre Elliott Trudeau's campaign for the leadership of the Liberal party was launched.

On April 4, when Liberals met in Ottawa, Trudeau was the clear favourite. He won on the fourth ballot. Pearson had expected a chance to say farewell to Parliament, but Trudeau dissolved it at once. Like Diefenbaker, he ran against his own party as much as against the opposition, but his style was utterly different from that of "the Chief." Trudeau teased and challenged audiences and invested them with his own sophistication and style. The pride and self-satisfaction of 1967 revived and found fulfilment in a leader who was literate, eloquent, and adventurous. In a battle of images, judged by the media, neither Stanfield nor the NDP's Tommy Douglas stood a chance. In the sole television debate they gave as good as they got, but most journalists covered for their new hero. In Quebec, separatists and conservatives grumbled about Trudeau, but Stanfield's complex remedies, tendered in painful French, were no substitute for pride in a local son. The rural, small-town base of conservativism was shaken by Diefenbaker's departure. Diefenbaker loyalists voted NDP as once they had voted CCF. On June 25, Trudeau won the majority that Canadians had denied Pearson, with 155 seats to Stanfield's 72, and 22 for the NDP. Even the West relented: the four western provinces gave 27 seats to Trudeau, 25 to the Conservatives, and 16 to the NDP.

Canadians had finally given a national mandate to a new leader in a new era.

PART V

A COUNTRY SHARED

I | LIBERATION

Since 1867, Canadians had been more willing than Americans to use the power of government to finance and administer great national undertakings, from the CPR to the nationwide health insurance program that took shape in 1968. Canadians also believed that they were more conservative, law-abiding, and moral than their neighbours. Sir Wilfrid Laurier, for one, proudly pointed to crime and divorce statistics to prove the happier state of Canadian society.

By 1968 the contrasts were blurred and, for some Canadians, a source of embarrassment. Personal liberation had become a watchword, cherished as fiercely by stockbrokers or separatists as by dropouts in the drug culture. Liberation ranged from long hair and blue jeans to unblushing acceptance of premarital sex and unmarried cohabitation. Members of religious orders demanded freedom from their vows. Censorship became intolerable. So were the burdens of child rearing and family. Liberated by Trudeau's amendments to the Criminal Code, homosexuals would soon begin to defy the "straight" majority to promote "gay rights." A birth-control pill ended the baby boom early in the 1960s. Maternity, once defended by feminists as the highest role of womanhood, became an interlude that could be avoided at will. Quebec's birth rate fell from the highest to the lowest in Canada, raising alarm over French-Canadian survival. Newfoundland shared the drop. Traditional barriers to the employment of women, even in mines and construction sites, crumbled. The composition of the Canadian labour force changed from one-quarter female to almost one-half female in a generation.

In itself, liberation was not new; the young had regularly challenged their elders. But seldom had the defenders of authority and tradition collapsed so abjectly. Clergy, educators, editors, and politicians hastened to meet demands for change. Claude Bissell, president of the University of Toronto, hurried home from a traumatic year at Harvard to impose drastic changes on his respected institution. Radicals abused him soundly for his pains. Electronic media disseminated a world-wide youth culture. Criminals, innovators, and rioters shared the psychic thrill of seeing themselves on television. Post-secondary education now embraced almost as large a share of the young as had the armed forces in two world wars. Colleges and universities became centres for the drug culture, popular music, and protest. Superficial exposure to the social sciences bred faith in Marx, in pop gurus like Charles Reich of Consciousness III or Timothy Leary, prophet of LSD, and in the shock-science offered by Greenpeace or, alternatively, Ayn Rand. A Canadian, Marshall McLuhan, joined the new Delphic oracles with his image of "a global village" and "hot" or "cold" media. Most ideas, from feminism to "participatory democracy," came from the United States and, less often, from Europe.

Fashions are never universal. Most Canadians avoided drugs, stayed married, and, for that matter, never voted for Pierre Elliott Trudeau. As a fashion, liberation was more conspicuous in British Columbia, big cities, and the middle class than in Manitoba, small towns, or among the poor. An unfashionable majority wondered why priests urged secularism in education, or why governments financed the counterculture through Opportunities for Youth. Many preferred more enlightened fads. Roland Michener, the third Canadian-born governor general, made himself a model of physical fitness for a sedentary nation by promoting jogging.

Environmental concerns united young and old, radical and conservative. Rage at polluting industries and the alleged hazards of nuclear power generation went hand-in-hand with an elitist disdain for the vulgarity and waste of mass affluence. The limits of growth would be reached more slowly if fewer people enjoyed nature's non-renewable resources of petroleum or silver. What united environmentalists with other crusaders of the age was a humourless intensity, often incapable of recognizing its own paradoxes. Legalization of marijuana could be urged by people who campaigned against smoking. A passionate concern for baby seals coincided with a desire to preserve the folkways of Newfoundland outports. Native people must be protected from white meddling, but not if they discriminated against women.

In Pierre Elliott Trudeau, the Liberals offered Canadians a symbol of the liberation generation. Debating Quebec's Daniel Johnson, Trudeau stressed individual rights over group rights. By promising "no more free stuff" in 1968, Trudeau condemned social programs that shared burdens collectively. Since liberation was often a matter of style, its disciples adored a prime minister who wore sandals in the House of Commons, slid down a banister at a Commonwealth conference, and told a political opponent (in Trudeau's own sanitized version) to "fuddle duddle."

At forty-nine, Trudeau was not Canada's youngest prime

minister, but he was the most inexperienced. Like many of the comfortable young Canadians who made him their hero in 1968, his wealth had been more the result of inheritance than of struggle. As a world traveller, outdoorsman, or critic of Duplessis in the 1950s, Trudeau had had the privilege of choosing his own challenges. So far, he had been spared the setbacks, frustrations, and personal financial insecurity that had taught caution and compromise to King, Laurier, or Macdonald.

As prime minister, Trudeau handled power with a firm and sometimes naive confidence. Pearson, the ex-bureaucrat, knew the power of deputy ministers and circumvented them. Trudeau simply switched them so frequently to new departments that they soon knew as little as their ministers. Cabinet meetings became seminars in which ministers tried to defend their policies and programs without officials to protect them. Verbal agility mattered more than dull common sense. The prime minister's own office expanded dramatically. Youthful aides took over the regional responsibilities of cabinet ministers. Trudeau and his confidants insisted that the change guaranteed a rationalization of the political process.

Eager for a capsule phrase to sum up Trudeau's goals, Liberals promised the "Just Society." But "justice" was not easily defined, and the phrase raised more hopes than it could satisfy. A 1969 white paper on Indian policy promised to abolish a perennial focus for native grievances, the Indian Act, replacing it with "full, free and non-discriminatory participation of the Indian people in Canadian society." The minister responsible, Jean Chrétien, retreated before cries of "cultural genocide." Indians wanted special status, not equality with whites. By 1974, native people had become a federally financed pressure group. White Canadians, who had imagined that land claims were ancient history, discovered that Indians and Inuit claimed the North and much else.

Pierre Elliott Trudeau was more successful in imposing his views in external affairs and defence, if only because his opinions were closer to a familiar Canadian political tradition. Trudeau had wondered aloud whether defence dollars would be better spent on foreign aid. Canadian armed forces had endured unification as the price for modern equipment. With Trudeau, that commitment died. Military manpower was slashed by a fifth, and Canada's NATO contingent was cut to half-strength – five thousand personnel. Outdated ships, tanks, and aircraft remained. Allies were not consulted. Trudeau had no respect for the pompous diplomats who lived in Pearson's shadow. The new priority for Canada's missions abroad was to be trade, not diplomacy. A collection of little booklets on Canada's new foreign policy insisted that self-interest, not self-importance, would be the guide. Even Trudeau's admirers were dismayed when he bluntly refused to devote himself to moderating the miseries of Nigeria's civil war. The prime minister, aides reminded them, was a man of contradictions.

Canada's relations with the United States were more important and more complicated than ever. Talk of special relations and undefended borders had worn thin. By criticizing American actions in Vietnam, Pearson had ignored the prudent doctrine that neighbourly differences were best discussed quietly. Anti-Americanism became a noisy feature of Canadian youth culture, fed by draft dodgers and émigré academics. The naive envy of the Kennedy years had become an equally naive antagonism. Issues, arguments, and even tactics echoed those in the strife-torn United States. Without the *Wall Street Journal* and the U.S. Freedom of Information Act, it would, for example, have been hard to document the alleged misdeeds of multinational corporations.

Nationalists in Liberal and Tory ranks and in a celebrity-studded Committee for an Independent Canada exercised a powerful influence on government. The youngest and most vociferous denounced "waffling" and moved from Trudeaumania to the NDP, in hopes of capturing it for true socialism. Nationalists targeted external policies and foreign takeovers of Canadian companies, and performers, publishers, and film producers were the main beneficiaries of their lobbying. Canada was made safe for *Maclean's* magazine by the belated elimination of *Time*'s Canadian edition. A new broadcast regulatory agency, the Canadian Radio-television and Telecommunications Commission (CRTC), imposed Canadian quotas for television programs and broadcast music. Anne Murray and Gordon Lightfoot led a flood of suddenly popularized entertainers.

Issues raised by economic nationalists like Walter Gordon, Mel Watkins, and later by Herb Gray, went to the heart of Canada's industrial weaknesses. Inefficient branch plants were vulnerable to the first serious economic downturn. Head offices kept research and development at home, charged artificial prices for their services, and discouraged export efforts that might compete with the parent company. Yet millions of Canadians depended on foreign companies for their jobs, most Canadian business leaders fervently defended foreign investment (it guaranteed a market when they sold out), and economists had no trouble proving that Canada's prosperity depended on a regular "fix" of foreign capital.

Canada's vulnerability was driven home in 1971. European prosperity and the policy of borrowing to finance its Vietnam war effort drove the United States into intolerable financial difficulties. The 1944 world of Bretton Woods, with an almighty dollar and gold at $35 an ounce, had ended. President Richard Nixon abandoned convertibility, sent gold prices soaring, and clamped down on exports of capital and imports of goods. With two-thirds of her exports bound for the United States, Canada was in a desperate plight. Nixon offered no exemptions. By dint of much humble pleading, Canada finally got partial relief from Washington at the price of Canadian agreement to U.S. programs to repatriate capital and increase industrial exports.

The 1971 crisis showed how the 1960s had changed the balance of power among western nations. As an American economic dependant, Canada was on the losing side. Europe offered no alternative market. Neither did China. Trudeau had fulfilled an election commitment to recognize the Peking government, but the mainland Chinese took that as their due; any brief economic advantage was promptly capped by President Nixon's overtures to China in 1971. Like Americans, Canadians began to lose interest in a world that seemed ungrateful and unfriendly. Affluence and cheap airfares allowed them to travel farther and more often, but they did so as tourists, not as world citizens. Some Canadians, secular missionaries from development agencies like the Canadian International Development Agency (CIDA) and Canadian University Studies Overseas (CUSO), lobbied for less developed countries, but most Canadians kept their sympathy and charity at home.

There was enough there to occupy them. Trudeau's single most substantive claim to power in 1968 was his strategy for keeping Canada united. In the euphoria of the election campaign his policies might be forgotten, but he had repeated them in French and English, even in the Interior of British Columbia. Trudeau angrily dismissed a "two nations" version of Canada or any special status for Quebec. Canada must be a truly federal state, with ten equal provinces. Canada must be a homeland for both French and English, without sacrifice of language or culture. The 1969 Official Languages Act was a legacy of Pearson, but it suited Trudeau. It offered bilingual districts "where numbers warrant" and a federal government and crown corporations where Canadians could find service and employment in either official language. Added to unification,

French-language units finally opened the armed forces to both major cultures. The act was endorsed by all parties and most MPs, with the exception of John Diefenbaker and a small rump of Tory supporters.

The liberation generation believed that history could be ignored or overturned. The Official Languages Act defined a vision of Canada which Cartier, Laurier, and the younger Henri Bourassa had sought but consistently failed to achieve. Trudeau set out to annul novelist Hugh MacLennan's description of Canada as "two solitudes." For a prime minister with a cosmopolitan education and easy fluency in French and English, it seemed simple enough. It was not. French Canada's nationalists now saw English as a deadly threat to French and demanded its repression in Quebec. In the West, Clifford Sifton's "national schools" had done their work. Generations of newcomers had sacrificed their languages for English; nothing in their perception of Canada gave special significance to French. In schools across Canada, letting students select their courses squeezed second languages from the curriculum. It was "oppressive" to compel students to learn what they found difficult or unrewarding.

Yet the alternative to Trudeau's vision was far more threatening to national unity. If French Canadians were to be at home only in Quebec, there would be no logical destiny for them but national independence, with instalments of "special status" easing the process. "Associate statehood," now urged by the Union Nationale, was a reversion to the double majorities of the 1860s, this time with a quarter of the population sharing equal voice with the rest. For all the grumbling about French on cereal boxes and the cost of making senior civil servants feebly bilingual, Trudeau's official languages program would persist.

The urgency was underlined by events in Quebec. In Montreal, nationalist riots became endemic. Trudeau's election victory was enhanced by his coolness in the face of a bottle-throwing mob at the 1968 Saint-Jean-Baptiste Day parade; in 1969, rioters simply demolished the procession. In March 1969, massed demonstrators marched on Montreal's venerable McGill University, demanding its conversion to French. In October, Montreal police and firemen struck; looters and rioting taxi drivers took over. Post-Expo Montreal was in economic trouble, but the inspiration came from revolutionary nationalists armed with a cause that drew grudging sympathy, even from conservative Québécois.

Quebec Liberals had been leaderless since the retirement of Jean Lesage. Trudeau imposed his choice, Robert Bourassa, a youthful economist who had married wealth and who possessed a computer-age image of competence. Bourassa's opposition was less the crumbling Union Nationale than a new Parti Québécois, René Lévesque's masterful merger of disparate, quarrelsome independence movements. To meet their fiery appeals for Quebec independence, Bourassa offered a "profitable Confederation" and a firm promise of a hundred thousand new jobs. Bourassa won easily in April 1970, but the PQ, with a fifth of the votes, took second place. Péquistes were bitterly chagrined by defeat and by Lévesque's loss of his partly English-speaking constituency.

Bourassa's victory was no prize. Quebec needed an economic wizard. The province was deep in debt. Too many of Quebec's industries – footwear, textiles, clothing – survived only because of mountainous federal tariffs. These were threatened by each step toward world trade liberalization. Quebec's hastily built education system seemed to be staffed by teachers as orthodox in Marxism as they had once been in Catholicism. Their graduates were well indoctrinated but unemployable. Foreign investment, needed to keep Bourassa's promise, was frightened by social turbulence and talk of revolution.

A challenge came quickly. On October 5, 1970, James Cross, British trade commissioner in Montreal, was kidnapped. It was a police matter, but the kidnappers had their *Front de Liberation du Québec* manifesto solemnly broadcast. Five days later, another FLQ cell kidnapped Pierre Laporte, Bourassa's labour minister. Panic and confusion reigned. Radicals, union leaders, and French-speaking students sympathized deliriously with the kidnappers. A rally chanted "FLQ, FLQ" in a downtown arena. A lawyer for the kidnappers held court before the admiring media. Claude Ryan of *Le Devoir* and René Lévesque of the PQ gathered prominent allies to offer advice and alternative leadership. Ottawa, they insisted, must not get involved.

It was too late. Bourassa had already asked for the army. Thousands of Canadian soldiers relieved the strain on competing municipal, provincial, and federal police organizations. At Quebec's explicit insistence, Trudeau went farther. Before dawn on October 16, the government declared that an "apprehended insurrection" existed in Quebec and proclaimed the War Measures Act. Ten thousand troops in battle order swept into Montreal, Quebec, and Ottawa. Police squads seized 468 people. Some were cases of mistaken identity; most had merely enjoyed the heady thrill of preaching and promoting revolution.

On October 17, Laporte's strangled body was found. Terrorists were no longer heroes.

The man elected in 1968 as the embodiment of liberation dissolved that dream in 1970. The fun went out of revolution. Canadians overwhelmingly approved of the War Measures Act: 88 per cent across Canada, 86 per cent in Quebec. Arrested nationalists would not forget their humiliation. Trudeau's erstwhile admirers were appalled by such a naked use of force. Trudeau's target was never the obscure terrorists of the FLQ, but the "self-appointed dictators," "the emergence of a parallel power which sets itself against the elected power in this country."

To Trudeau, the chanting crowds, the coffee-table conspira-
tors, even men like Ryan and Lévesque, constituted the "apprehended insurrection." Bourassa's government might seem feeble
and frightened, but it had been elected democratically. Police
rescued Cross and found Laporte's murderers. By December the
troops were gone. Dismayed by its lack of information, the
Trudeau government ordered the RCMP to spy on subversives
and discreetly averted its eyes from the amateurish consequences. Trudeau's critics also had a point. The War Measures
Act created martyrs. It furnished ugly precedents. It casually
shattered safeguards Canadians had taken for granted. Nor
could Trudeau or his colleagues, Jean Marchand and Gérard
Pelletier, publicly justify their role in the October Crisis without
explaining the intuitions gained in a lifetime of Montreal intellectual politics or without further hurting the credibility of
Robert Bourassa's government.

Trudeau's new Quebec enemies soon had revenge. Con-
fessing that he was opening Pandora's box, Trudeau returned to
the old chore of constitutional reform. To his surprise, he found
that the provincial premiers agreed on many issues, from
shared-cost programs to a provincial role in choosing Supreme
Court judges. In June 1971, he and the premiers met in Victoria,
wrapped up compromises, and adopted an amending formula
that limited veto rights to Ontario and Quebec. Proudly they
proclaimed a Victoria Charter. Bourassa agreed, but before his
plane reached Montreal, he changed his mind. A storm of
protest, much of it inspired by Ryan and *Le Devoir*, greeted him.
Bourassa had come home without Ryan's constitutional
panaceas: no special status, equal status, or associate status for
Quebec. On June 23, Bourassa declared that the deal was off.

Constitutional reform had a low priority for most Canadians;
economic management held no great interest for the prime
minister. The mismatch was unfortunate. For Canada, as for the

United States, the easy post-war years were over. Keynesian macroeconomic management was challenged by unacceptable levels of both inflation and unemployment. Canadian-born economist John Kenneth Galbraith blamed the combination of the price-setting power of great corporations and wage-fixing by strong unions. The remedy, as in wartime, lay with selective wage and price controls. In Canada, the problem and any solution were complicated by federal and provincial powers and by a belief that economic trends were irrevocably set by the American economy.

Economics mattered to the Trudeau government chiefly when national unity or regional problems took on an economic dimension. Trudeau-style federalism would have pushed Ottawa out of provincial fields like health, education, and welfare, but the provinces argued that Ottawa had pressured them into costly programs in post-secondary education and medicare, and retreat was not easy. In Trudeau's view, Ottawa was responsible for economic equalization among regions and even among individuals. In 1969, the government clustered its array of development agencies and programs in a new Department of Regional Economic Expansion (DREE) under Jean Marchand. By 1979, DREE was pumping half a billion dollars a year into Atlantic Canada and eastern Quebec with no conspicuous growth in local prosperity or contentment.

Unemployment insurance (UI), devised as a benefit for jobless factory workers, had been transformed through the Diefenbaker and Pearson years into an income subsidy for fishermen and loggers. In 1971, UI was changed again, into an income maintenance program for a wide range of Canadians, from artists to expectant mothers. To cover added costs, higher-income employees were brought into the scheme. Benefits were improved to guarantee "individual development" as well as survival. Suspicious citizens complained that government was subsidizing the idle, promptly translated as "welfare bums."

The 1968 slogan of a "Just Society" implied progress on a long list of overdue reforms. Kenneth Carter, appointed by Diefenbaker in 1962 to study Canada's tax laws, delivered twenty-six hundred pages of expertise and a simple proposition: a dollar of income should be taxed as a dollar, however earned. Wage earners agreed, but they carried no weight. By the time tax reform became law in 1971, lobbyists had done their work: a dollar earned by sweat was taxed at full value; a dollar added from a windfall was taxed as fifty cents; gambling winnings remained tax-free. The moral principle was clear. By 1975, lotteries in Canada were a billion-dollar government enterprise.

Business lobbies gutted tax reform, buried legislation threatening time-honoured price-fixing and monopoly practices, stalled the economic nationalists, and channelled Ottawa's anti-inflation campaign into a verbal assault on wages. But why even struggle with Ottawa? The Tories, bereft of business support since Diefenbaker, began to look more attractive.

In the West, Trudeau had a gift for making enemies. He could not be blamed for sagging world sales of grain in 1969 and 1970 nor for the hostile journalists who reported only his question to unhappy farmers – "Why should I sell your wheat?" – not his answer: that the Wheat Board was a federal agency. Still, Ottawa's programs for grain farmers regularly seemed to help the wrong people. Western Canada might have tolerated Trudeau's concerns for bilingualism and constitutional reform if the prime minister had shown much interest in their preoccupations. He seldom did.

In 1968, Liberals had achieved a western revival. It vanished like a May snowstorm. In June 1969, New Democrats under Ed Schreyer won a narrow victory in Manitoba. The extra votes came from provincial Liberals. Ross Thatcher's Saskatchewan Liberals defeated the CCF in 1964 and again in 1967, but his efforts to distance himself from Trudeau did not save Saskatchewan Liberals from Allan Blakeney and the NDP in 1971. Within three years, the oldest branch of prairie Liberalism was virtually dead. Next door in Alberta, Peter Lougheed, a young Calgary lawyer, replaced Social Credit conservatism with a younger, more imaginative Toryism. Remote from prairie grievances, Liberalism lasted longer in British Columbia, winning enough votes in 1972 to hand victory to Dave Barrett's NDP. The trauma of seeing socialists in power drove Liberals into Social Credit ranks, and the NDP fell before a right-wing phalanx in 1975.

Liberals could not entirely blame Trudeau. New Democratic Party success in the West encouraged right-wing polarization. Resource-based economies were as unstable politically as in their markets. The fact remained that Trudeau inherited a national following and a commitment to national unity. By 1972, Trudeau's support was in disarray and he seemed to be preoccupied with his marriage to Margaret Sinclair, the beautiful daughter of a famous British Columbia family. Advisers, influenced by Marshall McLuhan, proposed that Trudeau's re-election would be a "dialogue with Canadians," using the slogan "The Land is Strong." Who believed the opposition? Diefenbaker loyalists made misery for Robert Stanfield. David Lewis, architect of the CCF-Labour marriage, replaced Tommy Douglas, but the NDP was torn by the stormy politics of the liberation generation. With divided enemies, the Trudeau magic, and so much expertise, the Liberals could not lose.

They got a surprise. The NDP's Lewis denounced a "Just Society" that allowed huge firms – "corporate welfare bums" – to defer their taxes while ordinary citizens paid up. Lewis won few converts, but united troubled New Democrats. Then Tories took Lewis's theme and accused Trudeau of letting more conventional "welfare bums" live at ease. A lacklustre campaign became a cliffhanger. On October 30, Trudeau emerged with only 109 seats, Stanfield with 107, and Lewis's NDP with 31. Réal Caouette's Créditistes kept 15, and independents took 2.

In 1972, the media portrayed Trudeau as a spoiled brat, telling unemployed mail drivers to "*mange de la merde*" and dismissing journalists with icy aloofness. Perhaps he would now leave. Certainly defeat left him petulant: "Nine-tenths of politics appeals to emotions rather than to reason. I am a bit sorry about that, but this is the world we're living in, and therefore I've had to change."

Change he would. Quebeckers learned that it was Trudeau's devotion to their interests that had cost him votes elsewhere in Canada. Inspectors hunted (largely in vain) for welfare bums. When the Conservatives offered him no terms, David Lewis had to take what Trudeau offered or force an early and possibly fatal election. Armed with budget surpluses, the government spent its way back to modest popularity. Bread and milk subsidies offset inflation. A Food Prices Review Board unexpectedly denounced government marketing boards, not the supermarkets. That cued the new agriculture minister, Eugene Whelan, to champion farmers and their right to a good price.

By 1973, European and American economies had recovered from a mild recession. The long ordeal in Vietnam was approaching an end. Optimists boasted that the world would benefit from a "peace dividend." Canadian unemployment fell below 6 per cent and Liberal popularity climbed, even in the West. In the summer of 1973, David Lewis failed to persuade New Democrats to force an election.

Few Canadians noticed when major oil-exporting countries met to review their pricing policies. Even fewer realized that petroleum was the only significant commodity whose price was immune to inflation. Ontarians grumbled that Alberta crude cost three dollars a barrel while Iranian oil sold for fifty cents. Suddenly, those prices were memories. The Organization of Petroleum Exporting Countries (OPEC) raised world oil prices by 50 per cent in three months. In October 1973, Egypt launched an initially triumphant assault on Israel. Arab countries backed the war with an oil boycott of Israel's allies. By 1974, oil prices had quadrupled. A world accustomed to cheap energy struggled to readjust.

Canada was both supplier and importer. Alberta oil enjoyed a protected market in Ontario. Western states took about as much Canadian oil as the eastern provinces imported from abroad. Eager to justify exports, oil company forecasts insisted in 1971 that Canada had reserves for centuries. How odd that in 1973 the estimates suddenly shrank. Instead of immunity from the world crisis, Canadians learned that their energy reserves might vanish in a decade. Few sectors of the Canadian economy were more dominated by multinational corporations, and the large oil companies had not enjoyed great public respect.

An economic crisis brought political responses. Alberta and Saskatchewan, heavy oil producers, believed that they were entitled to the best available price for a non-renewable resource they had controlled since 1930. Depression-era memories haunted people in both provinces. Without energy wealth, those days would return. The western provinces would be accommodating, but, as Allan Blakeney insisted, no one had ever suggested that Ontario sell its resources to western provinces at less than the world price. The argument left the Trudeau government unmoved. Backed by the NDP and eager to show what government could do, the Liberals froze domestic prices; taxed exports to subsidize eastern oil imports; approved a pipeline to carry Alberta oil to Montreal; and created a crown corporation, Petro Canada, to give Canada a stake in the oil industry. Ottawa also began in earnest the development of Alberta's tar sands and a Mackenzie Valley pipeline to connect with expected Arctic oil deposits.

The program made electoral sense. Alberta would grumble, but it now had no Liberal seats. Others would see Ottawa protecting them from a crisis contrived by foreigners and oil companies. Americans would pay the export tax while Eastern Canadians, especially Quebeckers, would see new benefits in Confederation. Could even the West grumble when it was getting more than it ever imagined for its oil, and salting away the proceeds in bulging "Heritage" funds? Economists argued differently. The "hidden hand," even poorly concealed, must rule. World prices might be painful, but what else would shock Canadians into genuine conservation? Perhaps the National Energy Board should have checked the company estimates of reserves, but the gloomy truth had to be faced. New oil finds would be remote, heavy, and costly. Synthetic crude from the tar sands depended on expensive, water-wasting processes. Alberta got more money but not a world price. Most Canadians seemed pleased. Liberal fortunes revived.

In Newfoundland in 1972, Joey Smallwood finally fell to the Conservatives, but Nova Scotia Liberals regained power. In October 1973, Robert Bourassa tested his popularity with Quebeckers tired of public-sector strikes, labour violence, and militant speeches. The result was a Liberal landslide: 102 seats out of 110. (The sweep hid a more disturbing statistic: Parti Québécois electoral support rose to 30 per cent.)

As Liberal popularity revived, it seemed a good time to end minority government. An April budget distributed tax cuts and a dollop of corporate welfare designed to repel Lewis and the NDP. On May 8, 1974, to its total delight, the Trudeau government fell, and the NDP took the full blame. Robert Stanfield had decided that rising inflation was his issue. Unwisely, he also consulted experts and newspapers, and decided to offer a policy: a sixty-day wage and price freeze. Trudeau answered with sarcasm: "Zap, you're frozen," he shouted at audiences. They roared with pleasure. Good times and warm weather made Trudeau's audiences almost as forgiving as in 1968. He had changed, he told whistle-stop audiences across Canada: "I have a train, and I have Margaret." A beautiful young wife, gushing with adoration, was a definitive answer to critics who depicted the prime minister as cold and unfeeling.

On July 8, 1974, urban Ontario and British Columbia workers deserted the Tories and the NDP to restore Trudeau's majority: 141 seats to 95 for Stanfield and 16 for the NDP. The West gave Trudeau only 5 ridings, but Lewis lost his Toronto seat. The Italian Canadians who now dominated his district voted Liberal. So, for once, did their wives. A "Right to Life" movement persuaded them that Lewis favoured abortion.

The age of liberation was over. The counteroffensive had begun.

2 | AFFIRMATION

More than in 1968, Pierre Elliott Trudeau believed that his new majority was a mandate for his own approach to government. Ministers must now focus on long-term planning. A trusted friend, Michael Pitfield, took charge of the federal bureaucracy. A new jargon of policies and priorities permeated Ottawa. Rationality would surely follow. Instead, Trudeau and his colleagues rediscovered that political life is lived in short gasps. Two old enemies, inflation and unemployment, would not wait for the bureaucratic seminar to end. In the minority interlude, the Liberals had promoted the theory that Canadian inflation was largely imported and beyond Ottawa's control. Quadrupled oil prices affected more car owners; tomatoes cost more because greenhouses were heated by oil; so did plastic gadgets, since they began life in an oil-based feedstock. Almost everything in Canada was transported by road or rail. Oil-fired generators produced most of Atlantic Canada's electricity. Until its 1974 victory, the Liberal answer to inflation was to tie wages, pensions, and other payments to the consumer price index. Stealing one of Stanfield's

1972 election promises, John Turner, the finance minister, linked tax deductions to the price index. This was highly popular, though it cut Ottawa's revenue in a time when its expenses rose with inflation. Heavy spending on housing pleased the construction and real estate industries and satisfied young families eager for their own homes. However, spending sent house prices soaring. OPEC had fed the inflationary cycle, but so did Ottawa's policies.

Next to OPEC, oil companies, and Alberta's Premier Peter Lougheed, the obvious scapegoat for inflation was labour. Fixed contract periods, a proud feature of the Canadian industrial relations system, locked workers and employers into two- and three-year agreements. If lucky, unionized workers usually get one chance to raise their wages in any inflation cycle. Prices rise discreetly but often. Bent on catching up and protecting themselves from future inflation, union members demanded raises ranging from 30 to 80 per cent. Once politicians admitted that inflation was a problem, unions became convenient and outspoken villains. Since the public now employed some of the most militant unionists, notably in post offices, resentment was easily mobilized.

Before 1974, Trudeau preferred to lecture business and labour rather than following the short-lived American experiment with controls. After the Liberal victory, John Turner applied his undoubted charm to business and labour. Union leaders were tempted. The NDP had failed them in 1974; the Liberals had never seemed so attractive. What the government failed to see was that union members set bargaining demands. Canadian Labour Congress leaders might yearn to be statesmen, but their jobs depended on votes from union militants and from younger members who expected fast returns on their dues. Meanwhile, pressures for controls grew. Older government officials recalled the success of the Wartime Prices and

Trade Board. Former Canadian John Kenneth Galbraith lent his credentials to the cause. Richard Nixon's 1971 price control experiment looked better in retrospect than it had at the time. Turner blamed his failure to win voluntary restraint on the prime minister, whom he now loathed, and he left for a Toronto law firm. On October 13, Canadians could buy the current issue of *Maclean's* citing the prime minister's firm opposition to controls. They could also turn on their radios and hear Trudeau outline a program of mandatory wage and price guidelines enforced by an Anti-Inflation Board (AIB). Further details were complex, and they grew in complexity as their impact filtered through the economy.

Organized labour professed outrage. The brief flirtation with Liberals ended. Unionists who had signed agreements before October 13 pocketed their gains; others remained empty-handed. Anti-Inflation Board officials were not concerned by their plight. Serious collective bargaining ended for the duration of controls; the Canadian Labour Congress devoted itself to demonstrations, a court challenge, and, a year after Trudeau's announcement, a "Day of Protest" involving a million workers. Since such walkouts were illegal, some leaders lost their jobs. Unions resisted alone. While business slowly came to share union resentment at controls and their application, most Canadians (including union members) welcomed any policy that protected their savings.

True to his faith in long-range planning, the prime minister invited Canadians to contemplate a post-controls period when some kind of "social corporatism" might prevail. Union leaders surpassed business in their initial horror at the notion. Then some were attracted. For a few months, echoes of Mackenzie King's ideas of government, business, and labour tripartism, and Henry Wise Wood's theory of "group government," wafted among the CLC leadership and Liberal politicians, only to fade.

By 1978, the CLC leadership reaffirmed its commitment to the NDP, and ideas about industrial democracy were shelved.

Nowhere was labour protest angrier than in Quebec. The era when Taschereau or Duplessis could promise a cheap and docile labour force was gone. Eager to embarrass Bourassa's regime, Parti Québécois sympathizers in unions and the media gave political overtones to industrial conflict. The centrepiece of Robert Bourassa's economic strategy was a vast hydroelectric project on rivers leading into James Bay. Inflation and the price exacted by native bands for their land sent project costs soaring. Forcing workers to belong to Quebec's Federation of Labour was supposed to bring labour peace. Instead, workers rebelled against corrupt union bosses. In the winter of 1975, riots exploded on the construction sites and costly damage resulted. Despite his huge majority, Bourassa's government seemed to be in a perpetual state of siege.

Apart from a faltering provincial economy, Bourassa's worst problem was language. Both the Laurendeau-Dunton Report and the 1971 census had suggested that French was in danger. Immigrants, even in Montreal, learned English, not French. Worse, they earned more than *Canadiens*. In 1951 French Canadians formed 83 per cent of Quebec's population; by 1971 they dropped to 80 per cent. In 1969, riots had exploded in the Montreal suburb of Saint-Léonard because Italian immigrants preferred to send their children to English schools. Alarmists warned that francophones would soon feel like foreigners in an English-speaking Montreal. Nationalists had opposed the Union Nationale for refusing to end the right of parents to choose their child's language of education. While Trudeau urged bilingualism for Canada, nationalists demanded unilingualism for Quebec. The demand was widely popular.

Bourassa bought time with a commission of inquiry. Its report was moderate; its evidence should have been reassuring.

It was not francophones who were dwindling but Anglo-Quebeckers. The investment in French education in the 1960s was already giving francophones better jobs and higher incomes. Facts made no difference. In 1974, Bill 22 made French the sole official language of Quebec and abolished parental choice between French- and English-language schooling. To force immigrant children into French schools, toddlers were subjected to a language test. No one, from the Parti Québécois to the solidly Liberal English-speaking minority, seemed pleased. Elsewhere in Canada, foes of bilingualism added new arguments to their case.

In 1970 Jean Drapeau followed his Expo triumph with a fresh announcement: Montreal would be host to the 1976 Olympic Games. Outside the mayor's admirers, there was little joy. Drapeau's boast that the Games could no more show a deficit than he could have a baby reassured few. The Expo miracle did not recur. When the Games opened, an eighty-thousand-seat stadium was unfinished. Not even a new Canadian appetite for buying lottery tickets could cover the sky-high costs for the facilities. Despite a vivacious sports minister, Iona Campagnolo, and federal subsidies for athletes, Canada's Olympic record was mediocre. The Montreal Games left debts, unemployment, whiffs of corruption, and none of the euphoria of 1967.

Quebeckers yearned for a change of government; they did not want independence. Polls were unequivocal on both points. René Lévesque was a realist; so were his key advisers. Claude Morin and Jacques Parizeau were prominent veterans of the Quiet Revolution. The Parti Québécois promised to proceed step by step, first winning power and then submitting the independence issue to a referendum. Voting PQ would end Bourassa, not Confederation. It was a shrewd idea and the PQ advanced in the polls.

It needed a little more. A few hundred Quebec pilots and air traffic controllers, *les gens de l'air*, demanded to use French in the skies. Now the federal minister of transport, Jean Marchand, ordered that French as well as English could be used in Quebec skies. Other pilots and controllers, predominantly anglophone, insisted that English was the international language of the air. In June 1976, they backed their opinion with a strike. English-Canadian opinion leaders supported them. Ottawa retreated and Marchand quit. A pent-up flood of resentment at bilingualism burst and, just as suddenly, was gone. Most English Canadians forgot the issue and barely remembered a few years later when safety arguments were demolished and bilingualism returned. French Canadians did not forget and, on November 15, 1976, took their resentment to the polls. That night, amidst a vast, ecstatic crowd, René Lévesque stood triumphant. His PQ had soared from 6 to 71 seats. Bourassa lost his seat; his Liberals kept 26, and only 23 per cent of the votes.

Outside Quebec, Lévesque's victory was traumatic. The impossible had happened, and Canadians needed a leader. The earlier hostility to Trudeau had revived. In 1975, a fifth of the delegates at a Liberal policy conference favoured a leadership review. After Robert Stanfield gracefully resigned, the Tories chose a new leader. Despite a strange attempt by Diefenbaker to deliver the convention to Claude Wagner, an ex-Liberal from Quebec, and a hard run by another Quebecker, Brian Mulroney, delegates favoured a young, untried Albertan named Joe Clark. Few Canadians knew him, but by mid-1976 only 29 per cent wanted Trudeau.

Lévesque's victory changed that. "I say to you with all the certainty I can command," Trudeau reassured them, "that Canada's unity will not be fractured."

In February 1977, half the electorate would have voted Liberal. That spring, when Trudeau's wife left him for the role of media flower child, most Canadians sympathized with a lonely father left to raise three sons. As quickly as it materialized, support dissipated. Separatism seemed to be no threat. The Parti Québécois in power was more skilful than the Liberals and no more radical than a prairie NDP governments. Government auto insurance and a buy-out of the troubled asbestos industry hardly worried Bay Street. Bill 101, the PQ's language legislation, imposed French as the language of work, government, and even the signs on English bookshops, but Canadians outside Quebec were untouched, and Quebec's English-speaking minority won little sympathy. The minority itself was confused, divided, and moving out. As younger anglophones packed their bags, so did many of Montreal's head offices. Even Ottawa pleaded with businesses to stay. Sovereignists counted votes and quietly welcomed the exodus.

A referendum would come. Meanwhile, Trudeau and Lévesque competed for friends in New York and Washington – a discomforting reminder of where Canadian decisions were now made. A federal task force, headed by Jean-Luc Pepin of the Anti-Inflation Board and John Robarts, Ontario's retired premier, crossed the country, hunting for grievances linked to national unity. Canadians sadly returned to their economic preoccupations.

The 1973 price shock had pushed politicians to promise energy self-sufficiency. It was harder than it looked. Petroleum companies were discredited by their role in the oil price crisis, but they still controlled the industry. Most Western Canadians preferred the wisdom of the Calgary "Oil Patch," the local cluster of energy companies and their admirers, to the policies of a Liberal Ottawa. Their provincial governments controlled the resource. Only a huge public investment helped the new Syncrude plant at Fort McMurray to turn tar sands into oil. Two other vast projects stumbled through their planning stages while their private backers waited for the right price. Ottawa's proposed participant in the oil business, Petro Canada, looked too much like a concession to the NDP. Its mere existence contravened the American-style atmosphere of the oil industry.

North of 60 degrees and the provinces lay the fabled energy resources of the Northwest Territories, but the fable was unconfirmed, and testing it was enormously costly. Canadians complacently viewed the Territories as a remote, uninhabited wilderness, to be exploited at future convenience. Now was the time for a Mackenzie Valley pipeline to carry Arctic gas to southern markets. Belatedly, Canadians learned that the North had a fragile ecology and a newly outspoken native population, eager as anyone to profit from the energy crisis. Local protests led to an inquiry. Mr. Justice Thomas Berger visited a host of tiny communities, publicized problems threatened by the proposed line, and neatly aligned native leaders, their white allies, and a largely sympathetic Canadian public. By 1977, the pipeline seemed dead.

The pursuit of energy self-sufficiency was leisurely and sometimes fatuous. Canadians debated the merits of biomass and windmills, denounced the major achievement of Canadian post-war technology, the CANDU reactor, and paid less for gas than Americans. In 1975, Ottawa and Edmonton came to a reluctant agreement that Canadian oil prices would rise over four years almost to the level set by the OPEC cartel, $14.75 a barrel. Encouraged by the Iranian Revolution, OPEC chose that year to send prices zooming again. In a few months, the world price tripled. Canada's oil subsidy bill rose to $2.5 billion. With renewed fervour, the producing provinces demanded more money and the consuming provinces demanded protection.

Oil prices were one of several reasons for "stagflation," the combination of inflation and unemployment that infected most western industrialized nations. Keynesian ideas had either failed or proved too unpopular. Older economic orthodoxies appealed to the increasingly conservative mood that elected Margaret Thatcher in Britain in 1979 and sent Ronald Reagan to the White House. Unlike their Tory and Republican predecessors, both were happy to roll government and social policy back to the 1920s. Middle-class voters, educated, housed and rendered affluent by post-war policies, responded to lower taxes, less regulation, and lower-quality schools and health services because they never imagined needing them.

Inflation, said old-fashioned textbooks, happened when "too much money chased too few goods." "Monetarists" claimed that high interest rates would shrink a money supply inflated by excessive credit. "Supply-siders" insisted that lower taxes for the rich would liberate more investment capital. Money spent by governments was unproductive. Both doctrines benefited bankers and the wealthy; less affluent folk approved because nothing else had worked, and they wanted to be wealthy too.

In Canada, Pierre Elliott Trudeau had gone to Bonn in 1978 to join a summit with leaders of six other industrialized countries, and there he discovered the new orthodoxy. On his return he scrapped the Anti-Inflation Board, announced cuts in federal spending and programs, and promised tax reductions. Any beneficial effect on the economy and Liberal fortunes was slight. A cluster of by-elections in the fall of 1978 was disastrous for the government. Freed from wage controls, workers discovered that a recession was about to undermine their bargaining power. Canadian industrial incomes, second highest in the world in 1970, placed seventh by 1979 and would be fourteenth by 1982. Inflation had outpaced purchasing power since 1975, but economists insisted that wages had not shrunk enough. True to old orthodoxy, the Bank of Canada returned to tight money. As interest rates rose, Ottawa began borrowing to finance budgets that headed into deep deficit.

Since the war, Canadians had believed that Ottawa could manage the economy effectively if it chose to do so. The ingenious arrangement that allowed Ottawa to collect direct taxes for all but Quebec guaranteed fiscal leverage. That leverage had steadily dwindled. Instead of the 10 per cent of federal income tax revenue they received in 1947, wealthier provinces like Ontario took 44 per cent by 1977. Ottawa now proposed to limit increases in its share of post-secondary education and medicare costs to no more than the increase of the gross national product. Provinces, in return, could spend the money as they chose, setting local standards of health care and education.

Ottawa's fiscal plight was not understood. After modest surpluses turned into an annual deficit of almost $12 billion, the opposition complained of extravagance. Seizing a figure from the air, Joe Clark promised to wipe out sixty thousand government jobs. Homebuyers, he promised, would deduct mortgage payments from their taxable income (a revenue giveaway of $3.5 billion). Ottawa could have eliminated the deficit by cutting its direct spending, leaving $600 million for every federal expense, from the RCMP to lighthouse keepers. Or it could cut statutory programs that in 1978 paid out $14.6 billion to individuals, $10.5 billion to provinces, and $4 billion to businesses.

The problem was not insoluble. In contrast to the hopeless dilemmas facing other nations in a decade of harsh economic shocks, Canadians were as fortunate as they had ever been. Instead, the sour, resentful mood that brought Thatcher and Reagan to power invaded Canada.

A new selfishness was both an echo of liberation and a reaction to its disappointments. Freedom had brought pain and death. Between 1971 and 1978, abortions in Canada doubled. So did murder convictions. Once terrified by the drug culture, parents now worried that offspring would be swept into exotic religious cults. Long-established churches, eager for "relevance" in liturgy and theology, saw the faithful depart for fundamentalist or charismatic sects. A third of all marriages now ended in divorce, and the rate was rising. Victories for feminism in education, politics, and the workplace were undermined by the spread of pornography, sexual assault, and fear of unsafe streets.

Many Canadians found themselves in an amoral wasteland, cool to ideals or ideas. The old puritanism survived, but only when it stayed out of the line of fire. Lotteries, once illegal, became a multi-billion dollar business for governments seeking funds for political favours. Liquor consumption tripled. Montreal and Toronto filled out the seasonal cycle of spectator sports by acquiring major league baseball teams. Ontario politicians, guided by opinion surveys, had banned beer from the ballparks. In 1982, when opinion switched, so did the regulations.

Social commentators spoke of the "me generation," or worried about a selfish narcissism. Pierre Elliott Trudeau might have claimed the credit for such developments. He had written and spoken eloquently of individualism as an ideal higher than tribal or national loyalties. Few Canadians bothered to study his philosophy or to absorb the stoic demands of individual freedom. As in any age, the young wanted dreams greater than themselves, but they could not create them and none were provided. They wanted leadership, too. How badly, they would soon discover.

Outside Quebec, which now marched to a different political rhythm, Canadians were disillusioned by Trudeau and unimpressed by Clark. A pitiless media picked on Clark's appearance, his apparent clumsiness, and his lack of small talk. A world tour became a saga of lost baggage and Clark's inexperience. Tory strategists reprogrammed their leader to avoid "uncontrolled situations." Leadership had decided the 1974 election. Liberals hoped it would work again. When Trudeau called an election for

May 22, 1979, he presented a new image – a statesman, backed by a huge maple leaf flag, addressing high-school students stage-struck with celebrity. Clark spoke only to party faithful, behind an entourage of aides. If leadership had mattered, Ed Broadbent might have won. The latest NDP leader was an autoworker's son, a politics professor who looked like a game prizefighter. Voters liked him but not his socialism. They wanted change and, narrowly, they got it. The Liberals won more votes than the Tories, and they won all but 8 seats in Quebec. Elsewhere, they were trounced. NDP voters stopped a western Tory sweep and a Clark majority. In Canada's thirty-first Parliament, 136 Conservatives faced 114 Liberals, 26 New Democrats, and 6 Créditistes.

Clark had thought hard about being prime minister – perhaps too hard. Despite his efforts to become bilingual, Quebec ignored him, but he appointed Quebec ministers from the Senate. Diefenbaker loyalists were bypassed and the new cabinet was as competent as its Liberal predecessor. Trudeau had filled the civil service with his appointees; some left. Michael Pitfield departed in tears for Harvard; when the deputy minister of finance followed, bureaucratic rumbling stopped the decapitation process. A promise to move Canada's embassy in Israel from Tel Aviv to Jerusalem had not swayed Jewish voters, but it upset Arabs and their Canadian business partners. Robert Stanfield left for the Middle East to save the government's face.

Clark's favourite slogan, "a community of communities," had depicted a Canada free of Liberal-induced regional strife. That seemed easy to achieve. Yukon would become a province. Newfoundland's Tory government would control its offshore oil. Arthur Tremblay, Duplessis's old constitutional adviser, would offer similar wisdom to Clark. The prime minister would not intervene in the forthcoming Quebec referendum.

Energy issues were crucial. Clark had promised to abolish Petro Canada and bargain with Alberta. In power, both promises looked awkward. Eastern Canadians saw Petro Canada as a lonely defender against Arabs and Alberta. Clark and his ministers spent a long summer in interminable strategy sessions, studying their departments, and negotiating, no more successfully than Trudeau, with Alberta's government. His government, Clark explained, would act as though it had a majority. The numbers showed that it did not. Far from a honeymoon with gratified Canadians, polls showed a growing Liberal lead. On November 21, worried Tories relaxed: as expected, Trudeau announced his departure from politics. At sixty, with three motherless children, his political career was over. Delighted Tories surpassed Liberals in their effusive testimonials. As finance minister, John Crosbie made his first budget tougher than planned. Indeed, to the delight of bankers, monetarists, and his own party's noisy right wing, Crosbie revelled in toughness.

The outcome was utterly unexpected. Liberal members adjourned to a Christmas party, acquired substantial courage, and accepted the advice of their house leader, Allan MacEachen, that they should vote with the NDP, beat the government, and win the next election. Equally confident, Clark refused to cultivate Créditiste votes, sailed blithely into defeat, and pledged to repeat Diefenbaker's landslide of 1958. There were two modest differences: Joe Clark was not Diefenbaker, and polls put the leaderless Liberals twenty points ahead.

After waiting a few days to see which Liberals preferred John Turner, his detested rival, Trudeau resumed the leadership. Liberals could almost have campaigned without him. In Ontario, Premier William Davis denounced the Clark government's budget. Alberta's Peter Lougheed was dismissive of his former aide. Canadians would soon discover that Crosbie's eighteen cents per gallon excise tax on gas was modest; in the winter of 1980, Liberals portrayed it as intolerable. From beginning to end, opinion polls remained rocklike. On February 18, Ontario,

Quebec, and Maritime voters restored the Trudeau majority. Before polls closed in Manitoba, the Liberal victory was clear. Trudeau won 147 seats, Clark 103, Broadbent 32. Quebec wiped out the Créditistes and elected one Conservative; the West elected a sole Liberal. The new government had no nationwide mandate.

"Welcome to the eighties," Trudeau greeted his triumphant followers. He had gained a third majority government and he promised it would be his last. At gatherings of world leaders, Trudeau was now a survivor, longer in power than almost anyone. The leader of 1968, contemptuous of pompous diplomats and militarism, had learned painful lessons. Trade ties, not NATO, had forced re-equipment of Canada's forces in Europe. If Canada refused to buy suitable aircraft to patrol her shores or guard her skies, Americans would do it their way. Defence orders were placed, though the top criterion was job creation, not military requirements. In 1969, Trudeau had told Canadians to forget Pearsonian idealism. An older Trudeau had different dreams. In a globe divided between a developed north and a hungry south, Trudeau offered himself and Canada as intermediaries. If Canadians had carried their world responsibilities, the prime minister asked, would they have adopted the mean-minded regionalism of the 1970s?

Trudeau rejected his predecessor's indifference to the Quebec referendum. He sent Jean Chrétien, now the minister of justice, to take charge, because, to Trudeau's dismay, the man who had done more than most to bring down Robert Bourassa was now Liberal leader. Ryan's nationalism and his independence from Ottawa might be an asset against Lévesque, but his alternative to Quebec sovereignty was a feeble federal government controlled by the provinces, with a provincially appointed "federal council" as trustee.

Lévesque's referendum strategy was simple: Quebeckers would see a question to which the only possible answer was yes.

Market testing perfected the wording; would voters give their government a mandate to negotiate sovereignty-association with Ottawa? The outcome would lead to a second referendum. The PQ machine would muster *Yes* supporters; *No* voters would be organized by a coalition in which Liberals would quarrel with lesser allies and the stubborn Ryan would argue with almost everyone.

History is full of surprises. The *No* campaign was smoother and more persuasive than Lévesque expected; the *Yes* campaign was more fervid than planned. Lise Payette, a PQ minister and former broadcaster, provoked women No supporters by naming them "Yvettes," a French-Canadian "goody two-shoes" image. "Yvette" rallies were packed. However ingenious, the wording could not hide the meaning of the vote and no pollster ever found a separatist majority. On May 20, 1980, 88 per cent of Quebeckers voted: 40.5 per cent voted *Yes*; 59.5 per cent voted *No*. Even without solid anglophone opposition, francophones had said no too.

If Quebec voted no, Trudeau and Chrétien promised, the process of constitutional reform would resume. Of course, Quebeckers might believe that the reform would reflect Claude Ryan's desire for a highly decentralized Canada, particularly after his view was echoed in 1979 by the Robarts-Pepin task force. Trudeau had very different ideas. So did most provincial premiers. With Quebec secure, they felt free to demand whatever their province or ego desired. Since unanimity seemed to be the rule, each premier believed he had a veto and few of them liked Pierre Elliott Trudeau. Manitoba's Ed Schreyer had been closest in philosophy, but he was defeated in 1977. In 1978, Trudeau made him governor general. Richard Hatfield, who had made New Brunswick bilingual, and Ontario's William Davis, Tories both, backed Trudeau. Allan Blakeney, Saskatchewan's scholarly NDP premier, was a possible bridge to the region

Trudeau had long ignored. Saskatchewan's attorney general, Roy Romanow, joined Chrétien as cross-Canada negotiator, devising, promoting, and revising a shrinking list of constitutional proposals, but the momentum was gone. A week-long conference in September, televised across Canada, showed that federal-provincial unanimity, so close in 1971, had vanished.

The constitutional issue seemed dead, but Trudeau would not bury it. It was his personal cause, a symbol to mark long and seemingly sterile national leadership. In October 1980, Trudeau surprised the experts. Parliament would act alone on three issues: "patriation" of Canada's constitution, an amending formula, and a Charter of Rights and Freedoms. The Liberal majority guaranteed approval and the British could reject Canada's package at their peril. Hatfield and Davis approved and, after procedural compromises, so did the federal NDP. Eight provinces vociferously disagreed, and Clark prodded a reluctant Tory caucus into opposition. Manitoba and Quebec challenged Trudeau in their courts and lost; Newfoundland's judges ruled differently, forcing the issue to the Supreme Court of Canada.

On September 18, 1981, most of the Supreme Court's nine justices announced that while the government's procedure might be strictly legal, it defied the "conventions" or customs of the past. Provincial unanimity, they added, was not necessary. The "correct" convention was left unexplained since, as a dissenting Chief Justice Bora Laskin noted, it could not be found. The Court had simply revised history.

By the spring of 1981, dissenting premiers (including René Lévesque) offered their own meagre constitutional package, including an amending formula that allowed no province a veto. The proposal soon haunted its authors. After the Supreme Court decision, the NDP demanded a final federal-provincial meeting. Before dawn on November 5, 1981, the logjam broke.

Chrétien, Romanow, and nine premiers found a compromise: Trudeau would have his Charter, the premiers would have their preferred amending formula and the right to opt out of the Charter's less basic provisions.

Asleep in a hotel in Hull, Lévesque was not summoned. Surely he could have no complaints. But he did. Weary but triumphant premiers listened to his fury at their betrayal and his denunciations of the compromise, and ignored him. What politicians forgot was the role of constitutional reform in the Quebec referendum. Instead of feeling integrated, Trudeau's cleverness left many Quebeckers feeling excluded. Canada would have a rambling Charter of Rights to be defined by the judiciary and an amending formula that required unanimity for some changes and a majority of seven provinces with half the population for most others. Last-minute pressure from women, the disabled, and ethnic and native organizations brought revisions, but the debate was over. British politicians wrestled briefly with a residue of colonialism, undeterred by native protesters. The British North America Act was dead; on a cold, rainy April 17, 1982, the queen proclaimed the Constitution Act. Quebec was not represented.

INDIVIDUALISM | 3

The swift Liberal restoration in 1980 left the West deeply dissatisfied. By proclaiming a Trudeau triumph even before prairie votes were counted, electronics aggravated the sense of injury. Having done little but undermine Clark, Alberta's Peter Lougheed now had to disprove the Liberals' boast that they could get more from the West than the Tories. Liberals insisted that the accidents of Middle Eastern politics gave no part of Canada a right to absurdly inflated oil prices. Instead, Trudeau promised tax reforms, economic nationalism, and a comprehensive plan to Canadianize the oil industry. Ten months later, the energy minister, Marc Lalonde, unveiled a National Energy Program (NEP) designed to shrink foreign ownership and achieve Canadian oil self-sufficiency by 1990. Instead of tax incentives, the NEP let Ottawa decide who got money for exploration and how much. In November 1981, major tax reforms formed the centrepiece of Allan MacEachen's first budget as minister of finance.

The timing was not ideal. A decade earlier, Lalonde's NEP might have helped a stagnant, underpriced industry. It could have deterred some of the economic mishaps of the 1970s. If tax loopholes had been plugged in 1971, not 1981, business groups would have moaned as loudly, but Kenneth Carter's royal commission report on taxation had provided the arguments. The 1970s were over. In Washington, Ronald Reagan's administration slashed taxes, not tax breaks. In the halls of Congress, environmentalists scattered before oil company lobbyists. When exploration companies felt unwelcome in Canada, they moved their rigs south. Canadian companies, the intended beneficiaries of the NEP, sank in the undertow of a collapsing Canadian oil industry.

Good times make reform easier; in the early 1980s, times were not good. High interest rates, applied by President Jimmy Carter and intensified under Reagan, drove the United States deep into recession. Canada followed slowly and then plunged deeper than its neighbour. Interest rates reached 17 per cent in 1979. When mortgaged homeowners turned anger into votes, Clark lost. A year later, the prime rate reached 19 per cent. Canadians had always bought cars, refrigerators, and washing machines as well as homes on credit. Now they stopped buying. Farmers made old machinery last another year. The economy slowed; mass layoffs, bankruptcies, and reduced working hours were reminders from the past. By December 1982, close to one and a half million Canadians were hunting for work; many more had abandoned the search.

Canadians might have used post-war prosperity to build a stronger economy to sustain a comfortable standard of living. That was not their choice. Instead, Canada depended on a branch-plant economy with a stake in a continental automotive industry and a role as resource exporter to the world. Prairie farmers profited from poor Soviet and Chinese grain harvests. British Columbia was strip-mined to fuel Japanese industry. Mineral wealth financed imports from the United States.

Canadians who wanted creative challenges could take their talent elsewhere.

By the 1980s, the cost of post-war policies became more apparent, harder to pay, and even harder to avoid. Central Canada's economy faced particular problems. Industries in the St. Lawrence–Great Lakes corridor had thrived on cheap energy, skilled immigrants, and proximity to the industrial heartland of the United States. By the 1980s, energy was expensive, well-trained workers earned more in Europe, and U.S. industry had fled south and west, leaving a "rust belt" of sullen slums and ravaged landscapes. Sulphur dioxide, transformed into acid rain, threatened northern vegetation and freshwater fish.

For a time, the Canadian West grew. In the 1970s, only Alberta and British Columbia gained significant population. Though Toronto had surpassed Montreal as Canada's largest city, Calgary and Edmonton were boomtowns for a decade. Head offices fleeing Montreal for linguistic and political reasons sometimes bypassed Toronto and chose Calgary. Edmonton, metropolis of a newly rich Alberta, acquired the customary attributes of a subway, theatres, major league teams, and a supersized shopping centre, the West Edmonton Mall.

Prosperity made tax reform and the National Energy Policy unwelcome in the West. Lalonde argued that oil companies had a better deal in Canada than in Mexico, Australia, or the North Sea countries, but industry giants removed their rigs. To extract a new price agreement, Lougheed cut oil shipments to the East, but the OPEC cartel had cracked and petroleum prices tumbled. By 1983, the oil boom was a bust. Canadian firms spent billions on remote drilling sites on the Beaufort Sea or off Newfoundland, but the cost of any oil they found far exceeded a falling world price. Costs were human, too. In 1982, the *Ocean Ranger*, an offshore drilling rig, sank with all hands off Newfoundland.

In the 1980s, the average Canadian was older than in any decade since the 1930s. Canadians were also more diverse. In 1978, the Immigration Act finally dropped all racial restrictions. East Indians, Chinese, and West Indians had already joined the population mosaic. In Toronto and Vancouver, "visible minorities" became a collective majority in the twenty-first century. In 1978, for the first time since 1944, an average Canadian lost purchasing power, a trend continued in most ensuing years. A second income cushioned the impact on most families, but in 1990 double-income families were also worse off. Between 1951 and 1981, income distribution between rich and poor had scarcely changed; now, it began to shift slowly in favour of the affluent.

Most Canadians were still richer than their parents, and they enjoyed freedoms their parents had never imagined. More Canadians than ever before attended schools, colleges, and universities. Critics complained that years of schooling grew faster than the growth in learning and ignored the burden on teachers of replacing working parents. And without educational growth, would Canadian music, writing, and theatre have flourished as they did in the 1970s and 1980s – or the legal and accounting professions? Canada's new Charter gave legal substance to claims for greater freedom and individualism. Gays and lesbians challenged prejudice in the 1980s and sought greater action against the AIDS epidemic that initially seemed to target gay men. In 1988, Svend Robinson became the first MP to proclaim his homosexuality. He was re-elected in his Vancouver constituency that year and repeatedly thereafter.

Trudeau and his admirers applied social-scientific logic to most aspects of public policy, from postal administration to labour law, without, however, adding much to the sum of national happiness. The obvious beneficiaries were officials, consultants, and experts in new techniques of information management. The explosion of knowledge opened endless vistas of hope and fear. Like all humanity, Canadians again felt vulnerable to nuclear annihilation as means of mass destruction spread slowly from great powers to mere power-seekers. President Reagan expanded the U.S. war machine and assured Americans that a Strategic Defense Initiative could protect them from missile attack. Some Canadians revived the old campaign for unilateral disarmament, and Trudeau himself acted as an agent of peace and conciliation during a 1983 world tour. Allies received him politely.

At home Canadians were again out of love with Trudeau. The annual federal deficit, born in 1974 but barely noticed until 1979, reached $30 billion in 1982 but did little to curb a recession that left 1.3 million Canadians looking for work. As energy prices tumbled, Alberta and other producing provinces blamed the National Energy Program, not OPEC, for killing their dreams. Others complained that Trudeau was more preoccupied with constitutions and his world image than with the economic well-being of Canadians and their regions. Quebeckers had a further grievance: Trudeau's 1980 pledge to give them an acceptable constitution had resulted in a constitution acceptable to him.

Provincial elections provided a barometer. René Lévesque gained easy re-election in April 1981 on a record of reform and subdued nationalism. Newfoundland's Brian Peckford won a landslide by running against Ottawa. Other provincial premiers followed suit. Saskatchewan Tories flattened Allan Blakeney, partly for being too close to Trudeau on the constitution. Moreover, conservatism flavoured the response to the 1980s recession. Facing a budget crisis, Quebec's Péquiste government cut public salaries in 1982, straining the loyalty of teachers, civil servants, and other PQ militants. Quebec Liberals turned back to a more conservative Robert Bourassa and won a landslide in 1985. American-style neo-conservatism crossed the border:

faced with deficits, governments now cut spending, borrowed, and worried, but they dared not raise revenues to match needs. In British Columbia, Bill Bennett celebrated his 1983 re-election by abolishing the Human Rights Commission and kindred agencies and changed labour laws to undermine the province's union movement. When protesters united in a "Solidarity" movement, pollsters found that most British Columbians favoured Bennett. Union leaders compromised. They had read the public mood. In 1986, Bennett's successor, Bill Vander Zalm, won an increased majority.

To reverse their 1980 humiliation, the Tories chose a fresh face. The decent, luckless Joe Clark had won his leadership review, but he yielded to pressure for a full-scale contest. Brian Mulroney, a Montreal lawyer and corporate executive, had bided his time since 1976, professed loyalty, and discreetly encouraged anti-Clark Tories. On June 11, 1983, Conservative delegates made Mulroney their leader. Born and bred in the little company town of Baie-Comeau, Mulroney was handsome, smooth-tongued, and easily colloquial in French and English. A veteran of backroom politics and a telegenic veteran of a Quebec royal commission into labour racketeering, Mulroney also managed to close down much of the Iron Ore Company of Canada for its American owners without enraging unions or investors. Beyond restoring harmony to the Canadian federation, improving relations with Reagan's White House, and "jobs, jobs, jobs," Mulroney was enigmatic about his priorities. He distanced himself from the francophobia of Manitoba Tories and public-sector bashing by British Columbia's Bill Bennett, and assured anyone who asked that Canada's social programs were "a sacred trust." Tory fortunes rose.

Then, with Trudeau's departure, they plummeted. On February 29, 1984, the prime minister went for a walk in an

Ottawa snowstorm and returned to announce his retirement from public life. Most Liberals had convinced themselves that there could be only one successor, the handsome former finance minister and covert Trudeau critic, John Turner. Though lesser contenders emerged, only the brash populist Jean Chrétien posed a real alternative. On June 16, 1984, Liberal delegates chose Turner; by June 30, he was prime minister.

With Liberals in power, a lead in the polls, and both a royal tour and Canada's first papal visit to add to his profile, Turner was confident of victory. Some backers urged him to take time before calling an election so that voters could see the benefit of his pro-business policies and forget the lavish patronage Trudeau had insisted on for his cronies. Others warned that his majority might drain away. Turner decided to act. Only then did he learn how penniless and disorganized the Liberals were. Years in a Toronto law firm, shooting sly barbs at Trudeau, had eroded his political skills. In a televised debate, Mulroney pinned him with the blame for approving many of Trudeau's recent appointees. "I had no choice," mumbled Turner. His campaign sank.

By autumn, the Tories had a lead in English-speaking Canada, but they expected little from Quebec. Without Trudeau or Chrétien in the race, however, Mulroney had sole claim to be "*un des nôtres.*" Quebec's federal Liberals, discredited by the 1982 constitution, proved helpless. Armed with Mulroney's pledge to "bring Quebec into the Constitution with honour and enthusiasm," Conservative candidates rode a wave. In the West, fears that Mulroney and Turner were "Bobbsey twins" for eastern business helped save the NDP from oblivion. On September 4, 1984, Mulroney swept Canada from coast to coast, nearly matching Diefenbaker's 1958 landslide: 211 Tories to 40 Liberals and 30 New Democrats. More out of pity than conviction, an affluent Vancouver riding allowed Turner the only Liberal seat west of Ontario.

Some Tories claimed a mandate for massive "privatization," downsizing government, deregulation, slashing social programs, even a return to hanging and an end to the metric system. The new finance minister, Michael Wilson, burned with zeal to slash the $30 billion federal deficit. As energy minister, Vancouver's Pat Carney would kill the National Energy Program. A flotilla of "task forces" promised business-pleasing policies for every problem from Indian affairs to unemployment insurance. Mulroney warned civil servants that all they could expect was "a pink slip and running shoes."

In fact, Mulroney was not a right-wing ideologue. His private goal was to be prime minister. A voluble man with an urge to please, Mulroney wanted Tories to supplant the Liberals as Canada's natural governing party. That was why he had culti-vated Quebec. Wilson's plan to cap old-age pension payments was dropped when French-Canadian seniors protested. Business logic would have awarded a billion-dollar aircraft repair con-tract to a Winnipeg firm; political instinct gave it to Montreal. Like Maurice Duplessis, the political idol of his youth, Mulroney believed in gratitude and loyalty. Unlike Duplessis, he cultivated media affection. Ottawa's traditional frugality, forgotten in the Trudeau years, became a more distant memory. The city swarmed with lobbyists, their task made easier because the Tories surrounded their ministers with political staff. Tax changes soon gave the wealthy more to spend. When affluent and influential voters showed no taste for tax increases and little for spending cuts, the deficit issue faded. Most of Wilson's early budget savings were sacrificed in 1985 to compensate depositors in two ill-managed, and worse-regulated, Alberta banks. By the summer of 1986, six ministers in a forty-member cabinet had departed under a shadow of failure or corruption.

"Good relations, super relations with the United States, will be the cornerstone of our foreign policy," Mulroney promised the *Wall Street Journal* in 1984. When Ronald Reagan came to Quebec City in 1985, the two leaders charmed the audience with a joint rendition of "When Irish Eyes Are Smiling." Mulroney sent early signals to Washington that Canada would meet Reagan's elaborate defence expectations. The obsolete DEW line became a modernized North Warning System, the Liberal order for six new patrol frigates was doubled, and Canada's brigade in Germany was reinforced. When a 1987 defence white paper suggested that nuclear-powered navy submarines patrol Canada's Arctic frontier, Pentagon opposition killed the proposal by 1988 and the offending minister was switched to a harmless department.

Mulroney's honeymoon was soon over. As usual, provincial elections set the trend. In 1984, eight of ten provincial governments were Conservative or sympathetic. Ontario's forty-two-year Tory dynasty had survived Diefenbaker but not Mulroney. A belated commitment to full funding for Catholic schools and a rightward tilt by Bill Davis's successor helped topple the Tories, and David Peterson formed a Liberal minority government based on the NDP's more popular policies. Peterson won his own majority in 1987. In Manitoba, Gary Filmon's Tories beat an NDP government in 1986, but ultra-Tory Alberta promptly made the NDP its official opposition. Joe Ghiz's Lebanese roots were no obstacle to a 1986 Liberal revival in Prince Edward Island, and Liberals won every seat in the New Brunswick legislature in 1987, ending Richard Hatfield's seventeen-year rule. Nowhere was Mulroney an issue, but nowhere was he an asset. By 1987, his unpopularity rivalled Trudeau at his lowest.

Good times returned to southern Ontario and Quebec by 1985, though the recession persisted grimly in much of Atlantic Canada and remained as a cruel affront in the recently buoyant West. Ottawa badly needed new ideas.

At the depth of his recession, Trudeau had appointed a royal commission on the economic problems of the Canadian federation headed by his ex-finance minister, Donald S. Macdonald. Academic economists urged an aged nostrum on the commission: free trade with the United States. Only within a guaranteed, protected North American market could Canadian exports compete with the goods and services of European and Asian trading blocs. Since Americans would protect their own shrinking industrial base, Canadians must get inside the U.S. wall or be cut off from the buyer of 80 per cent of their exports.

When Macdonald presented his commission's report to Mulroney in 1985, he provided the Tories with a policy agenda. During his leadership campaign, Mulroney insisted that one item was not on his agenda: free trade. That, he declared had been settled in 1911. As prime minister, Mulroney could change his mind. Finally, with certified Liberal backing, he had a policy. Business elites and the Reagan White House could rejoice.

Once launched, there was no turning back. Ottawa negotiators might have won better terms if Mulroney's desperation for a deal had been less obvious. On September 23, 1987, Canada's tempestuous chief negotiator, Simon Reisman, walked out of the talks. Mulroney promptly used his direct line to the White House. After a few cosmetic concessions, the deal was settled on October 4, 1987. Within ten years, all tariffs would disappear. Americans would have equal access to Canada's natural resources and to financial and other service industries. Breweries and so-called "cultural industries" were protected, but Ottawa buried plans to protect Canada's film industry.

Free trade gave Mulroney an election issue. Was it a vote-getter? Most Canadians were opposed or at least suspicious. Formidable pressure groups, from feminists to trade unionists, lined up against the deal. So did John Turner and the NDP's Ed

Broadbent. However, Mulroney had friends, too. Big business, once solemnly protectionist, wanted bigger markets and a Canada whose unions and social legislation would soon be "harmonized" with Ronald Reagan's America. Once a stronghold of protectionism, Quebec wanted to sell its electricity to the United States, and its opinion-leaders imagined that its new *goût des affaires* would turn the U.S. into Quebec's oyster. Other provinces agreed, with the exception of Liberal Ontario and P.E.I. Special clauses persuaded farmers that their marketing boards were safe, and the sick and elderly that social programs were still "a sacred trust." Even the hesitant wondered what alternatives the anti-free-traders could offer.

By the time Mulroney announced an election for November 8, 1988, his party's coffers were bulging and his popularity was reviving. Quebec's Robert Bourassa was an ally, as were most moderate nationalists. An old friend, Lucien Bouchard, had won a by-election for the Conservatives. Twelve billion dollars in pre-election promises, from daycare to a heavy oil upgrader for Saskatchewan, made friends. So did an apology to Japanese-Canadians for their wartime internment and $21,000 for each survivor. Just before Mulroney called the election, his scandal-plagued Nova Scotia allies narrowly won re-election. Suddenly, being a Conservative was not a liability.

John Turner, in contrast, spent much of the pre-election period avoiding his critics. Canadians opposed to free trade had to choose between a discredited Liberal or an NDP that insisted that other issues mattered too. For a moment in the televised leaders' debate, Turner seized the lead, charging Mulroney with destroying Canada's national identity. Liberal fortunes rose, but the moment passed. By staging the debate early in the campaign, the Tories and business could overcome the setback and win the contest. Turner became a personal target. Simon

Reisman called him a traitor. Mr. Justice Emmett Hall, the former proponent of medicare, was brought from retirement to insist that health insurance was safe.

On November 21, 1988, the Tories won 170 seats with only 43 per cent of the vote, virtually sweeping Quebec. The two main opposing parties won 53 per cent of the vote, but the split gave the Liberals 82 seats and the NDP 43, too few to stop free trade even if both parties had attempted a coalition. Brian Mulroney was the first Conservative prime minister since Sir John A. Macdonald to win back-to-back majorities. He was free to create "the level playing field" of free trade.

Attentive voters could note a Tory promise of a new Goods and Service Tax, a Canadian version of a European-style value-added tax. Set at 7 per cent and covering everything but food, rent, and the cost of financial services, the GST was awkwardly in place by January 1, 1990. It was not welcome, least of all in Alberta, where oil wealth had so far spared residents from any sales tax at all. Alberta anger had lasting consequences. In May 1987, a clutch of disgruntled right-wing westerners met in Winnipeg to create the latest of a long string of protest parties. To lead their new Reform party, they chose Preston Manning, son of a former Alberta Social Credit premier, and a man of evangelical faith and business orthodoxy. Manning lost to Joe Clark in 1988, but the GST was a gift. Rage at the new tax, linked to old anger at bilingualism, bureaucracy, the NEP, the appointed Senate, and a score of regional grievances, brought Reform a hundred thousand members by 1992. Another bonus was Mulroney's attempt to keep his constitutional promise to Quebec.

PAYING THE PRICE | 4

Whatever their reservations about Trudeau's actual policies, many Canadians were captivated by his vehicle for a single national citizenship. The Charter of Rights and Freedoms promised that, as Canadians, they enjoyed individual rights rather than privileges due to their collective political influence. Once their new constitution and Charter were ratified in 1982, Canadians soon began testing its limits. Judges, many of them appointees from the Trudeau years, proved eager to use their new powers, striking down criminal sanctions against abortion, upholding francophone rights in Alberta and Saskatchewan and anglophone rights in Quebec, and even lifting a ban on appearing topless in public. Courts gave generous significance to the 1982 constitution's commitment to "aboriginal rights." A "notwithstanding" clause allowed governments to suspend judgements for a few years, but only Quebec used the clause widely, and its citizens could turn to Quebec's own charter.

Trudeau hoped to transcend the narrow defensiveness of groups and regions by what some called "Charter nationalism."

He was most successful in the West, where his other policies had little impact. No region was more ethnically mixed, none had welcomed John Diefenbaker's vision of "unhyphenated Canadians" more, and none had less allegiance to old ideas about Canada. On the other hand, Trudeau largely failed with his fellow Quebeckers. His Quebec caucus had supported his vision, but Quebec's national assembly had voted unanimously in opposition. For over a century, Quebeckers had idealized their relationship with Canada as a partnership: the "compact" of Confederation gave them an equal voice with the majority. The idea was almost unknown in the rest of Canada and ridiculed by most historians and lawyers, but in Quebec it was the prevailing orthodoxy. Sovereignists insisted that the compact had been irreparably broken; Quebec federalists insisted that it could be re-established.

The constitutional compromise with aboriginal peoples gave them a special status Trudeau had denied to French Canadians. Whatever "aboriginal rights" meant to the colonizing majority, to aboriginal leaders the words meant that the lands and sovereignty of the original inhabitants of Canada were intact. Driven to the margins of Canadian society and at times close to extinction, natives found in the new constitution the exciting prospect of exercising power alongside the invaders. Soon they identified themselves as "First Nations," with full implications of self-governing sovereignty.

Trudeau insisted that Quebec would accept Canada's new constitution; Mulroney believed otherwise. In 1984, Robert Bourassa's Liberals joined sovereignists to sweep Trudeau MPs from Quebec's francophone constituencies. Mulroney's constitutional pledge, drafted by Lucien Bouchard, had made the difference. Once Bourassa regained power in 1986, Mulroney could complete what he and most Quebeckers saw as unfinished constitutional business. After marathon sessions at the government's Meech Lake conference centre, Mulroney and ten premiers reached agreement on April 30, 1987. After more changes and an Ottawa meeting on June 3, Mulroney kept his 1984 promise. Mulroney and the premiers accepted what Trudeau had refused: in a "Meech Lake Accord," senators and Supreme Court justices would be chosen from provincial nominees; "major" constitutional amendments would need provincial unanimity; provinces that opted out of federal programs in health, education, welfare, and other provincial domains could claim full compensation; and Quebec would be recognized as a "distinct society."

Supporters saw the accord as a milestone; to a growing number of critics, it undermined their view of Canada. Supporters assumed that the three-year wait imposed by the 1982 amending formula was a formality. They were wrong. Trudeau denounced the accord as a sellout to the provinces and to separatists. Parti Québécois leaders agreed that they must kill the accord or be killed by it. Natives were angry that governments could agree on Quebec's demands but not on theirs. Interest groups, from feminists to the disabled, complained that there was nothing in the accord for them.

Opponents of the accord benefited from post-1988 hostility to Mulroney. The free-trade election left scars among Canadian nationalists, including outrage that Quebec nationalists had backed the deal enthusiastically. The new Goods and Services Tax (GST), made even more enemies, especially after Mulroney used a little-known constitutional procedure to appoint enough senators to overcome Liberal appointees. By 1990, free trade coincided with a harsh new recession. Almost a million Canadians saw their well-paid factory jobs disappear. Mulroney was to blame. If the prime minister favoured the Meech Lake Accord, many reasoned, it must be bad. Those who read the accord could expect weaker central government, more powerful provinces, and an undefined "special status" for Quebec. In 1988, Bourassa gave a troubling meaning to that status. In his 1986 campaign he had promised to modify Bill 101, to allow more English. Assailed by language crusaders, Bourassa retreated. Outside Quebec, most Canadians had ignored Bill 101; now they were affronted. Why bother with French immersion at school and bilingual signs at the airport if Quebec played by different rules? Bourassa's answer was unapologetic: "*Deux poids et deux mesures.*" Preserving French was vital to Quebec; in the other provinces, it was merely beneficial. If that was what "distinct society" meant, many Canadians were angered by it.

The Meech Lake Accord was in trouble. Frank McKenna, the new premier of officially bilingual New Brunswick, demanded that the deal be reopened. Manitoba's new Tory premier, Gary Filmon, was uncomfortable. Newfoundland voted Liberal in 1989, and the new premier, Clyde Wells, a former Trudeau aide and a believer in Charter nationalism, told his legislature to reject the accord. As the ratification deadline of June 28, 1990, approached, Meech Lake was not an accord but a problem. Beset by nationalists in his caucus and by Jacques Parizeau of the PQ, Bourassa would not budge. Mulroney sent a junior minister, Jean Charest, to seek compromises. His old friend and Quebec lieutenant, Lucien Bouchard, called the prime minister a traitor, quit, and became leader of a handful of indignant Liberal and Tory Quebec MPs who formed the Bloc Québécois. If Canada could not accept Meech, he claimed, Quebec sovereignty was inevitable and even overdue.

A seasoned labour negotiator, Mulroney kept trying. On June 3, he summoned premiers and territorial leaders to dinner. The few hours turned into a week of meetings. At one point Alberta's premier, Don Getty, a former football player, rose to stop Clyde Wells from leaving. Bourassa once withdrew in despair. Somehow Mulroney kept the sessions going until, near midnight on June 9, a complex parallel agreement was announced to a national television audience.

Was the accord saved? It seemed so. Then the *Globe and Mail* printed a self-serving interview with the prime minister. He had "rolled the dice," boasted Mulroney, and the premiers had lost. Insulted and angry, Clyde Wells withdrew his grudging consent. Newfoundland's House of Assembly would vote, but his position would be clear. A speech by Mulroney made no difference. Manitoba's three party leaders accepted the compromise but found solid hostility back home. Elijah Harper, a Cree member of the legislature, saved them. Claiming that the accord slighted aboriginal rights, Harper tied up the legislature until a pre-arranged adjournment on June 22. The Meech Lake deadline was June 23. His allies boasted that a Cree had killed the Meech Lake Accord: never again could the First Nations be overlooked. Others grumbled that he had also killed Canada's tradition of compromise.

Many celebrated the defeat. Feminists denounced constitution-making by "eleven middle-class men in suits." In September 1990, the NDP's Bob Rae defeated Ontario premier David Peterson. While Ontario's acute recession was a key reason, Peterson's efforts on behalf of the Meech Lake Accord had made enemies. Western fury at Meech added support for Preston Manning's Reform party. English-speaking indignation at the accord was matched by Quebec fury at its rejection. Having described the deal as a betrayal, sovereignists switched sides to portray its fate as a fresh humiliation. Support for independence soared to 60 per cent. Parizeau congratulated separatists on the "serene certainty" that independence was now inevitable. Bourassa declared that he would never again meet with other premiers. Instead, a commission jointly chaired by prominent businessmen Jean Campeau, a sovereignist, and federalist Michel Bélanger would advise Quebeckers on their future.

Quebeckers were less serene about another Meech Lake aftermath that summer. Elijah Harper had forced Canadians to heed aboriginal concerns; so did Mohawk communities near Montreal. During the spring, a violent dispute over gambling shattered the peace of Akwasasne, a Mohawk reserve that straddled the borders of Quebec, Ontario, and New York State. Across the Ottawa River, near Oka, armed Mohawks built a roadblock as part of a campaign to regain lands granted after the American Revolution. After months of legal wrangling, on July 11, Quebec police attacked the barricade. A police officer died in a fusillade; his comrades fled. At Kahnewake, opposite Montreal, other Mohawks blockaded a bridge and closed a major commuter route across the St. Lawrence. That summer, natives across Canada blocked roads and rail lines and toppled an occasional hydro pylon, but it was events in Montreal that gave television a summer-long focus. The dispute fed on constitutional issues: Indian affairs were federal; law and order was provincial. The Mohawks spoke English and won sympathy from journalists and civil libertarians outside Quebec; their angry neighbours spoke French. After Bourassa asked for troops, soldiers and equipment from Valcartier and Gagetown camped for a month at Oka and Kahnewake. With patience developed in peacekeeping, soldiers slowly pushed the natives back. After some tense moments, resistance folded on September 25.

To clarify issues that had become dense and urgent, the government appointed a royal commission jointly chaired by Georges Erasmus, grand chief of the Assembly of First Nations, and Quebec judge René Dussault. Despite ample evidence of a tragic relationship between natives and Canadians, most people lost interest. Like Meech Lake, Oka was a local distraction from the increasingly brutal struggle to earn a living in a drastically altered world.

The 1989 collapse of the Berlin Wall heralded the sudden,

unpredicted end of the Cold War. In 1987, a defence white paper had demanded a major effort to arm Canada against Soviet military threats; now abruptly the Soviet regime ended. From the Baltic to central Asia, satellites and Soviet republics overthrew Communist dictatorships, proclaimed independence, and professed devotion to democracy and free enterprise. Had a new world order begun? Was capitalism triumphant or merely less exhausted than its rival? One answer came when Iraq, backed alternately by East and West in its aggression against Iran, suddenly seized its oil-rich neighbour, Kuwait. With a deference to the White House that some critics condemned, Mulroney despatched a destroyer, an elderly frigate, and a supply ship to the Gulf, later followed by a squadron of CF-18s. After a few weeks of bombing and a few days of ground fighting, the Gulf War ended in late February 1991. The former rulers returned to a devastated Kuwait. By April 1991, when its ships and aircraft had come home, Canada's fifth war in the century had been its least bloody: not one Canadian had died, though some carried the symptoms of a debilitating "Gulf War syndrome."

More trouble followed. Yugoslavia, a mountainous Balkan federation that had maintained a precarious neutrality during the Cold War, shattered along ethnic lines in 1991. Amidst the televised horrors of civil war, soldiers from Canada's NATO contingent negotiated truces and blocked contending killers in Croatia and later in Bosnia-Herzegovina. Thousands of young Canadians endured the crossfire of ethnic slaughter as both the UN Security Council and European powers argued over what might be done. Canadian peacekeepers flew to Cambodia, Namibia, Central America, and Haiti to help bring peace, manage elections, and train civil police.

In Somalia, warring militias killed aid workers, stole food, and left the population to starve. Television forced the United States to intervene. Canada dutifully followed, though Ottawa insisted that its mission was "peacekeeping." A Canadian air-borne unit, trained to be tough and ruthless, occupied Belet Huen, guarded its perimeter, and shot intruders. Some soldiers tortured and killed a teenaged Somali thief, while a soldier's video camera recorded the crime. Canadians were appalled. The search for scapegoats climbed the heights of a military hierar-chy that had certainly resisted sharing horrifying news. Soon after, in Rwanda, the Canadian UN commander, Major-General Roméo Dallaire, sent desperate early warning of Hutu genocide against the Tutsi minority. The response was feeble. After Somalia, peacekeeping had lost its attraction. Only after eight hundred thousand died were significant forces sent to Rwanda.

Recession interfered with idealism. Between 1990 and 1992, three hundred thousand manufacturing jobs vanished in Ontario alone. Experts blamed an underperforming economy, high taxes, and low productivity. Like the Great Depression, the 1990s recession was part of a predictable boom-bust cycle, weighted by wild speculation, corporate greed, and business myopia. A speculative fever in the 1980s had allowed solid com-panies to be purchased, plundered of capital, and left vulnera-ble to global competition and the costly changes of a digital world. As the recession deepened, long-established companies collapsed, merged, or endured drastic "downsizing," emptying whole floors of computer-literate information handlers.

In Toronto, Vancouver, and other large cities, property values had soared in the 1980s. Now they tumbled, taking the develop-ment and construction industries with them, and leaving banks and trust companies dangerously exposed. In the 1980s, ques-tioning the real value of Paul and Albert Reichmann's world-wide property developments had risked lawsuits; the recession wiped out their Olympia & York holdings. Quebec's confidence in its new business acumen survived the collapse of company acquisitor Robert Campeau – he was from Sudbury, after all –

but such erstwhile powerhouses as Provigo, a supermarket
chain, and Lavalin, a multinational engineering giant, had to be
rescued by the province's huge pension-based investment fund,
the Caisse de dépôt. Interest rates fell, inflation faded, and
unemployment killed consumer spending. Shops began Boxing
Day sales before Christmas. Huge warehouse stores, branches of
American parent companies, opened in the suburbs and
emptied malls of customers. Long-established retail chains
sagged into liquidation. Woodward's and, in 1999, Eaton's
massive department-store chains died.

Resource industries were in trouble too. Years of overfishing
off the Atlantic coast by domestic and foreign fleets, com-
pounded by changes in water temperature, reduced fish stocks,
perhaps beyond recovery. Years of warnings by scientists,
denials by the industry and its workers, and political evasion
meant that Canada had to ban most offshore fishing, beginning
with Newfoundland's northern cod and soon extending to the
entire Atlantic coast. Not only the economic staple of the region
but also a way of life, fishing was over for hundreds of communities for a decade, perhaps forever. Soon, the Pacific faced a
similar fate as salmon stocks dwindled. Meanwhile, prairie
wheat growers watched prices fall below the cost of production
in the early 1990s. The U.S. and the European Community could
afford the subsidies of a grain price war; Canada could not.
Supply management agreements, exempted from the Canada-
U.S. free trade pact, were threatened by the World Trade
Organization. Egg, poultry, and dairy producers, chiefly in
Quebec and Ontario, faced ruinous competition, which only
huge corporate production units could survive.

In the 1930s, John Maynard Keynes had urged governments
to spur the economy by spending and to tax and save in periods
of prosperity. But when was Canada so completely prosperous
that it could impose a cycle of saving? Even wealthy provinces

had hinterlands where jobs were scarce and incomes low. Had the economy of Atlantic Canada ever "overheated"? In the prosperous 1980s, government deficits had deepened because Canadians insisted on benefits and services but resented paying for them. When employers and payrolls vanished, so did tax revenues. The 1990 GST replaced a higher but hidden manufacturers' sales tax, but it hit a larger range of products and services, depressing the economy at a time when it needed stimulus.

Neo-conservatives insisted that Keynes was wrong: the state had no role in economic management. Individuals, not governments, should save or spend. John Crow, governor of the Bank of Canada, insisted that inflation and excessive public debt were bigger problems for Canada than a short-lived recession. Most politicians and even many voters agreed. After Keynesian stimulation sent Ontario's deficit soaring, Bob Rae forced his NDP government to cut public spending. As deficits continued, Rae enraged his union allies by imposing wage cuts and unpaid holidays as an alternative to layoffs. A labour movement dominated by public-sector unions turned its back on its party, and Rae's government would go down to defeat in 1995. In Saskatchewan, it was Conservatives who had brought the province close to ruin. Elected in 1991, the NDP's Roy Romanow inherited the heaviest per capita debt load of any province. His cuts included many small but cherished local hospitals. British Columbia's Asian markets spared it most of the recession. Fed up with Bill Vander Zalm's mingling of personal and public business, voters took another chance on the NDP. Premier Mike Harcourt faced a bruising struggle for compromise between the province's most profitable industry and its powerful environmental movement, notably over logging of "old-growth" forests. British Columbia remained Canada's most prosperous, fastest-growing province until Asian economic problems hit in the late 1990s, but the NDP steadily lost friends.

Tough times meant unpopular choices, disillusionment with politicians, and reduced faith in government. That was certainly Brian Mulroney's conclusion as he headed into 1992, a possible election year. Never had pollsters found a more unpopular prime minister. The third year of recession and of dropping real incomes, the GST, and the elimination or privatization of public enterprises from Canada Post to Air Canada had made him few friends. Family allowances, born in 1945, died in 1992 in favour of a tax credit supposedly targeted at the needy. The 1988 promise of a national daycare system was formally scrapped. Child poverty grew.

Helpless to end the recession or to relieve regional miseries, Ottawa went back to the constitution. It had little choice. Quebec's Bélanger-Campeau commission had agreed on very little, but it advised Bourassa to set October 26, 1992, as the deadline for a referendum on whatever constitution Canada offered. And there was no offer. Shaping one seemed impossible.

A government task force sent to take the national pulse found Canadians united chiefly in their distaste for politicians and their reluctance to "kowtow" to Quebec. Elijah Harper had ensured that the First Nations would be consulted, but they came in four competing groups: "status" and "non-status" Indians (those who lived on and off reserves), Métis, and Inuit. The territories had to be included, but Quebec refused to be part of any negotiations until the rest of Canada recognized that Quebec was not a province like the others. Two provinces, British Columbia and Alberta, now required province-wide referenda to approve any constitutional amendment. They also insisted on a "Triple-E Senate" – elected, equal, and effective. Instead of a quarter of the Senate seats, Quebec or Ontario would have no more than Prince Edward Island, and the new senators would be much more powerful. Native leaders insisted that any new constitution must recognize their "inherent" – and hence

undebatable – right of self-government. Provinces, though not
necessarily their citizens, demanded transfer of federal powers.

For six months, committees struggled to produce an acceptable package. Mulroney put Joe Clark in charge of gaining consensus from nine premiers, two territorial leaders, four
aboriginal groups, a host of pressure groups demanding a place
or at least influence, plus Quebec, eloquent in its absence. To
give himself leverage, Mulroney adopted referendum legislation. He now hoped that the provinces would deadlock. Then he
could devise a package acceptable to Quebec, wage a referendum campaign with or without the premiers, and offer himself
in this third federal election as a national saviour. To Mulroney's
dismay, Clark proudly announced a consensus. In return for an
equal, elected, but less-effective Senate, and more seats in the
House of Commons for bigger provinces, Ontario's Bob Rae
had persuaded western provinces to accept aboriginal demands.
All agreed to entrench their commitment to social programs.
Even Clyde Wells accepted that Quebec was a distinct society.
For his efforts, Clark got a scolding from the prime minister for
allowing an agreement to form that Quebec would find hard to
swallow. However, Robert Bourassa joined the discussions,
more intense negotiation ensued, and a largely symbolic visit
to the "Cradle of Confederation" on August 28 led to the
Charlottetown Accord.

Those enmeshed in the process shared a miraculous mani-
festation of the spirit of compromise Canadians preached to a
conflict-strewn world. A "Canada clause" would remind judges
that Quebec's distinctiveness, the Charter, linguistic duality,
social justice, and regional redistribution would all be part of
the national fabric. A Triple-E Senate, with power over key
federal appointments, resource taxes, language, and culture,
would be balanced by a larger House of Commons in which
Quebec, thanks to deft wording by Saskatchewan's Roy

Romanow, would always have a quarter of the seats (about its normal share). Aboriginals could thank themselves and Bob Rae for inclusion of their "inherent right to self-government." Scores of issues were settled in a document that, in its final version, was as thick as a small telephone book.

This was Canada's proposal. Quebeckers would decide its fate on October 26. And so would the rest of Canada. Using his new referendum law, Mulroney could satisfy the widespread demand for individual participation. Those who supported the Charlottetown Accord, or rejoiced at a seeming nation-saving compromise, or even liked one or more of the provisions, could vote Yes. They included every premier, three national parties, business and labour leaders, and most newspaper editors. On the other side, Quebec's Lucien Bouchard and Jacques Parizeau insisted that the accord offered too little. After some hesitation, Reform's Preston Manning decided that the accord gave Quebec too much. Aboriginal groups, promised much in the accord, split when dissidents demanded more. Pierre Elliott Trudeau emerged to offer a thunderous denunciation of those who would wreck his handiwork. Charter nationalists responded. Opposition was reinforced by a host of Canadians who resented all that had befallen them in the Mulroney years, from the GST to the recession. September polls suggested that the new accord could win even Quebec; by October 26, support had collapsed. Only Newfoundland, Prince Edward Island, New Brunswick, and, by the narrowest margin, Ontario voted Yes. Six provinces, both territories, and 54 per cent of Canadians voted No. Commentators identified the outcome as a rebellion against elites. In Quebec, support for independence rose; outside, most politicians agreed that it would be suicide to discuss the constitution for a long time to come.

Despite record unpopularity, Mulroney believed he could win another election. He regularly reminded his loyal caucus that he had survived the depths of 1987. Recession would not last forever; indeed, early in 1993, officials announced it was over. Completing Reagan's 1980 vision of a three-nation North American Free Trade Agreement (NAFTA) promised the Tories a winning argument with business backers: new markets, cheap labour, and minimal environmental standards. A divided opposition would do the rest. In 1990 the NDP chose Yukon MP Audrey McLaughlin as Canada's first female federal party leader. Later that year, the Liberals chose Jean Chrétien. The media dubbed him "yesterday's man," and Quebeckers remembered the man who echoed Trudeau on the Meech Lake Accord. Right-wing Liberals, mindful of business, had favoured Paul Martin, a corporate executive whose loyalty to his father's memory did not stretch to social reform.

Tories agreed they could win, though not with Mulroney. After lavish patronage for his friends, a mawkish farewell tour of world capitals, and a delay to make sure Joe Clark quit first, Mulroney announced his retirement on February 24, 1993. "This is a beautiful view," he told reporters at his residence on Sussex Drive, "but it ain't free." With 3082 days in office, Brian Mulroney had outlasted all but four Canadian prime ministers. He had forced through free trade with the United States, slashed the civil service, employed his friends, won admiration in Africa by opposing apartheid, and doubled the national debt.

When prominent Tory lieutenants announced their departure, the leadership seemed destined for a forty-five-year-old Vancouver woman Mulroney had appointed as defence minister only weeks earlier. Kim Campbell was attractive because she was much that Mulroney was not: a westerner, twice divorced, witty, a newcomer elected in 1988, untied to Tory old-boy networks. It was not clear that Campbell had many friends, but she suddenly had a bandwagon with hundreds of ambitious Tories clambering aboard. The media and some Tories had second thoughts. Jean

Charest, an impeccably bilingual environment minister from Sherbrooke, was the beneficiary. But he came too late. On June 13, 1993, Campbell took the Tory leadership on the second ballot, and on June 25 she became Canada's nineteenth prime minister.

Like Trudeau in 1984, Mulroney gave his successor little time to get known. Unlike Turner, Campbell took all the time she could, with a summer of friendly cross-country travel, handing out promises as she went. The deficit would vanish in five years, with no cuts to social programs. As defence minister, she had approved the purchase of a sophisticated helicopter; to win votes, she cut the order. If Quebec wanted to run job training, it could have the money, too. Campbell's summer almost put her ahead of the Liberals. Tory hopes rose. With twenty-four parties in the race, five of them serious contenders, a good campaign could make all the difference. In Alberta that fall, a new leader, Ralph Klein, rescued Don Getty's moribund Tories and almost wiped out the opposition.

Canada was not Alberta. The Tory campaign was not effective. Campbell's admission that she could not overcome serious unemployment much before the year 2000 was true, but her offhand manner suggested that it did not matter very much. A Tory ad focusing on Chrétien's facial paralysis, the legacy of a childhood disease, backfired. Instead, the Liberal leader issued, and then ignored, a "red book" full of pledges, promised "jobs, jobs, jobs," and benefited from low expectations. The hated GST would be replaced; Canadians would keep their endangered health and social programs. Long before 1993, support for McLaughlin's NDP had sunk to a miserable 7 per cent. It never rose. Preston Manning's Reform party spread from the West and split votes in rural and small-town Ontario, while Lucien Bouchard's Bloc Québécois simply absorbed Mulroney's former Quebec voters. A week before election day, the outcome was obvious. It also seemed impossible.

On October 25, the Tories elected only two members (one of them Jean Charest). The NDP saved 9 of the 43 seats it held at dissolution. Liberals swept the Maritimes, took 98 of Ontario's 99 seats, and won a generous scattering of western ridings. Chrétien's 177 seats made him prime minister. With 51 seats from the West and one from Ontario, Preston Manning's Reform became a major party, while Lucien Bouchard's 54 Quebec seats made a sovereignist leader of Her Majesty's Official Opposition. It was not his intention to live in the official residence, explained Bouchard; he did not intend to stay in Ottawa long.

The Liberals swept into office like new brooms. Chrétien allowed only twenty-three ministers; each would have five aides, not the twenty allotted in the Mulroney era. Jocelyn Bourgon replaced the short-tempered and pro-business Glen Shortliffe as top civil servant. A $500 million deal to privatize Toronto's Pearson International Airport, signed two weeks before the election, was cancelled. The principals had included former Tory fundraiser Don Matthews. Exasperated by Tory patronage, most people applauded, though the courts forced generous compensation.

Chrétien soon reported that the Tories had left him a $40 billion deficit, 1.4 million unemployed, and a major recession. Deficit-cutting would be his government's sole preoccupation in the first term. Finance Minister Paul Martin, Jr., would pay the price in popularity, but both men were as fiscally conservative as self-made millionaires usually are. Both realized that middle-class Canadians wanted national finances balanced by any means short of higher taxes. If the poor complained, the NDP, like the Tories, now lacked enough seats to be an official party. Slashing public spending would rob Manning of his best issue, and other Reform policies would look extreme.

As for Liberal promises, who could deny that circumstances had changed? National daycare, the elimination of the GST, home care for the sick, and stable funding for the CBC were ideas from another day. Cheap promises could be kept. A judge, a journalist, and a militia colonel investigated the Somalia scandal and, soon after, the suspected cover-ups. Indian affairs minister Ron Irwin declared that Canada would give natives full authority over their affairs, starting in Manitoba. Claims that the Red Cross had distributed blood contaminated with HIV in the mid-1980s were handed to a royal commission to investigate. Many Canadians wanted tighter control of firearms. There were many horrible stories of crimes involving guns, but the worst was the slaughter of fourteen women students by an anti-feminist gunman at Montreal's École Polytechnique in 1990. Justice Minister Allan Rock would deliver.

At a newly named Department of Foreign Affairs and International Trade (DFAIT), André Ouellet's priority was creating jobs. High-profile trade promotion justified a series of "Team Canada" excursions, in which the prime minister led provincial premiers and business executives on tours of Asia and Latin America. Meanwhile, American sympathy for Ottawa in the Quebec-Canada debate was not to be jeopardized by any needless national assertion. When they found the Americans planning bilateral trade deals with other western-hemisphere countries, the Liberals promptly embraced the Reagan-Mulroney notion of a three-nation North American Free Trade Agreement with Mexico.

At Marrakesh on April 15, 1994, Canada helped replace the post-war General Agreement on Tariffs and Trade (GATT) with a 131-member World Trade Organization (WTO), with expanded powers to end dumping and subsidies and enhance "fair trade." Canada promptly joined the United States in challenging a European Union ban on cattle raised with growth hormones. Better known were WTO rulings against Canada's protection of its domestic magazines, and a 1999 decision condemning the 1965 Canada-U.S. Auto Pact.

Not all disputes went to formal tribunals. Faced with evidence of Spanish overfishing on the Grand Banks, fisheries minister Brian Tobin had the trawler *Estai* seized and hauled into St. John's. Spain threatened gunboats; the European Union, sweeping trade sanctions. Tobin displayed the illegal Spanish nets to New York media, and a Canadian submarine discreetly went out to await Spain's navy. However embarrassing to diplomats, Tobin's war "to save the last lonely turbot, clinging to the Grand Banks by its fingernails," gave unholy joy to Canada's Peaceable Kingdom. There were no such victories when Americans insisted that salmon spawned in British Columbia waters were theirs for the taking.

Over time, even cheap initiatives exact a price. The tainted-blood inquiry lasted for almost four years while victims died. Opponents of gun registration, backed by the U.S. National Rifle Association, won western, rural, and aboriginal support. Allegations, shared with Swiss authorities, that Mulroney had dealt with a German "fixer" forced the government to apologize and compensate the former prime minister. The Somalia inquiry embarrassed Liberals more than Tories, cost the defence minister and the chief of defence staff their jobs, and was wound up in 1996 after seeking further extensions. Robbed of a daily circus, the media protested. Meanwhile, underpaid, poorly housed service members confessed that they frequented food banks and delivered pizza to support their families. Not surprisingly, the military failed a Charter-based requirement to recruit women for 20 per cent of its combat positions. A new defence chief promised to do more, though by the late 1990s fit young women and men could easily find better-paid work.

The deficit remained Chrétien's cornerstone issue. In his 1994 and 1995 budgets, the finance minister, Paul Martin, broke with the tradition his own father had helped establish forty years before. Martin squeezed benefits from affluent pensioners and, despite the recession, cut unemployment benefits and made them harder to get. The chronically unemployed, living most of the year on a few months' work, got training, counselling, or just a rude shock. By 1996, the UI commission had a new name – Employment Insurance (EI) – and a new role: turning payroll taxes from workers and employers into a rich income source for Martin's budget-balancing. Martin forced privatization of Canadian National Railways, Petro Canada, and airports and their traffic-control systems, shut down military bases, and closed two of three military colleges.

The finance minister's biggest target was transfers to provinces for such Liberal-inspired policies as medicare and the Canada Assistance Plan, each of which fostered nationwide standards. Having rolled the transfers into a single Canada Health and Social Transfer, Martin used his 1995 budget to cut $4.2 billion from annual payments to the provinces. The provinces scrambled to cut costs, raged at Ottawa, and warned that national standards would shatter. Since provinces had seldom shared credit with Ottawa for funding programs, could they blame the federal government for cuts? Provincial politicians did their best.

When Ontario's NDP protected public-sector jobs and sustained welfare benefits that experts insisted were already too low, it plummeted in the polls. A June 1995 provincial election bypassed the Liberals and gave Tory leader Mike Harris 85 of 125 seats. Harris's "Common Sense Revolution" promised wholesale neo-conservatism: a 30 per cent cut in income tax, forced labour for welfare recipients, a shrunken government, privatization, landlord power, employer-friendly labour laws – but no cuts to health care. Guided by a coterie of young ideologues, Harris closed or merged hospitals, cut grants to schools, colleges, and universities, and reduced welfare benefits by 22 per cent. The Tories transferred responsibility for welfare to municipal government, gutted school boards and gave their powers to the province, rewrote school curricula, and prepared Ontario Hydro for privatization. Storms of protest erupted and dissipated, and Harris won easy re-election in 1999. If prosperity and tax cuts continued, insiders boasted, the Tories could run Ontario for another forty years. And why not? Canadians wanted balanced budgets and lower taxes. Most were healthy, employed, and long past paying tuition fees.

Pressed by federal cuts and their own shrinking revenues, almost every province tried some neo-conservative policies, whether the government was NDP (in Saskatchewan and Manitoba), Conservative (in Alberta and Saskatchewan), or alternating Liberal or Tory (in most of Atlantic Canada). They closed hospitals, cut convalescent care, and slashed welfare rates below levels already condemned as inadequate. Most cut support to colleges and universities, let tuition fees rise, and told university students who couldn't pay to borrow the money. Experienced teachers and nurses took early retirement and governments sought cheaper replacements. Classes were crowded; weaker students got shorter shrift. Post-secondary students carried bigger debts when they graduated, and many feared that they would never earn enough to pay them off. Governments closed offices, fired employees, and responded to business complaints with deregulation. Opinion leaders argued that Canada had not gone half as far as it must. If unemployment was twice the American rate, surely it was because government handouts were still too generous.

After the deficit, Chrétien's second preoccupation was Quebec. Never before 1993 had the province rejected one of its own. The Bloc's success in Quebec preceded a PQ victory in the next provincial election. Mortally ill from cancer, Bourassa retired early in 1994. His successor as head of the Quebec Liberals, Daniel Johnson, was a son of the former premier and brother of Lévesque's successor as PQ leader. His popularity had been exhausted by years as finance minister and the September 12 election was predictable: Jacques Parizeau won 77 seats to the Liberals' 47. Did the popular vote prefigure a referendum result? The PQ gained 44.7 per cent, with 44.3 per cent for Johnson. Eight per cent supported the soft-sovereignist Action Démocratique.

A *pur et dur* separatist, Parizeau set himself to prepare a province-wide vote. In October, his charismatic rival, Lucien Bouchard, almost succumbed to a severe bacterial infection. He survived, albeit without a leg, after all Quebec prayed for his life. Bouchard favoured caution; Parizeau charged ahead. Special commissions toured Quebec's regions to prepare the way. To Parizeau's dismay, they came back with grievances about roads and local government. Parizeau's budget warned of higher taxes if Quebec voted No. Optimistic studies of post-sovereignty Quebec appeared; others were suppressed for "bad methodology." In June, Parizeau reluctantly involved Bouchard and Action Démocratique's young leader, Mario Dumont. Quebeckers would vote on sovereignty, they agreed, but only after a year of trying to get equal partnership with Canada. A new referendum question emerged:

> Do you agree that Quebec should become sovereign, after having made a formal offer to Canada for a new economic and political partnership, within the scope of the bill respecting the future of Quebec and of the agreement signed on June 12, 1995?

Once they had voted Yes, Parizeau told diplomats, Quebeckers would be like lobsters in a trap, compelled to suffer the heat. Privately, colleagues pleaded with Parizeau to stop; polls showed 40 per cent support for separation and not much more for the softer notion of "sovereignty." "Monsieur" was unmoved. The campaign opened in August in Bouchard's hometown of Alma. In early September, Gilles Vigneault and Marie Laberge read an emotional prologue claiming to harvest "the fields of history." The No side had less to say. Unable to promise much after Meech and Charlottetown, federalists could only warn of chaos. The Yes side began growing. It spurted in October when, with obvious reluctance, Parizeau invited Bouchard to be Quebec's negotiator with Canada and a full referendum campaigner. Jettisoning old scripts, Bouchard claimed that after a Yes vote, Canadians would come on their knees to make a deal with Quebec. Quebec had enough Canadian dollars to control their value. Above all, Quebeckers must vote with pride, not fear.

Ottawa's polls now predicted trouble. Five days before the vote, flanked by Daniel Johnson and Tory leader Jean Charest, the prime minister intervened. In a Verdun arena, Chrétien promised to fight for the changes Quebec had lost in 1990 and 1992. Polls showed a No revival until "the rest of Canada" finally got involved. A mass rally in Montreal on October 27, packed by people from English-speaking Montreal and from other provinces, pleased No voters but annoyed the undecided. If the English really cared, where had they been in 1990 or 1992? By Monday, the rally and inflammatory francophone coverage were forgotten. The results were exciting enough: out of 4.7 million voters, 90 per cent of those eligible, 49.4 per cent said Yes, 50.6 per cent said No. The difference was smaller than the number of spoiled ballots.

Earlier in the day, Parizeau was confident enough to share plans for a quick declaration of independence. That evening he blamed "money and the ethnic vote" for his defeat. The French-speaking majority, he said, "will have our own revenge, and we will have our own country." Next day, he resigned. Early in 1996, a PQ convention chose Lucien Bouchard as his successor. The man of short-tempered clarity was gone; the man of profound but prudent emotion had arrived.

After the referendum, problems ignored earlier surged forward. The referendum question had been ambiguous. Could half the Quebec electorate dissolve Canada? If Canada could be divided, why not Quebec? Did northern Cree and Inuit have the right to remove their original territory? What about anglophones west of Montreal or along the Ottawa River? Was separation even legal? A former sovereignist, Guy Bertrand, took the issue to court. After Quebec insisted that, since 1982, there was no Canadian constitution, Ottawa joined the suit.

Critics attacked Chrétien for failing to derail the separatists, though no one had anything clever to suggest. Committed to change but reluctant to revive a sterile debate, Chrétien announced that Quebec could use Ottawa's veto if it opposed a constitutional change. So could Ontario, Atlantic Canada, and the West. Suitable outrage won British Columbia a distinct veto. Chrétien could do no less – or more, as voters denounced any scheme to conciliate Quebec. The best Chrétien could manage was a statement of "Social Union," conceding provincial primacy in social policies. For a moment, even Quebec seemed ready to join, until Bouchard found a pretext to refuse.

Would Quebec leave? Most Quebeckers thought so, but not soon. Seventy per cent hoped it would not happen. Outside Quebec, many in the political elite insisted that it was time for a "Plan B": the means, gentle or brutal, to settle the issue. Narrowly reprieved, English Canadians showed no signs of embracing a Bouchard-style partnership. As premier, he insisted that he would wait for "winning conditions," probably when the late-1990s economic recovery had restored prosperity.

5 | NEW CHOICES

Canada had begun the twentieth century under the Liberals; it would end the century the same way. Since 1993, Jean Chrétien's Liberals had stayed far ahead in the polls. Paul Martin claimed that a balanced budget was almost in sight, and insiders added that only the finance minister's caution delayed a victory proclamation. Unemployment at 10 per cent was a problem, but new jobs were emerging as the economy recovered. Meanwhile, the opposition was in trouble. The Bloc replaced Bouchard with a dull school administrator who, in turn, was replaced by Gilles Duceppe, an abrasive ex-Communist from downtown Montreal. Reform's Preston Manning acquired contact lenses, well-cut suits, and a better haircut, but some able Reformers had quit, and polls raised Liberal hopes of a few gains in the West. When opponents and journalists complained about a June election, Chrétien only felt more confident.

In fact, the election was not a sure thing. Competent enough in office, Chrétien proved uninspired as a campaigner, unable even to explain why he was calling an early election. Manning benefited from a polished campaign, skilful sound bites, and his promise to cut taxes after the deficit vanished. The mid-campaign TV debates were won, in both French and English, by the new young Tory leader, Jean Charest. Audiences loved his ringing pledge to keep Canada united for the sake of his children. When Jacques Parizeau released his memoirs in mid-campaign, revealing that even a tiny Yes margin would have led him to proclaim independence, voters recalled a Chrétien failure. A Reform ad denouncing Quebec's monopoly on federal party leaders appealed to westerners but probably hurt Manning in Ontario, where it seemed discriminatory. The ad also helped revive a struggling Bloc, as did Chrétien's warning that a margin of 50 per cent plus one was not enough for independence. The NDP's Alexa McDonough won real interest only in her own Atlantic region.

On election day, June 2, 1997, Canadians in 301 ridings had twelve staggered hours to vote. This time, westerners would not hear the results before they voted. Forty-five per cent of voters stayed home; the rest reflected how their own region had interpreted the campaign. Liberals took 155 ridings, all but two Ontario seats, and 25 mostly English-speaking seats in Quebec. The Bloc faded a little, to 44 seats and 11 per cent of the vote, the same as Alexa McDonough's NDP. Most of her 21 seats came from the West, but eight were won in Nova Scotia and New Brunswick. Charest's 20 seats also came largely from Atlantic Canada and his native Quebec. The Tories' 18 per cent share of the vote almost matched Reform's 19 per cent. Could a united right have won? The temptation was obvious.

Jean Chrétien offered neither repentance nor resignation. An eight-seat majority was better than none. His four opponents had no more common ground than the Bloc and Reform in 1993, and each was deeply repugnant to some Canadians. Chrétien was imperfect but he was the first choice of a lot of

Canadians. His was not a high road but, as the poet Frank Scott had once observed, that was not the route Canadians chose. Meanwhile, the Liberals would have money to spend, a Supreme Court decision on Quebec to resolve, and a millennium celebration to enjoy.

Perhaps the major Canadian development of the 1990s was the altered status of First Nations. Oka was not unique. In 1995, months of armed stand-off at British Columbia's Gustafson Lake and a deadly confrontation between Ontario police and natives at a former army camp on Lake Huron were fresh reminders of potential violence between an impoverished minority and other Canadians. At a cost of $60 million, the Royal Commission on Aboriginal Peoples (RCAP) gave Canada five volumes of advice and information on issues the country could no longer abandon to backwoods or slums. The commission proposed that natives gain the power and resources to be self-governing.

By 1998, the federal government made a formal apology for the earlier policy of residential native schools and approved a $350 million "healing fund." Six thousand lawsuits by former students threatened to bankrupt the four Christian denominations that had run the schools. But without a land settlement, insisted the RCAP, there could be no beginning. British Columbia had never acknowledged native land claims, even though First Nations claimed 70 per cent of its area. In 1994, its NDP government broke precedent by promising to negotiate a native land base. After the Supreme Court ruled that Delgamuukw, a native of the Gitskan and Wet'suwet'en people, had a clear claim to his ancestral land, costly, complicated negotiations began. In July 1998, Ottawa, Victoria, and the Nisga'a agreed to Nisga'a ownership of 2000 square kilometres of the Nass Valley and surrounding territory and recognized the band as a third order of government with municipal-level powers. The Reform and the B.C. Liberal party pledged to overthrow the treaty if elected. In 1999, after Donald Marshall was charged with fishing for eel out of season, the Supreme Court decided that the constitution's aboriginal-rights clause guaranteed Marshall's Mi'kmaq people the right to make "a moderate living" from traditional resources. Non-natives protested the loss of control of logging and the offshore fishery. Meanwhile, across Canada, thousands of young natives began to provide their communities with lawyers, teachers, social workers, and health professionals as well as chiefs and councillors.

On April 1, 1999, Nunavut became a third territory, and 25,000 people – 21,000 of them Inuit – won control over half the Northwest Territories, or a third of Canada. Nunavut Tunnagavit, an Inuit-owned economic development corporation, received the $1.6 billion Ottawa had paid to settle land claims. The forty thousand people of the remaining Northwest Territories, evenly divided between natives and whites, would govern themselves from Yellowknife. Celebration of a new regime momentarily diverted attention from Nunavut's average income of $11,000, 25 per cent unemployment level, high living costs, and major drug and alcohol addiction problems. Many hoped that an Inuit tradition of consensual government would solve problems that defied southern experts. Others were sceptical.

Politically, a surplus could be a bigger problem than a deficit. Chrétien announced that half the surplus would be spent on programs and the rest on tax cuts. New money would target reform in health care, education, and research. Tax changes would make business more effective in a global economy. Provincial premiers simply demanded a reversal of Martin's 1995 cuts; they would do any reforming themselves. Business echoed Reform's message: all the surplus belonged to the taxpayers. Without tax cuts, business and Canada's best and brightest young professionals would flee to the United States. It was an old argument, which divided even the government itself, and which, on the whole, the progressive wing lost.

Canada became more conservative, but Canadians still enjoyed idealism in the world. They took pride in peacekeeping, teenager Craig Kielburger's crusade against child labour, and Foreign Affairs Minister Lloyd Axworthy's campaign against land mines. If China, Russia, the United States, and other major users did not sign Axworthy's land-mine protocol, who could blame Canada for trying? Economic globalization presented harder choices. Potentially, supporters claimed, it would promote human rights, gender equality, and social justice. Meanwhile, it meant doing business with all kind of regimes. Late in 1997, Chrétien welcomed a cluster of dictators and democrats to the Asia Pacific Summit in Vancouver. When police used pepper spray to control protesters, Chrétien felt the heat. Still, foreign policy could give the Liberals a more liberal look. Axworthy denounced the use of child soldiers, supported an international court, and called for the release of Cuban political prisoners. When Cuba ignored the demand, relations cooled with the aging Fidel Castro, and Washington was pleased.

Axworthy's human-security agenda led Canada into more conflicts abroad. After UN peacekeepers failed to protect unarmed Bosnians from a Serb massacre at Srebrenica in 1995, NATO moved in with troops committed to protecting Serbia's neighbours. Late in 1989, when civil war broke out in the Serb province of Kosovo, Kosovar nationalists succeeded in gaining a U.S.-led NATO intervention. In March 1999, Canadian CF-18 fighters joined American and British jets in devastating Serb infrastructure. After a month, Serbia pulled out its forces and 850 Canadians joined NATO's occupying army in Kosovo. In September 1999, Indonesia ended its occupation of East Timor with devastation and massacres. Ottawa sent aircraft, a supply ship, and a few infantry to diversify a UN-approved but largely

Australian security force. Canadians strongly approved of their forces, though barely seven in ten wanted to pay for the necessary weapons and equipment.

The Supreme Court decision on Quebec referenda called for action. The Liberals pushed legislation through a reluctant Parliament. The Bloc opposed any meddling with Quebec "self-determination"; other opponents denounced a law that envisaged Canada's break-up. "I never thought I'd see the day the Liberal party came down in favour of disunity of the country," an ailing Michael Pitfield protested. "Our country makes sense only if based on mutual consent," responded Intergovernmental Affairs Minister Stéphane Dion.

In the 1990s, Canada embraced a new economic model. Much as the Great Depression transformed a generation, the economic disaster of the early 1990s changed its victims. Trends away from resource industries and manufacturing and toward information and global connections became realities. In a global marketplace, people were producers, consumers, and commodities – not members of a socialist Society of Friends. Recovery began when laid-off workers accepted minimum-wage jobs without benefits, seniority, or overtime. Security in a job well done – a fundamental of civilized life for much of the century – vanished, even in the public service. To a global corporation, worker loyalty was meaningless. Sometimes Canadians rebelled. When four of Canada's five big banks, Montreal and the Royal, followed by the Canadian Imperial Bank of Commerce and the Toronto-Dominion, proposed mergers, public and political protest interfered, but mostly business did as it pleased.

The 1990s devastated the manufacturing, service, and resource industries of Canada. Links to Asia protected British Columbia for a time, making it a prosperous island of exceptions. As the rest of Canada recovered, Asia's financial collapse made a victim of the West Coast. Markets for wood, coal, and fish faded; even Asian tourists lacked the means to visit. Symptomatic of change, MacMillan-Bloedel, a historic forest giant, became a fiefdom of Weyerhaeuser, its old American rival.

The decade was rich in hinterland gloom. Newfoundland's ancient cod stocks and the salmon of British Columbia were devastated. Less noticed, other species replaced the cod and, at the end of the decade, Atlantic fishers landed some of their biggest catches in years. Caught in a world subsidy war only the United States and the European Union could win, western grain farmers faced ruin. The alternative, factory-farming livestock with cheap feed grain, risked pollution of the region's fragile water supply.

Much else changed for Canadians: "plastic" replaced cash, electronic databanks penetrated personal privacy, and the Internet simultaneously linked and isolated people in front of their computer screens. Secularism and the profit motive undermined the Lord's Day Act ninety years after Parliament had made it law. Sunday became another holiday, available for shopping, sleeping, entertainment – and earning.

Was the state another anachronism? Would state pensions and health insurance ever serve younger citizens? Popular ideologues told them not to believe it. Why, therefore, should they put their faith in civic loyalty or any public good?

Chrétien's Liberal government achieved a reversal of much that previous Liberals had done. Most Canadians approved. An older belief that government was a means for social justice faded, as did its main standard-bearers, unions and the NDP. An opposing, American-style conservatism had gathered about one voter in five. Multi-millionaire Conrad Black acquired much of Canada's daily press and created a new national daily, the *National Post*, to promote a "unite-the-right" agenda. Item one was uniting Reform and the Tories. Preston Manning responded by reorganizing his Reform Party as a "Canadian Alliance" to target eastern Progressive Conservatives. A new party, he belatedly discovered, demanded a new leader. Tom Long, Mike Harris's former chief handler, was too eastern; Manning carried too many memories. The Alliance choice was Alberta's treasurer, Stockwell Day, a handsome former Pentecostal preacher who opposed abortion, espoused "family values," and had introduced a flat-rate income tax for Alberta.

Having lost Jean Charest to the Quebec Liberals in 1998, the endangered Tories chose former prime minister Joe Clark to save them. By the summer of 2000, Day was moving up in the polls. Could he also pass Jean Chrétien? Right-wing Liberals wanted Paul Martin, Jr., as a leader more acceptable to business and perhaps even to Quebec. How better to bury the scandals and failures that mar any government's record? Leadership was much on the public mind with the death of Pierre Trudeau on September 28, and slighting comments on the quality of his political heirs were much in fashion. At sixty-six, Chrétien, Trudeau's chief lieutenant, saw no need to yield power while polls and prosperity promised an easy Liberal victory – as they had in 1997. Almost two years early, critics complained, he called a general election for November 27, 2000.

With four opposition parties, and half a dozen smaller groups, from Marxist-Leninists to a Marijuana Party, the anti-Chrétien clamour was almost deafening. The prime minister was denounced for sins ranging from calling an unnecessary election to denying Paul Martin a chance at power. The Liberals left the West to the Alliance, used their surplus to win back support in Quebec and Atlantic Canada, and, with a little help from the Alliance's platform and spokesmen, portrayed Stockwell Day and his policies as a threat to moderate, middle-of-the-road Ontarians.

Though campaign polls showed the Liberal lead evaporating, Chretien's bold strategy was vindicated. Liberals lost a few seats in the West, gained more in Quebec and the Maritimes, and emerged with 172 MPs and a higher popular vote than in their two previous victories. Stockwell Day's Alliance took 66 seats, but the hoped-for breakthrough in Ontario amounted to only two seats and 80 second-place finishes in Ontario. The chief losers in the Liberal tide were the Bloc, with 38 seats, the New Democrats with only 13, and Clark's Progressive Conservatives with 12, barely meeting the cut-off for official parties in the House of Commons. Only an anti-Alliance coalition won Joe Clark a seat in Calgary. In Quebec, Chrétien won a higher popular vote than the Bloc, and he joined King, Laurier, and Mackenzie King among prime ministers who had won their parties three consecutive majorities.

One early consequence was the departure of Lucien Bouchard. Frustrated by the erosion of sovereigntist support, dismayed at the prospect of a new battle with his party's hardliners and ethnic nationalists, conscious that his years with his young family were limited, sovereignty's most popular advocate retired on January 11, 2001. His movement, of course, was not dead, and economic adversity might well revive it.

Another consequence was a belated look at Canada's democratic system. Not for a century had more eligible voters stayed home. Some blamed the adoption of a permanent list; others a five-week campaign of personal abuse and policy obfuscation; still others the enormous power of the prime minister in Canada's system of responsible government.

Canadians ended the nineteenth century in 1900; they buried the twentieth century a year earlier, in 1999. Had Laurier's 1904 claim that it would be "the Century of Canada" come true? Four times in the 1990s, the UN labelled Canada the world's best place to live. Thousands of homeless people – many mentally ill and some of them mothers with children – found that hard to believe. So did natives sharing Third World conditions in remote communities or urban slums. Canada's rich had grown richer since 1978 and the poor poorer. Americans, of course, were even richer and poorer, and their economic freedom less trammelled. Like others, Canadians have been envious. United Nations human development indices are comparative and selective: literacy matters more than wealth.

Canada's climate and scenery make it a good place to live, but more important is what people have done together. Canadians live in relative peace with each other, and they practise, imperfectly, virtues of neighbourliness and compromise that the rest of the world envies. In 2000, satisfaction is surprisingly widespread, among French and English, old-stock immigrants and newcomers, and even among native peoples. Quebec sovereignists intend significant association with Canada and expect to carry its passport. More conservative than their elders about social policies, younger Canadians ignore differences of colour, culture, and customs. They are well adapted to the smaller globe and greater diversity of the twenty-first century.

Torn between old heritages and regional identities, Canadians have always wondered who they are. Such tensions can be more interesting than painful. Céline Dion is both Québécoise and *Canadienne*; the novelist Margaret Atwood is a Canadian from Toronto who summers in the north woods; born in Sri Lanka, Michael Ondaatje chose to be Canadian and to teach other Canadians about the art of writing and themselves.

History is another word for experience, not a form of prophecy. The past tells Canadians that they live in a tough old country with a tradition of compromise, an aversion to violence, and a gift for survival. Only the Swiss and the Americans have older federal systems, and Canada's federation has outlived many gloomy prophets. Whatever the temptations, geography makes it hard to live apart. Under a shell of cynicism and self-deprecation, Canadians are as proud of their land as any people on earth. Make no mistake about it.

INDEX